Cooking Light®

REAL familyfood

Simple & Easy Recipes   Your Whole Family Will Love

Cooking Light®

REAL familyfood

Simple & Easy Recipes · **Your Whole Family Will Love**

BY AMANDA HAAS

Oxmoor House®

ISBN-10: 0-8487-3700-8
ISBN-13: 978-0-8487-3700-9
Library of Congress Control Number: 2012941514

Printed in the United States of America
First Printing 2012

Be sure to check with your health-care provider before making any changes in your diet.

Oxmoor House
VP, Publishing Director: Jim Childs
Editorial Director: Leah McLaughlin
Creative Director: Felicity Keane
Brand Manager: Michelle Turner Aycock
Managing Editor: Rebecca Benton

Cooking Light Real Family Food
Senior Editor: Heather Averett
Assistant Designer: Allison Sperando Potter
Director, Test Kitchen: Elizabeth Tyler Austin
Assistant Directors, Test Kitchen: Julie Christopher,
   Julie Gunter
Recipe Developers and Testers: Wendy Ball, RD; Victoria E. Cox;
   Stefanie Maloney; Callie Nash; Leah Van Deren
Recipe Editor: Alyson Moreland Haynes
Food Stylists: Margaret Monroe Dickey; Catherine Crowell Steele
Photography Director: Jim Bathie
Senior Photo Stylist: Kay E. Clarke
Photo Stylist: Katherine Eckert Coyne
Assistant Photo Stylist: Mary Louise Menendez
Assistant Production Manager: Diane Rose

Contributors
Project Editor: Perri Hubbard
Designer and Compositor: Cathy Robbins
Copy Editors: Jacqueline Giovanelli, Kate Johnson
Proofreader: Julie Bosche
Indexer: Mary Ann Laurens
Nutritional Analyses: Wendy Ball, RD; Keri Matherne, RD
Interns: Erin Bishop; Mackenzie Cogle; Jessica Cox, RD;
   Laura Hoxworth; Alicia Lavender; Anna Pollock; Ashley White
Recipe Developers and Testers: Martha Condra, Tamara Goldis,
   Erica Hopper, Kathleen Royal Phillips
Photographers: Johnny Autry, James Carriere, Beth Hontzas,
   Mary Britton Senseney
Photo Stylists: Mary Clayton Carl, Mindi Shapiro Levine,
   Caitlin Van Horn
Food Stylists: Ana Price Kelley, Robyn Valarik

Time Home Entertainment Inc.
Publisher: Richard Fraiman
Vice President, Strategy & Business Development:
   Steven Sandonato
Executive Director, Marketing Services: Carol Pittard
Executive Director, Retail & Special Sales: Tom Mifsud
Director, Bookazine Development & Marketing: Laura Adam
Publishing Director: Joy Butts
Finance Director: Glenn Buonocore
Associate General Counsel: Helen Wan

Cooking Light
Editor: Scott Mowbray
Creative Director: Carla Frank
Executive Managing Editor: Phillip Rhodes
Executive Editor, Food: Ann Taylor Pittman
Special Publications Editor: Mary Simpson Creel, MS, RD
Senior Food Editors: Timothy Q. Cebula, Julianna Grimes
Senior Editor: Cindy Hatcher
Assistant Editor, Nutrition: Sidney Fry, MS, RD
Assistant Editors: Kimberly Holland, Phoebe Wu
Test Kitchen Director: Vanessa T. Pruett
Assistant Test Kitchen Director: Tiffany Vickers Davis
Recipe Testers and Developers: Robin Bashinsky,
   Adam Hickman, Deb Wise
Art Directors: Fernande Bondarenko, Shawna Kalish
Senior Deputy Art Director: Rachel Cardina Lasserre
Designers: Hagen Stegall, Dréa Zacharenko
Assistant Designer: Nicole Gerrity
Photo Director: Kristen Schaefer
Assistant Photo Editor: Amy Delaune
Senior Photographer: Randy Mayor
Senior Photo Stylist: Cindy Barr
Photo Stylist: Leigh Ann Ross
Chief Food Stylist: Kellie Gerber Kelley
Food Styling Assistant: Blakeslee Wright
Copy Chief: Maria Parker Hopkins
Assistant Copy Chief: Susan Roberts
Research Editor: Michelle Gibson Daniels
Production Director: Liz Rhoades
Production Editor: Hazel R. Eddins
Assistant Production Editor: Josh Rutledge
Administrative Coordinator: Carol D. Johnson
CookingLight.com Editor: Allison Long Lowery
Nutrition Editor: Holley Johnson Grainger, MS, RD
Associate Editor/Producer: Mallory Daugherty Brasseale

To order additional publications, call
1-800-765-6400 or 1-800-491-0551.

For more books to enrich your life, visit
oxmoorhouse.com

To search, savor, and share thousands
of recipes, visit **myrecipes.com**

Cover: Pulled Barbecue Chicken and Coleslaw Sandwiches (page 203)
   and Black Bean Soup (page 237)
Front Flap: Chicken Soft Tacos (page 163)
Back Cover: Turkey Sausage Lasagna (page 233) and Banana Split
   Sundaes (page 273)

food is love—at least, for me it is! Eating it;

cooking it as an expression of gratitude and care for the important people in my life; and sharing it with my family and friends at the dinner table all add up to some of my best memories. I think great things can happen when people sit down together to break bread—even if it's just for a few minutes. We connect, we nourish our bodies, and we hear about the important things in each other's lives.

So why has it become so difficult to keep good food and the family dinner ritual in our daily lives? I have a couple of theories: The advent of TV dinners may have started it, but increased demands on our time, nonstop social media in our homes, and the onslaught of kids' activities in the middle of the evening compete for our family's attention. No matter what our reasons, most of our kids have become so used to eating quick, packaged foods on the run that sitting down together for dinner seems foreign to them.

The positive effects of gathering at the table for a shared meal a few times a week are proven: Children are happier, less likely to do drugs, and have higher self-esteem. Also, the nutritional benefits of eating healthier foods around a dinner table are significant: Childhood obesity rates drop; children learn moderation in eating; and they begin to set the stage for good nutrition that will last a lifetime. My own beliefs around food, which have slowly morphed into "One Family One Meal," center on this one concept: Children can and will eat the same meals grown-ups eat. "But," I hear you saying, "My child is so picky. He would never sit down for a real meal. He only eats chicken nuggets/pizza/fill in the blank. He would never eat broccoli/green beans/fill in the blank." I love showing parents that if given the chance, their kids will eat things other than processed foods. Beginning on page 13 of this book, I will teach you that cooking doesn't have to be expensive, time consuming, or difficult.

Let's get cooking!

Amanda

contents

ONE FAMILY ONE MEAL

the one family one meal plan

Giving your family a chance to connect around good food is something I believe is more important than anything else you can give them. To achieve that, I created the One Family One Meal Plan, which focuses on the following key attributes: menu planning, budgeting, making a grocery shopping list, and ultimately, creating simple meals. I know I can't get rid of soccer practice in the middle of the dinner hour, but I do hope I can give you the next best thing—bringing joy into your kitchen and around your family table when possible. Here's how it's done:

MEAL PLANNING

Meal planning has always seemed like drudgery to me. But once my kids arrived, I realized that if I didn't have a plan, I would be missing key ingredients and wouldn't have the energy to go back to the store. And as I studied other moms, I saw that the only ones who were actually cooking were the ones who had a game plan each week. If I wanted to create simple, healthy meals in a hurry, I knew I had to get serious about meal planning. Once I started, I couldn't stop. It saved us a ton of money, and I was no longer throwing away food at the end of the week. Also, knowing that I can come home and have what I need to make dinner has created a sense of calm for me. Here's what I do:

1. Make a chart that has a spot for every meal you'll be cooking at home for the week.
2. Flip through the cookbook and find all the recipes you'd like to make for the week. I like to change it up a bit, choosing maybe a fish recipe, a few starch or vegetarian-based recipes, a chicken recipe, and usually a beef recipe. Then I look at which lunches and breakfasts we'll need, and I add those to my menu plan. Tip: Look at your dinner recipes and see if any of them could provide leftover ingredients for lunches or breakfasts. For example, take the leftovers from Simplest Roast Chicken Ever (page 235) and toss them into your Crunchy Chinese Chicken Salad with Wonton Chips (page 121) for lunch, or

wrap them in the Chicken Soft Tacos (page 163).
3. Make your shopping list.
4. Check against your budget and adjust the recipes as needed.

BUDGET

The challenge I made to myself and all my friends in 2008 was this: that I could buy enough food for 20 meals a week, snacks, and a few moderately priced bottles of wine or decadent items for $200. The other kicker was that I had to be able to shop at my favorite Whole Foods Market because I wanted to buy organics as much as possible. No one believed I could do it, so the challenge was on! I learned that if I took 20 minutes to plan meals, make my list, and budget, I could save $50 to $100 a week in the store and consistently spend about $200 a week. (Believe me, when you have a website telling people this is how you live, they are watching over your shoulder at the grocery store. (I can literally get my bill within a buck or two of $200 every time.) Here's how:

1. After I make my shopping list, I write in an approximate price next to each item. Yes, this does take practice, but if you notice the prices of items the next time you go to the store, you can commit them to memory. First focus on the common things you buy: milk, eggs, cheese, produce, meat, chicken...you'll be amazed.

2. Tally up your totals at the bottom of your shopping list. If it's a lot more than you budgeted, change out a few of the recipes for ones that don't require expensive cuts of meat, fish, or poultry. Fresh produce, beans, legumes, and pasta recipes always seem to bring down the cost. Also, seasonal produce is less expensive than out-of-season produce. (As you continue to plan menus, you'll naturally get a better feel for balancing your weekly menus with recipes that are more expensive and less expensive.)
3. Practice makes perfect. The more you shop and pay attention to prices, the easier it will be. I know how much my favorite cuts of meat cost, so it's easy to budget those recipes in advance. And if you always shop at the same store, it's even easier.

GROCERY SHOPPING LIST

I never used to go to the store with a list, and I'd walk out having spent a few hundred dollars with nothing to show for it. That all changed when the economy tanked, and I had to take a hard look at my spending. I realized I was throwing out $40 to $50 worth of food every week because I hadn't planned how to use it. Once I started menu planning, I devised a little map of my grocery store and turned that into my list. Your store is, of course, different from mine, so you can make your list to match your store, but you get the gist.

Here's what I do:
1. I compile the recipes I've chosen for the week (or go to my site and do it).
2. I fill in my ingredients from the shopping list according to those recipes. If I'm not sure if I have something, I write it on my list and put a question mark next to it.
3. I fill in extras: wine, chocolate, household goods, etc.
4. I double-check to see if I already have any of the items in question. If so, I mark them off (things like olive oil, salt, pepper, and spices often get crossed off the list).

5. Go shop. I have two approaches: buy everything for my recipes, along with snacks and a big heap of fruits and veggies, at once and be done with it. Then I cook the recipes that call for perishable items first. The other option is to go twice a week: once for the main staples, and a second time for perishable things like fish or extra fruits and vegetables for snacking.

GETTING STARTED

If your kids are used to eating frozen foods or calling the shots for dinner every night, the idea of getting them to eat what you eat probably sounds terrifying. It won't happen overnight, but here are my tips to get your entire family to eat the same meal:

1. Start slowly. Flip through this book and find five recipes you think they'll try based on ingredients you know they'll eat. Good ones to start with are recipes that allow them to have some control (i.e. they can make their own burritos, top their tacos, etc.). Giving them some control is half the challenge. Once you've found a few recipes they like, start to play off those.
2. Only offer great choices (remove the bad ones). If you're offering sweet potatoes, chicken, and a crunchy romaine salad one night, it's OK if they only eat one or two of them (they're all good choices). This is a hard concept for some parents to grasp. "What if they don't eat?" they ask. When you remove the bad choices, children tend to gravitate toward better ones. If you're looking to change habits, keeping the old foods around will only make it more difficult. And if you're really desperate, turn to chicken tenders (page 161), tacos (page 163), or pizza (pages 217 through 223).
3. Don't worry if they don't eat everything on their plates. Again, if you're only offering them good choices to start with, they'll find a balance throughout the week. Given time, most hungry kids will pick one thing and eat it up. But if you throw the chicken nuggets back in as a choice the second they turn up their noses, watch out.
4. My dinner table is not a battleground. My son doesn't want to eat his pesto tonight? Oh well. I am convinced that many children are simply trying to assert their independence when turning down foods, so I try not to panic when they reject them. It's like paying attention to a tantrum—the

more attention you give it, the bigger deal it becomes. If I've served them three nutritious items, I'm OK if they ignore one of them (with the exception of rule 5 below). And if they excuse themselves from the table and say they're hungry an hour later, they get to choose from the same things.
5. Try the "no thanks" bite. Sometimes I like to try things I know my kids don't care for because I want them. So I tell them they can have a "no thanks" bite. If they try one bite and don't like it, they don't have to eat any more. Here's the interesting part—children might try something up to a dozen times before deciding whether they like it or not. By not making a big deal out of a rejection and reintroducing the food later, you increase the chance they'll change their minds.
6. Eat real foods. If you're cooking with fresh ingredients, your entire family will feel better.
7. Get cooking, and then get them cooking with you. Again, so many of our childrens' food choices come down to their need to feel in control. Asking them to choose what they'd like to make for dinner, and then allowing them to help cook it is empowering. I always get much better buy-in when my children play a part in preparing the meal.
8. Commit to sitting down together a few nights a week. People hear that we do this nightly and think we're crazy. It's the one thing we've always committed to do as parents. Just like anything new, it takes practice to make it a priority. Once you do, you may be surprised at what a nice part of your day it becomes.
9. Try your best. If you're a family who's used to fast food or plain pasta, miracles won't happen immediately. Finding even three or four meals that your whole family will agree on can make a world of difference to your health. Good luck, and enjoy!

USING THE ICONS IN THIS BOOK

I've provided some icons to help you easily pin down what you'd like to cook. Here's how they work:

 Gluten free. Because I can't have gluten, this is a big one for me. This icon means the recipes have no gluten. There are wonderful gluten-free versions available these days for bread, pasta, soy sauce, and even pizza dough.

 Dairy free. (Pretty straight up!)

 Vegetarian. Implies a purely vegetarian recipe.

Easy entertaining. This means a recipe can come together quickly and easily be doubled to serve a crowd.

Make ahead. These recipes can be made in advance, cooled, and refrigerated to be served later. They're the ones I like to cook over the weekend so we have things to eat all week. Also, they usually taste better if you make them ahead and let them sit for a day or two.

15 minutes or less. These recipes take less than 15 minutes to prepare. (Let's give them a round of applause, shall we?)

 KIDS CAN HELP

Whenever you see this icon you'll know the kids can help in the kitchen. From measuring ingredients to mixing and stirring, the kids will love to help.

the real family food pantry

A well-stocked pantry is key to cooking delicious food quickly. Keeping the basics around prevents you from going for takeout when you're in a pinch, which saves money and helps you eat better food. Here's a list of staples. Most of these ingredients are easy to find, but see the resources (page 288) for finding trickier items like gluten-free flour.

BAKING
- [ ] Agave nectar (my favorite sweetener for drinks)
- [ ] Baking powder
- [ ] Baking soda
- [ ] Brown sugar: dark and light
- [ ] Dark chocolate bars
- [ ] Gluten-free flour (Cup4Cup)
- [ ] Granulated sugar
- [ ] Honey
- [ ] Powdered sugar
- [ ] Regular all-purpose flour
- [ ] Semisweet chocolate chips
- [ ] Whole oats

FREEZER
- [ ] Chicken—whole or breasts
- [ ] Ground beef or turkey
- [ ] Organic berries, mango, and pineapple for smoothies
- [ ] Spinach

FRUIT
- [ ] Bananas
- [ ] Clementines
- [ ] Lemons
- [ ] Limes
- [ ] Organic Fuji apples

PANTRY
- [ ] Couscous
- [ ] Fish sauce
- [ ] Garlic
- [ ] Ginger
- [ ] Olive oil: regular and extra-virgin (Olio Santo and Whole Foods Market oils are my favorites.)
- [ ] Onions: red and yellow
- [ ] Organic canned beans: black, cannellini, kidney, and pinto
- [ ] Organic canola oil
- [ ] Pasta: fusilli (regular and gluten-free), lasagna, orzo, penne, and spaghetti
- [ ] Rice: Arborio or Vialone Nano, brown, and jasmine
- [ ] Tamari and/or lower-sodium soy sauce (Note: Most tamari is gluten free and easily replaces soy sauce in recipes.)
- [ ] Vinegars: apple cider, balsamic, red wine, and white wine
- [ ] Wine (for cooking and for drinking!)

REFRIGERATOR
- [ ] Almond milk
- [ ] Bacon
- [ ] Carrots
- [ ] Celery
- [ ] Dijon mustard
- [ ] Ketchup (I love Heinz Organic.)
- [ ] Mayonnaise
- [ ] Milk
- [ ] Mozzarella and cheddar cheese
- [ ] Organic, free-range eggs
- [ ] Parmigiano-Reggiano cheese
- [ ] Prepared polenta
- [ ] Romaine lettuce
- [ ] Unsalted butter

SPICES
- [ ] Allspice
- [ ] Black peppercorns
- [ ] Chili powder
- [ ] Cinnamon
- [ ] Cumin
- [ ] Curry powder
- [ ] Fennel seeds
- [ ] Ginger
- [ ] Kosher salt
- [ ] Oregano
- [ ] Paprika
- [ ] Turmeric
- [ ] Whole nutmeg

amanda's favorite tools

Nothing replaces the quality and agility of a great knife, and high-quality pots and pans will change your life. I try to buy the good stuff and keep it forever. (My pots and pans are 18 years old, and they are in great shape.) If you're just getting started, here are tools I think every cook should own:

- 10- and 12-inch skillets
- 3-qt. sauté pan
- 5- to 6-qt. sauté pan
- 8- to 10-qt. stockpot or Dutch oven (I use mine interchangeably.)
- Risotto pan or 3- to 4-qt. stockpot
- 3-qt. saucepan
- Nonstick: I buy only the highest-quality, nontoxic nonstick pans. I like a 10-inch nonstick skillet for eggs and pancakes and that's it.
- Cast-iron skillet or griddle: Cast iron is the original nonstick. When seasoned properly, you can cook practically anything in it. It's heavy and a bit hard to handle, but it is inexpensive and will last forever.
- Knives: Quality matters so much. Make sure to take care of them with a sharpening steel. Any knives that are dishwasher safe are not the ones you want to buy. Look for knives that are hand-forged out of solid metals like stainless steel. The handles should be comfortable in your hand, so make sure to hold them before you buy. My go-to knives are:

- 8-inch chef's knife
- 3- to 4-inch paring knife
- 8-inch slicing knife
- Japanese Santoku knife
- Serrated "tomato" knife
- Serrated bread knife

- Slotted spoon and regular spoon for stirring
- Tongs (Hands down the tool I use the most.)
- 8- or 10-inch whisk
- Colander
- Ginger grater
- Cheese grater
- Blender
- Food processor
- Stand mixer
- Juicer
- Muffin pan
- Sturdy baking sheets or sheet pans

- Parchment paper
- Silpat baking sheets (You put them on your baking sheets, and nothing sticks to them.)
- Stainless steel measuring cups and spoons
- Zester for citrus, nutmeg, and Parmigiano-Reggiano cheese
- Meat pounder
- Pastry brushes
- Ice-cream scoop (great for cookies, meatballs, etc.)

a note about organics

People always ask me how we can afford organics on a budget. I live in a place where there are many organic farms nearby, so it costs less to buy organic foods that are in season. It depends on where you live and what you can access, but my rule is just to eat as organically as you can. The Environmental Working Group produces a list of foods that contain the most pesticides called "The Dirty Dozen," so if you want to start incorporating organics into your life, here are the most important ones to start with:

Apples • Celery • Peaches • Strawberries • Domestic Blueberries • Imported Nectarines • Sweet Bell Peppers • Spinach/Kale/Collard Greens • Cherries • Potatoes • Imported Grapes • and Lettuce.

They have also created a list called "The Clean 15" that contains foods that show little to no traces of pesticides and are safe to eat in nonorganic forms. (Phew!) They are:

Onions • Avocados • Sweet Corn • Pineapples • Mango • Sweet Peas • Asparagus • Kiwifruit • Cabbage • Eggplant • Domestic Cantaloupe • Watermelon • Grapefruit • Sweet Potatoes • and Mushrooms.

One great trick to incorporating more organic foods into your diet while on a budget is to buy them frozen. I purchase organic frozen fruit for smoothies and organic frozen rice for weeknights, and the prices are very close to the nonorganic versions.

THE BASICS

Quick and convenient, these vinaigrettes are a must-try. They take five minutes to make. Plus, they're healthier than store-bought dressings, which tend to be loaded with sugar and sodium.

APPLE CIDER VINAIGRETTE

HANDS-ON TIME: 5 MINUTES | TOTAL TIME: 5 MINUTES

¼ cup apple cider vinegar
¼ cup white wine vinegar
1 tablespoon Dijon mustard
2 tablespoons agave syrup
¼ teaspoon kosher salt
¼ teaspoon freshly ground
    black pepper
½ cup canola oil
1½ tablespoons minced shallots

1. Combine first 6 ingredients in a small bowl, stirring with a whisk. Gradually add oil, stirring constantly with a whisk; stir in shallots. Serves 9 (serving size: 2 tablespoons)

CALORIES 130; FAT 12.5g (sat 0.9g, mono 7.9g, poly 3.5g); PROTEIN 0.1g; CARB 5g; FIBER 0g; CHOL 0mg; IRON 0g; SODIUM 94mg; CALC 1mg

HONEY-LIME VINAIGRETTE

HANDS-ON TIME: 5 MINUTES | TOTAL TIME: 5 MINUTES

1½ teaspoons grated lime rind
½ cup fresh lime juice
2 tablespoons honey
1 tablespoon Dijon mustard
¼ teaspoon kosher salt
¼ teaspoon freshly ground
    black pepper
½ cup olive oil
1½ tablespoons minced shallots

1. Combine first 6 ingredients in a small bowl, stirring with a whisk. Gradually add oil, stirring constantly with a whisk; stir in shallots. Serves 9 (serving size: 2 tablespoons)

CALORIES 127; FAT 12g (sat 1.7g, mono 8.8g, poly 1.3g); PROTEIN 0.1g; CARB 5.6g; FIBER 0.1g; CHOL 0mg; IRON 0.1g; SODIUM 94mg; CALC 3mg

SHALLOT AND DIJON VINAIGRETTE

HANDS-ON TIME: 5 MINUTES | TOTAL TIME: 5 MINUTES

½ cup red wine vinegar
1 tablespoon Dijon mustard
¼ teaspoon kosher salt
¼ teaspoon freshly ground
    black pepper
½ cup olive oil
1½ tablespoons minced shallots

1. Combine first 4 ingredients in a small bowl, stirring with a whisk. Gradually add oil, stirring constantly with a whisk; stir in shallots. Serves 8 (serving size: 2 tablespoons)

CALORIES 126; FAT 13.5g (sat 1.9g, mono 9.9g, poly 1.4g); PROTEIN 0.1g; CARB 1g; FIBER 0g; CHOL 0mg; IRON 0.2g; SODIUM 107mg; CALC 2mg

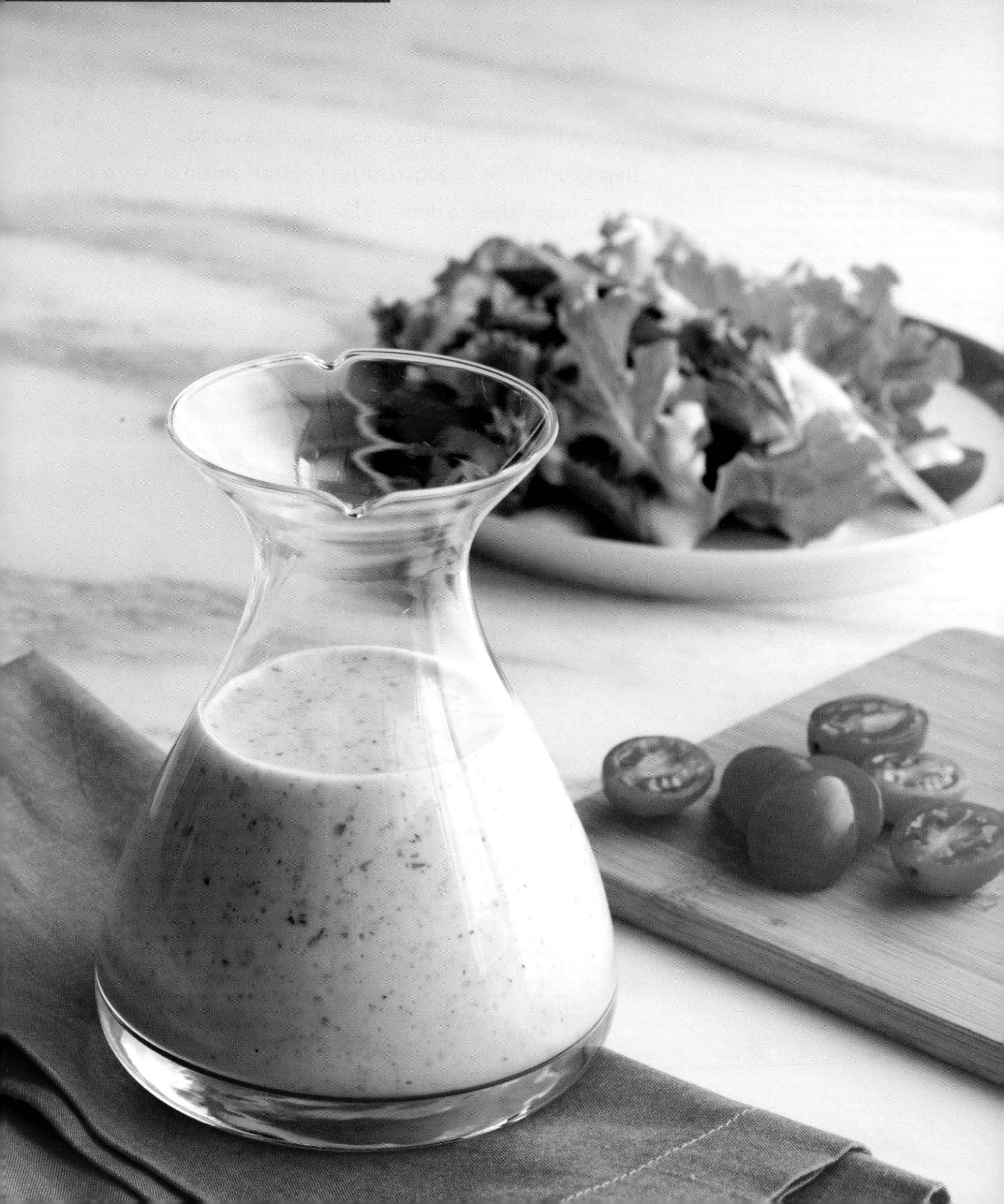

I always thought of creamy dressings as junk food, until I started using Greek yogurt instead of sour cream or regular mayonnaise. Use the dressing like you'd use any ranch or Green Goddess dressing—on salads, as a dip for veggies, or as a sauce for anything your kids claim they won't eat. It can also be used as a marinade, on top of baked potatoes, or served as a dipper for your oven fries. Now you can serve creamy dressings without the guilt.

GREEK GODDESS DRESSING

HANDS-ON TIME: 10 MINUTES | TOTAL TIME: 10 MINUTES

²/₃ cup nonfat buttermilk
¹/₂ cup plain 2% reduced-fat
  Greek yogurt
¹/₄ cup canola mayonnaise
1 tablespoon thinly sliced shallots
1 tablespoon chopped fresh
  tarragon
1 tablespoon finely chopped
  fresh chives
1 tablespoon finely chopped
  fresh flat-leaf parsley
1 tablespoon fresh lemon juice
¹/₂ teaspoon kosher salt
¹/₄ teaspoon freshly ground
  black pepper
1 small garlic clove, peeled

1. Place all ingredients in a blender; process until smooth. Cover and store in refrigerator up to 1 week. Serves 13 (serving size: about 2 tablespoons)

CALORIES 43; FAT 3.6g (sat 0.4g, mono 1.9g, poly 0.9g); PROTEIN 1.3g; CARB 1.5g; FIBER 0g; CHOL 2mg; IRON 0mg; SODIUM 120mg; CALC 23mg

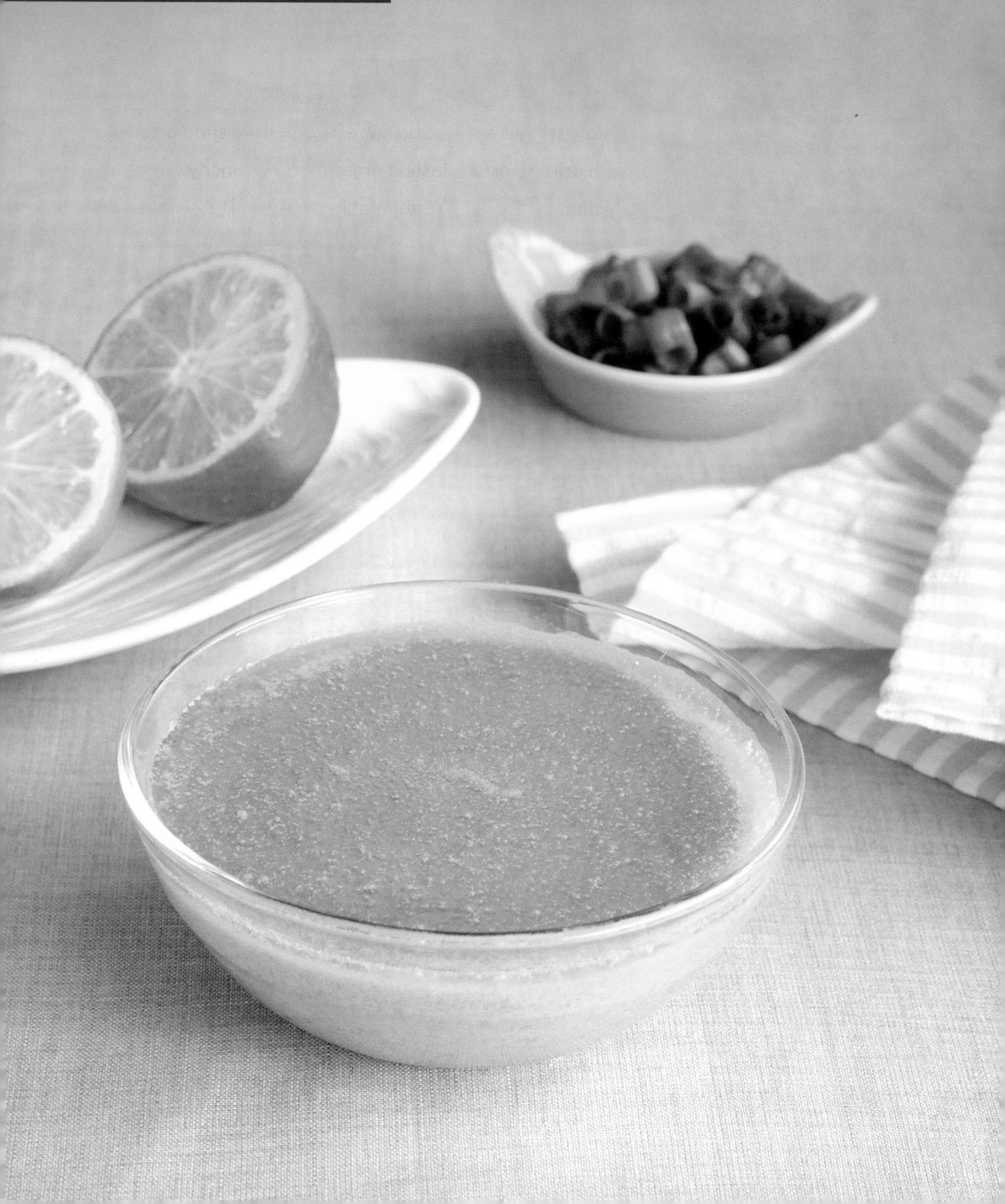

This dressing is so delicious. We joke that we should serve it as a drink! Besides tasting amazing on Crunchy Chinese Chicken Salad with Wonton Chips (page 121), it's also tasty served over grilled chicken or tossed with rice noodles and green onions as a simple side dish.

PEANUT-LIME DRESSING

HANDS-ON TIME: 5 MINUTES | TOTAL TIME: 5 MINUTES

2 tablespoons brown sugar
¼ cup canola oil
¼ cup fresh lime juice
3 tablespoons dark sesame oil
2 tablespoons creamy
   peanut butter
½ teaspoon kosher salt
2 green onions, cut into
   2-inch pieces
1 garlic clove, peeled

1. Place all ingredients in a blender; process until smooth. Cover and chill up to 3 days. Serves 6 (serving size: 2½ tablespoons)

CALORIES 197; FAT 18.8g (sat 2.2g, mono 8.6g, poly 5.5g); PROTEIN 1.5g; CARB 7.1g; FIBER 0.5g; CHOL 0mg; IRON 0.2mg; SODIUM 187mg; CALC 10mg

KIDS CAN HELP

Kids can measure the liquids and add them to the blender. They can also squeeze the lime juice, peel the garlic, and snip the onions with a pair of scissors.

There are some foods we all just assume are icky. Take anchovies, for example. Have you ever met a kid who thought they'd like anchovies? Anchovies add a depth of flavor to sauces that is indescribable. So the next time you make pizza or just want to jazz up some pasta, take kids outside their comfort zone and try this sauce.

MY SECRET TOMATO SAUCE

HANDS-ON TIME: 25 MINUTES | TOTAL TIME: 25 MINUTES

2 tablespoons olive oil
4 canned anchovy fillets in oil, drained
3 garlic cloves, minced
½ teaspoon kosher salt
½ teaspoon dried oregano
½ teaspoon freshly ground black pepper
2 (14½-ounce) cans no-salt-added whole tomatoes, undrained and finely chopped

1. Heat a medium saucepan over medium-high heat. Add oil; swirl to coat. Add anchovy fillets and garlic. Cook 2 minutes, pressing anchovy fillets with the back of a spoon until smooth; stir constantly.

2. Stir in salt and remaining ingredients. Bring to a simmer; cook, uncovered, 15 minutes or until you reach the desired consistency, stirring occasionally. Serves 6 (serving size: 2½ tablespoons)

CALORIES 40; **FAT** 2.4g (sat 0.3g, mono 1.7g, poly 0.3g); **PROTEIN** 1g; **CARB** 3.5g; **FIBER** 0.6g; **CHOL** 1mg; **IRON** 0.5mg; **SODIUM** 137mg; **CALC** 16mg

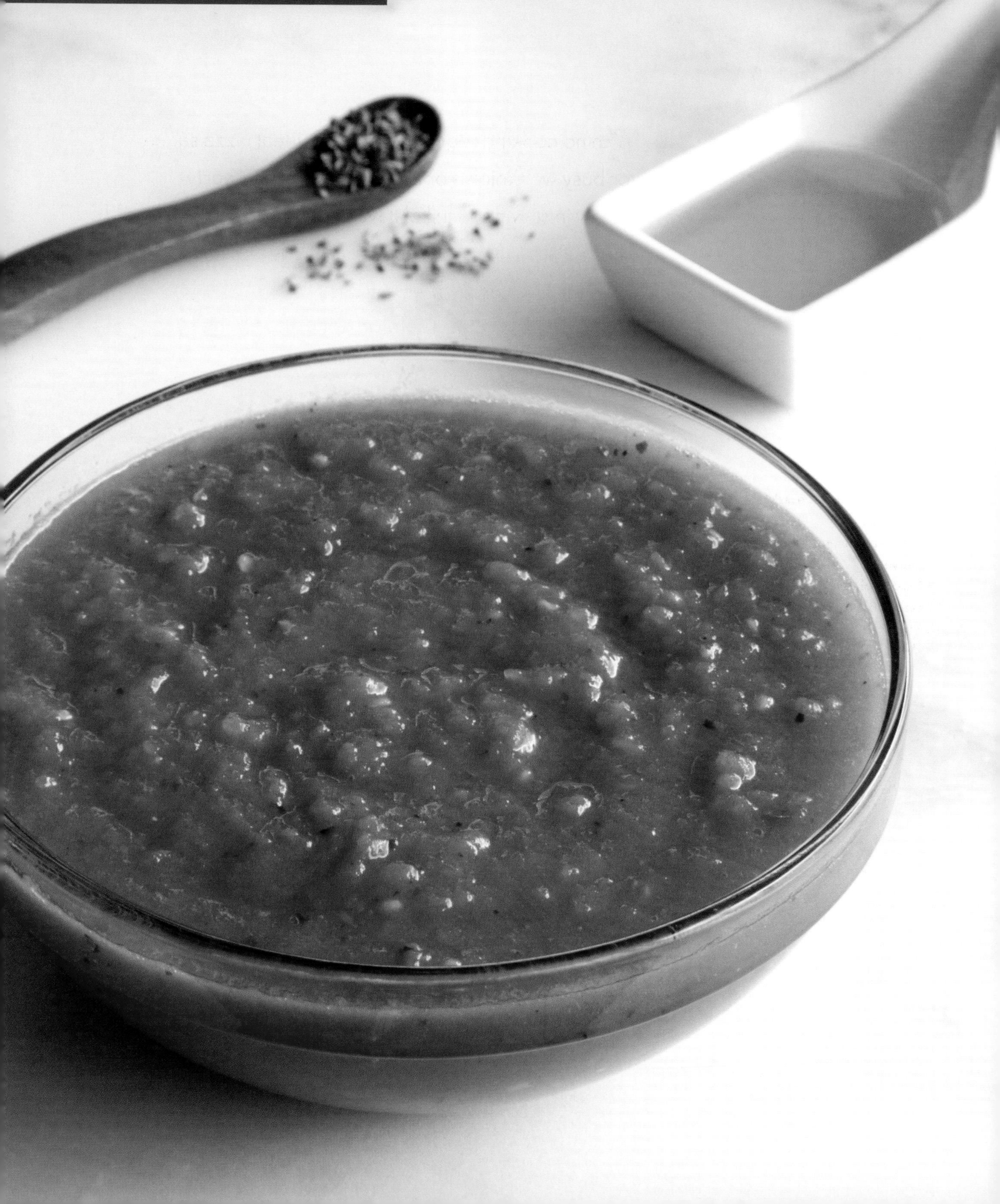

With no cooking required, this is the ideal pizza sauce for busy weeknights or an impromptu pizza party. It's low in sugar and full of flavor, and even the pickiest eaters will eat it. Freeze ½-cup portions in freezer-safe containers for up to three months.

PIZZA SAUCE

HANDS-ON TIME: 5 MINUTES | TOTAL TIME: 5 MINUTES

1 (28-ounce) can diced tomatoes, drained
2 tablespoons extra-virgin olive oil
1 teaspoon dried oregano
1 teaspoon kosher salt
½ teaspoon freshly ground black pepper

1. Place all ingredients in a blender or food processor; process until you reach the desired consistency. Serves 16 (serving size: 2 tablespoons)

CALORIES 24; FAT 1.8g (sat 0.3g, mono 1.4g, poly 0.2g); PROTEIN 0.3g; CARB 1.7g; FIBER 0.3g; CHOL 0mg; IRON 0.2mg; SODIUM 199mg; CALC 7mg

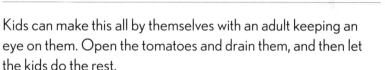

Kids can make this all by themselves with an adult keeping an eye on them. Open the tomatoes and drain them, and then let the kids do the rest.

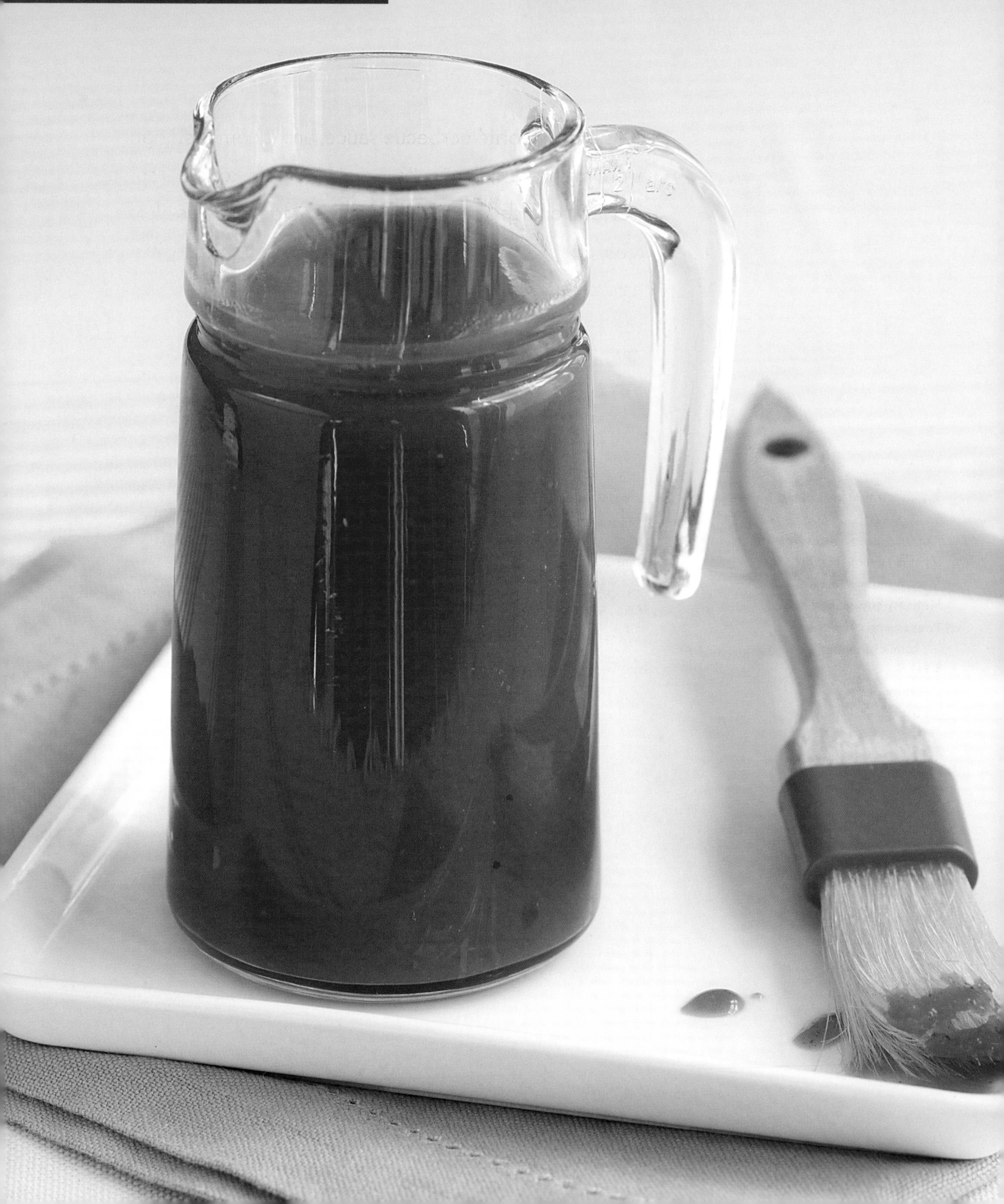

This is my favorite barbecue sauce, and it comes straight from my mom's kitchen. It's sweet with just a touch of spice, perfect for kids and adults. If you want to make this gluten free, check the label on your Worcestershire sauce; it may contain gluten.

BARBECUE SAUCE

HANDS-ON TIME: 2 MINUTES | TOTAL TIME: 30 MINUTES

1 cup organic ketchup
1 cup water
¼ cup packed light brown sugar
¼ cup Worcestershire sauce
¼ cup cider vinegar
¼ teaspoon celery seeds
1 teaspoon chili powder
⅛ teaspoon salt
⅛ teaspoon freshly ground black pepper
⅛ teaspoon hot pepper sauce

1. Combine all ingredients in a small saucepan, stirring with a whisk until smooth. Bring to a boil; reduce heat, and simmer 25 minutes, stirring occasionally. Cool completely. Cover and store in refrigerator up to 2 weeks. Serves 15 (serving size: 2 tablespoons)

CALORIES 40; FAT 0g; PROTEIN 0g; CARB 9.9g; FIBER 0g; CHOL 0mg; IRON 0.3mg; SODIUM 279mg; CALC 9mg

Tip: I have gone a bit crazy trying to get high-fructose corn syrup out of my kids' diet, so I've started buying organic ketchup, which doesn't have any. It's delicious.

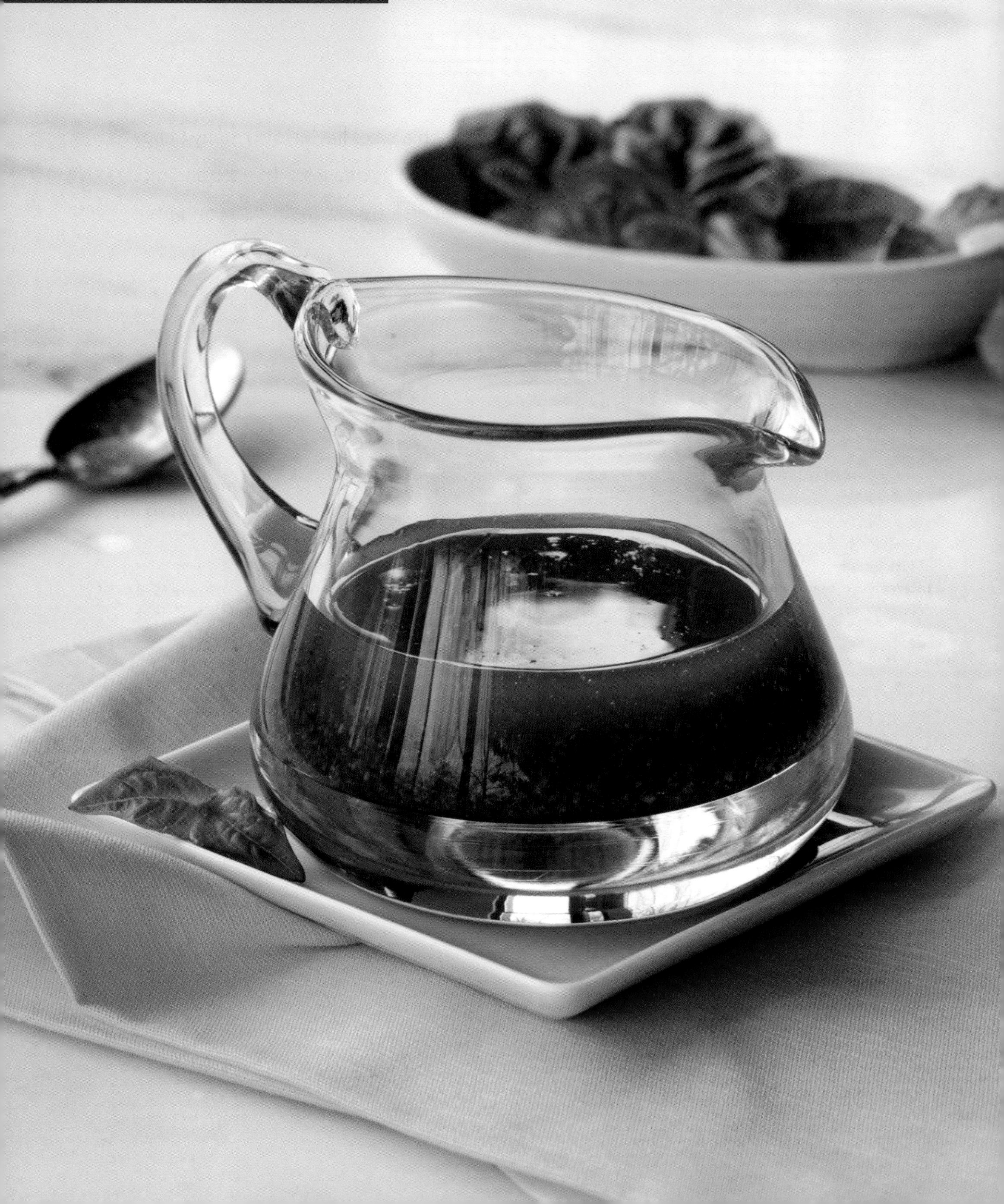

Fresh basil can add such a hit of flavor to so many things: soups, grilled chicken, panini, or a fresh tomato and mozzarella salad. If you've found fragrant, fresh basil, or have grown your own, use it in this oil. Freeze extra oil in ice-cube trays.

BASIL OIL

HANDS-ON TIME: 4 MINUTES | TOTAL TIME: 4 MINUTES

½ cup fresh basil leaves,
  tightly packed
½ cup olive oil
¼ teaspoon kosher salt
⅛ teaspoon freshly ground
  black pepper
1 tablespoon grated fresh
  Parmesan cheese

1. Place first 4 ingredients in a food processor; pulse 5 times or until pureed. Add cheese; process until blended. Serves 24 (serving size: 1 teaspoon)

CALORIES 41; FAT 4.6g (sat 0.7g, mono 3.3g, poly 0.5g); PROTEIN 0.1g; CARB 0g; FIBER 0g; CHOL 0mg; IRON 0.1mg; SODIUM 23mg; CALC 4mg

Tip: People ask all the time how to keep their basil green and fresh. When you buy a bunch of basil, trim the ends and place it in a glass (stems down) with an inch of water at the bottom. Cover the glass with a plastic bag and leave it on your countertop. You won't believe how long it stays green.

Basil is so fragrant. Kids seem drawn to it. Making this recipe is an opportunity to teach them how to pick the leaves off the stems.

"I can't believe I like green pasta!" —Brock, age 6

I've managed to convince more than a few children that pesto rocks. If you'd like to make it a few days ahead, place the pesto in a small container and pour a layer of olive oil over it before refrigerating. The oil acts like a sealant and helps keep the green color of the pesto. Just be sure to scrape off the oil before serving.

FAVORITE PESTO

HANDS-ON TIME: 15 MINUTES | TOTAL TIME: 15 MINUTES

2 garlic cloves, peeled
3 cups fresh basil leaves
2 tablespoons pine nuts, toasted
1 tablespoon fresh lemon juice
1 teaspoon kosher salt
1 teaspoon freshly ground
    black pepper
¼ cup extra-virgin olive oil

1. Place garlic in food processor; process until minced. Add basil and next 4 ingredients (through pepper). With processor on, slowly pour oil through food chute; process until smooth, scraping sides. Serves 9 (serving size: 1 tablespoon)

CALORIES 74; **FAT** 7.6g (sat 1g, mono 5.2g, poly 1.3g); **PROTEIN** 0.8g; **CARB** 1.1g; **FIBER** 0.4g; **CHOL** 0mg; **IRON** 0.6mg; **SODIUM** 214mg; **CALC** 28mg

Tip: If you don't have pine nuts, you can substitute other nuts such as unsalted and toasted walnuts or cashews. All nuts add their own unique flavor to pesto.

Hands-down, this is the most requested sauce on my website. I hear from parents everywhere that their kids love it! Most people serve it with Skirt Steak (page 243). It's so versatile. You can spoon it over chicken and fish, or even offer it as a dip for veggies.

CHIMICHURRI SAUCE

HANDS-ON TIME: 5 MINUTES | TOTAL TIME: 5 MINUTES

1 garlic clove, peeled
½ cup fresh parsley leaves
⅓ cup fresh cilantro leaves
⅓ cup fresh mint leaves
2 tablespoons extra-virgin olive oil
1 tablespoon Dijon mustard
1 tablespoon fresh lime juice
1½ teaspoons drained capers
½ teaspoon freshly ground
    black pepper

1. Place garlic in food processor; process until minced. Add parsley, cilantro, and mint; process until coarsely chopped. Add remaining ingredients; process until finely chopped. Serves 6 (serving size: 1 tablespoon)

CALORIES 49; **FAT** 4.7g (sat 0.7g, mono 3.6g, poly 0.4g); **PROTEIN** 0.3g; **CARB** 1.6g; **FIBER** 0.4g; **CHOL** 0mg; **IRON** 0.4mg; **SODIUM** 85mg; **CALC** 13mg

KIDS CAN HELP

Kids can pick the herbs or chop the tops off of them with a safe knife. They can also measure the ingredients for you. With your help, let them pulse the ingredients in a food processor.

Such an easy twist on guacamole, this creamy condiment is my secret weapon on fish tacos and in burritos.

AVOCADO CREMA

HANDS-ON TIME: 8 MINUTES | TOTAL TIME: 8 MINUTES

1 garlic clove, peeled
2 ripe avocados, halved and pitted
½ cup reduced-fat sour cream
1½ tablespoons fresh lime juice
½ teaspoon ground cumin
½ teaspoon kosher salt

1. Place garlic in food processor; process until minced. Scoop pulp from avocados; add to food processor. Add remaining ingredients; process until smooth. Serves 12 (serving size: about 2 tablespoons)

CALORIES 59; **FAT** 5g (sat 1.2g, mono 0g, poly 0g); **PROTEIN** 1.3g; **CARB** 3.5g; **FIBER** 0.9g; **CHOL** 5mg; **IRON** 0.3mg; **SODIUM** 86mg; **CALC** 18mg

After you remove the pits from the avocados, kids can help scoop out the flesh with a large spoon.

GUACAMOLE

I'm a purist—I don't like to gunk up my guacamole with a bunch of random ingredients. So here's a super-simple recipe and an upgraded version. Double them, if you want. The simple version is a great place to start kids on avocados. The second option is for the guacamole lovers in your home.

GUACAMOLE

HANDS-ON TIME: 5 MINUTES | TOTAL TIME: 10 MINUTES

2 ripe avocados, halved and pitted
1 tablespoon fresh lime juice
½ teaspoon kosher salt

1. Scoop pulp from avocados; place in a small bowl. Pour juice over avocado. Sprinkle with salt; mash with a fork until almost smooth. Serves 8 (serving size: 2 tablespoons)

CALORIES 63; **FAT** 5.6g (sat 0.6g, mono 0g, poly 0g); **PROTEIN** 1.3g; **CARB** 3.9g; **FIBER** 1.3g; **CHOL** 0mg; **IRON** 0.5mg; **SODIUM** 120mg; **CALC** 0mg

Tip: Place a layer of plastic wrap directly on the surface of the guacamole, and it will keep its green color.

ROASTED CORN AND ONION GUACAMOLE

HANDS-ON TIME: 10 MINUTES | TOTAL TIME: 10 MINUTES

Cooking spray
½ cup fresh corn kernels
    (about 1 ear)
Guacamole (recipe above)
1 tablespoon minced
    red onion
2 teaspoons chopped
    fresh cilantro
¼ teaspoon freshly ground
    black pepper

1. Heat a large skillet over medium-high heat. Coat pan with cooking spray. Add corn kernels to pan; sauté 3 minutes or until corn begins to brown. Remove from pan; cool 2 minutes. Place Guacamole in a medium bowl; stir in corn, onion, cilantro, and pepper. Serves 8 (serving size: about 3 tablespoons)

CALORIES 72; **FAT** 5.7g (sat 0.6g, mono 0g, poly 0.1g); **PROTEIN** 1.6g; **CARB** 5.9g; **FIBER** 1.6g; **CHOL** 0mg; **IRON** 0.5mg; **SODIUM** 122mg; **CALC** 1mg

This is one of those recipes that only takes 15 minutes to make and tastes a million times better than anything from a jar. If you don't have the time to dice the tomatoes, you can pulse them a few times in a food processor. The salsa won't look as pretty, but it will taste just as fabulous.

FRESH SALSA

HANDS-ON TIME: 15 MINUTES | TOTAL TIME: 15 MINUTES

3 cups diced seeded tomato
1 cup diced onion
**¹/₃ cup diced seeded jalapeño pepper
   (1 large)**
¹/₄ cup chopped fresh cilantro
2 tablespoons fresh lime juice
¹/₂ teaspoon kosher salt

1. Combine all ingredients in a medium bowl. Cover and chill until ready to serve. Serves 13 (serving size: ¹/₄ cup)

CALORIES 13; **FAT** 0.1g; **PROTEIN** 0.5g; **CARB** 3g; **FIBER** 0.8g; **CHOL** 0mg; **IRON** 0.2mg; **SODIUM** 76mg; **CALC** 7mg

Tip: Adults should dice the jalapeños and onions in this recipe to avoid teary-eyed kids.

Think your kids won't eat fish? Try grilling salmon or halibut and topping it with this delicious salsa.

You'll enjoy this pineapple salsa for extra kick on tacos. When you can find a fragrant, ripe mango, throw that in as well—it's a refreshing combination. Kids will love topping foods such as tacos and grilled chicken with this gorgeous mix.

PINEAPPLE SALSA

HANDS-ON TIME: 14 MINUTES | TOTAL TIME: 14 MINUTES

3 cups finely diced fresh pineapple
½ cup finely diced red bell pepper
¼ cup chopped fresh cilantro
¼ cup finely diced red onion
3 tablespoons fresh lime juice
⅛ teaspoon kosher salt
2 tablespoons finely diced
   seeded jalapeño pepper
   (optional)

1. Combine first 6 ingredients in a bowl. Stir in jalapeño, if desired. Serves 16 (serving size: ¼ cup)

CALORIES 19; **FAT** 0.1g; **PROTEIN** 0.3g; **CARB** 4.9g; **FIBER** 0.6g; **CHOL** 0mg; **IRON** 0.1mg; **SODIUM** 16mg; **CALC** 5mg

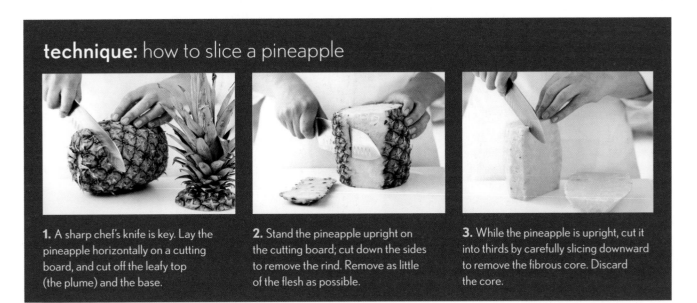

technique: how to slice a pineapple

1. A sharp chef's knife is key. Lay the pineapple horizontally on a cutting board, and cut off the leafy top (the plume) and the base.

2. Stand the pineapple upright on the cutting board; cut down the sides to remove the rind. Remove as little of the flesh as possible.

3. While the pineapple is upright, cut it into thirds by carefully slicing downward to remove the fibrous core. Discard the core.

Store-bought pizza dough is perfect in a pinch, but sometimes there's nothing like homemade. If you make this once, you'll make it again and again.

PIZZA DOUGH

HANDS-ON TIME: 10 MINUTES | TOTAL TIME: 1 HOUR AND 5 MINUTES

**1 package dry yeast
(about 2¹⁄₄ teaspoons)
¹⁄₂ teaspoon sugar
2 cups warm water (100° to 110°),
divided
23.63 ounces all-purpose flour
(about 5¹⁄₄ cups), divided
1 tablespoon extra-virgin olive oil
¹⁄₂ teaspoon kosher salt
Cooking spray**

1. Dissolve yeast and sugar in ¹⁄₂ cup warm water in a large bowl; let stand 5 minutes, or until bubbly.
2. Weigh or lightly spoon flour into dry measuring cups; level with a knife. Stir remaining 1¹⁄₂ cups water into yeast mixture. Add 21.38 ounces (about 4³⁄₄ cups) flour, oil, and salt; beat with a mixer at medium speed until smooth. Turn dough out onto a floured surface. Knead until smooth and elastic (about 5 minutes); add enough of remaining 2.25 ounces (about ¹⁄₂ cup) flour, 1 tablespoon at a time, to prevent dough from sticking to hands (dough will feel sticky).
3. Place dough in a large bowl coated with cooking spray, turning to coat top. Cover and let rise in a warm place (85°), free from drafts, 45 minutes or until doubled in size. (Gently press two fingers into dough. If indentation remains, dough has risen enough.) Punch dough down; cover and let rest 5 minutes.
4. Divide dough into 4 equal portions; shape each portion into a ball. Roll out dough according to recipe directions, or place in a bowl coated with cooking spray; cover and refrigerate up to 2 days. Makes 2 pounds

CALORIES 108; **FAT** 0.9g (sat 0.1g, mono 0.5g, poly 0.2g); **PROTEIN** 3g; **CARB** 21.5g; **FIBER** 0.8g; **CHOL** 0mg; **IRON** 1.3mg; **SODIUM** 41mg; **CALC** 5mg

Tip: For longer storage, coat dough balls with cooking spray; place each in a large heavy-duty zip-top plastic bag. Seal bags tightly and freeze up to 1 month. Thaw dough in bag in refrigerator overnight. Remove dough from bag. Reshape dough into a smooth ball. Place in a bowl coated with cooking spray. Cover and let rise in a warm place (85°), free from drafts, 1 hour or until doubled in size. (Gently press two fingers into dough. If indentation remains, dough has risen enough.) Punch dough down; cover and let rest 5 minutes. Proceed as directed in recipe.

An amazing treat on its own, this has
to be the easiest fancy food trick I know.

These crisps are terrific to float on top of Creamy Tomato Soup (page 185) or Creamy Broccoli Soup (page 187) for an extra kick of flavor.

PARMESAN CRISPS

HANDS-ON TIME: 5 MINUTES | TOTAL TIME: 33 MINUTES

2 ounces grated fresh Parmesan cheese (about ½ cup)
¼ teaspoon freshly ground black pepper

1. Preheat oven to 400°.
2. Line a large baking sheet with parchment paper. Spoon cheese by tablespoonfuls 2 inches apart on prepared baking sheet. Spread each mound to a 2-inch diameter. Sprinkle mounds with pepper. Bake at 400° for 6 to 8 minutes or until crisp and golden. Cool completely on baking sheet. Remove from baking sheet using a thin spatula.
Serves 11 (serving size: 1 crisp)

CALORIES 31; **FAT** 2g (sat 1.2g, mono 0.6g, poly 0.1g); **PROTEIN** 3g; **CARB** 0.3g; **FIBER** 0g; **CHOL** 6mg; **IRON** 0.1mg; **SODIUM** 108mg; **CALC** 78mg

Let kids sprinkle the grated cheese onto the baking sheets.

Here's a scrumptious way to dress up any simple dessert, such as ice cream, berries, or Banana Split Sundaes (page 273).

DARK CHOCOLATE SAUCE

HANDS-ON TIME: 4 MINUTES | TOTAL TIME: 4 MINUTES

½ cup sugar
⅓ cup unsweetened dark cocoa
¼ teaspoon ground cinnamon
1 cup fat-free milk
2 ounces dark chocolate, chopped
1 teaspoon vanilla extract

1. Combine first 3 ingredients in a small saucepan; stir with a whisk until blended. Add milk, stirring with a whisk until blended. Bring to a boil; reduce heat, and simmer, stirring constantly, 1 to 2 minutes or until sugar dissolves.
2. Remove from heat. Add chocolate and vanilla, stirring until sauce is smooth. Serve warm or at room temperature. Serves 12 (serving size: 2 tablespoons)

CALORIES 67; FAT 1.6g (sat 0.9g, mono 0g, poly 0g); PROTEIN 1.4g; CARB 13.9g; FIBER 0.3g; CHOL 1mg; IRON 0.2mg; SODIUM 40mg; CALC 26mg

BREAKFAST & LUNCH

My son Connor had an amazing after-school teacher when he was in kindergarten. On top of keeping 50 kindergartners entertained for hours on end, she cooked with them regularly (Can you imagine?). With this recipe, Mrs. Inada managed to sneak in some whole-wheat flour as well, pleasing both parents and kids. The recipe makes two dozen muffins, so I freeze half of them and then microwave them for 20 to 30 seconds.

PUMPKIN MUFFINS

HANDS-ON TIME: 12 MINUTES | TOTAL TIME: 38 MINUTES

7.1 ounces whole-wheat flour (about 1½ cups)
4.5 ounces all-purpose flour (about 1 cup)
1¼ teaspoons ground cinnamon
1⅛ teaspoons ground nutmeg
¾ teaspoon ground cloves
½ teaspoon ground ginger
1½ teaspoons baking soda
1¼ teaspoons kosher salt
1½ cups sugar
⅔ cup canola oil
½ cup water
3 large eggs
1 (15-ounce) can pumpkin

1. Preheat oven to 350°.
2. Place 24 paper muffin cup liners in muffin cups. Weigh or lightly spoon flours into dry measuring cups; level with a knife. Combine flours, cinnamon, and next 5 ingredients (through salt) in a medium bowl, stirring with a whisk. Make a well in center of mixture. Combine sugar and next 3 ingredients (through eggs), stirring with a whisk. Stir in canned pumpkin; add to flour mixture, stirring just until moist. Divide batter evenly among prepared muffin cups.
3. Bake at 350° for 25 minutes or until a wooden pick inserted in center comes out clean. Serves 24 (serving size: 1 muffin)

CALORIES 168; **FAT** 7.2g (sat 0.7g, mono 4.2g, poly 1.9g); **PROTEIN** 2.8g; **CARB** 24.4g; **FIBER** 2g; **CHOL** 26mg; **IRON** 1mg; **SODIUM** 189mg; **CALC** 12mg

Pumpkin Bread: Spoon batter into 2 (9 x 5–inch) or 4 (5 x 3–inch) loaf pans coated with cooking spray. Bake large loaves at 350° for 1 hour; bake small loaves at 350° for 25 minutes. Loaves are done when a wooden pick inserted in center comes out clean. Cut each large loaf into 12 slices; each small loaf into 6 slices. Serves 24 (serving size: 1 slice)

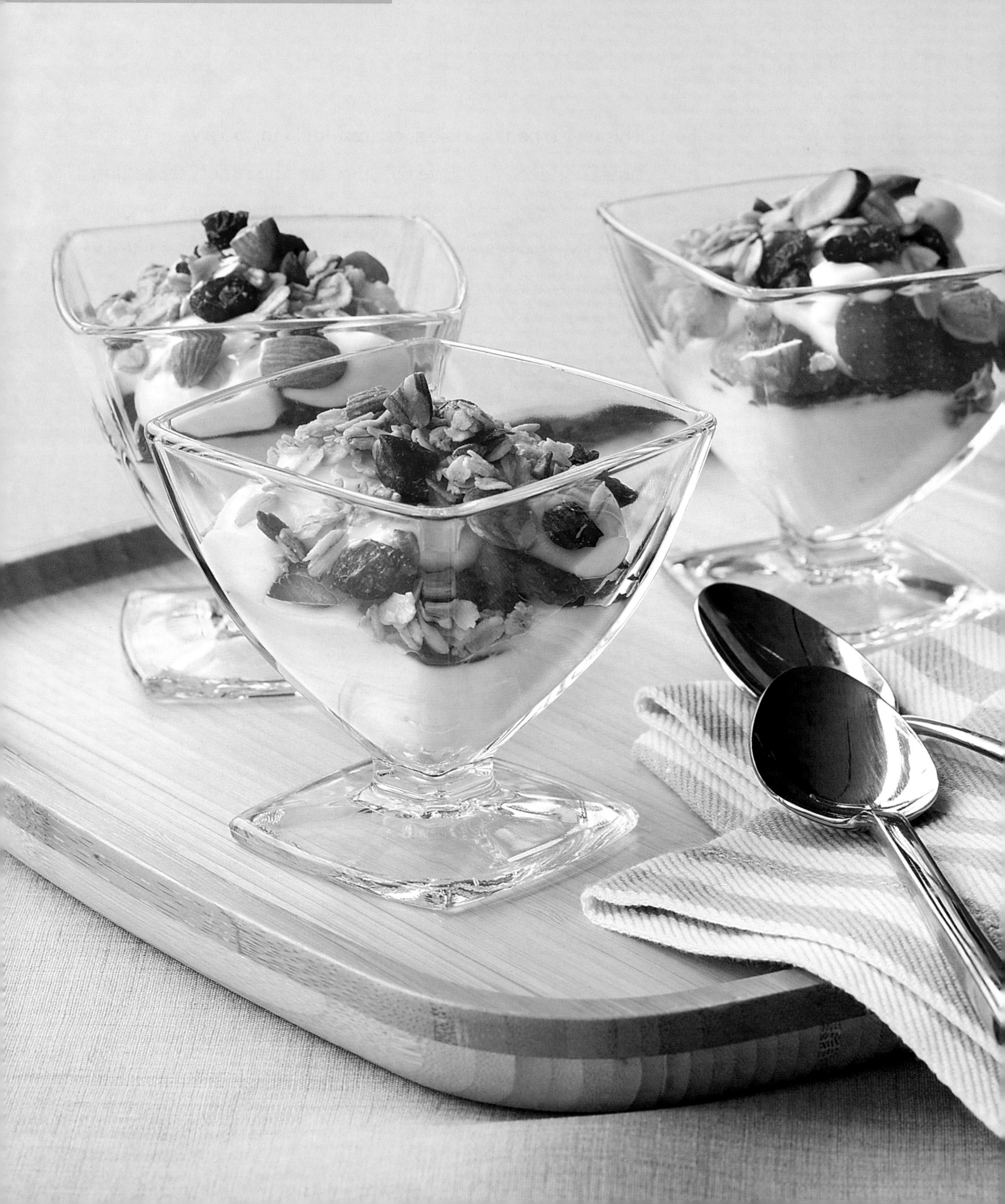

This has to be the easiest, coolest-looking, most well-rounded breakfast ever. Kids love the color and the variety of textures. Plus, they can make their own, which always helps them buy in! I suggest using Crunchy Maple Granola (page 63), but store-bought granola is a nice alternative, too.

YOGURT SUNDAES

HANDS-ON TIME: 7 MINUTES | TOTAL TIME: 7 MINUTES

2 cups vanilla fat-free yogurt
1 cup blueberries, raspberries,
    or sliced strawberries
¼ cup Crunchy Maple Granola
    (page 63)

1. Spoon ¼ cup yogurt into each of 4 parfait glasses. Top each with ¼ cup berries, ¼ cup yogurt, and 1 tablespoon Crunchy Maple Granola. Serves 4 (serving size: 1 sundae)

CALORIES 159; **FAT** 2.1g (sat 0.5g, mono 0.9g, poly 0.5g); **PROTEIN** 7.2g; **CARB** 27.2g; **FIBER** 1.5g; **CHOL** 4mg; **IRON** 0.4mg; **SODIUM** 91mg; **CALC** 238mg

KIDS CAN HELP

Set out the granola, yogurt, and berries so kids can make their own breakfast. I like to use measuring cups for scooping the granola and fruit so they learn how to serve themselves a portion.

French toast doesn't have to be a junky breakfast. In fact, with the protein from the eggs and some fresh strawberries, it can be an energizing start to the day. Serve a small amount of syrup on the side if you want to control how much sugar your kids are getting. They'll love dipping the "soldiers" into the syrup. You can also make this a gluten-free breakfast by choosing the right bread. I've used Udi's bread with great results.

FRENCH TOAST SOLDIERS

HANDS-ON TIME: 10 MINUTES | TOTAL TIME: 18 MINUTES

1 teaspoon vanilla extract
½ teaspoon ground cinnamon
⅛ teaspoon kosher salt
3 large eggs
1 cup 2% reduced-fat milk
6 (1.35-ounce) slices Italian bread,
    halved lengthwise
Cooking spray
¼ cup maple syrup
1 cup hulled strawberries
1 tablespoon powdered sugar
    (optional)

1. Preheat oven to 250°. Place a baking sheet in oven.
2. Combine first 4 ingredients in a medium bowl, stirring with a whisk. Add milk; whisk until well blended. Working in batches, dip bread strips in milk mixture, turning gently to coat both sides.
3. Heat a large skillet over medium-high heat. Coat pan with cooking spray. Add 6 coated bread strips to pan; sauté 1 to 2 minutes on each side or until lightly browned. Place on preheated pan in oven to keep warm. Repeat procedure with cooking spray and remaining bread strips.
4. Place syrup and strawberries in a food processor; process until smooth. Serve with French toast strips. Sprinkle each serving with powdered sugar, if desired. Serves 6 (serving size: 2 strips and 2 tablespoons syrup)

CALORIES 207; FAT 3.8g (sat 1.4g, mono 1.2g, poly 0.7g); PROTEIN 8.7g; CARB 34.5g; FIBER 1.5g; CHOL 100mg; IRON 2.1g; SODIUM 337mg; CALC 86mg

I used to make Mexican Breakfast Burritos (page 71) or poached eggs almost every morning—until I went to New York several times last year for work. Every time I go, I stay at the W Union Square hotel, where my friend Todd's restaurant, Olives, is in the lobby. I'm such a creature of habit—I quickly got hooked on the asparagus-and-ham frittata. I skip the ham and substitute spinach for the asparagus when I'm at home, but you can get creative with your combos. This frittata easily feeds all four of us.

SPINACH, ONION, AND SWISS FRITTATA

HANDS-ON TIME: 8 MINUTES | TOTAL TIME: 32 MINUTES

2 teaspoons canola oil
2 cups vertically sliced onion
4 cups baby spinach leaves
8 large eggs, lightly beaten
¼ teaspoon salt
¼ teaspoon freshly ground
   black pepper
3 ounces shredded Swiss cheese
   (about ¾ cup)

1. Preheat oven to 400°.
2. Heat a 10-inch ovenproof skillet over medium heat. Add oil; swirl to coat. Add onion; sauté 10 minutes or until tender. Add spinach; cook 2 minutes, stirring just until spinach wilts.
3. Combine eggs, salt, and pepper. Pour egg mixture over vegetables in pan; cook until edges begin to set, about 2 minutes. Gently lift edge of egg mixture, tilting pan to allow uncooked egg mixture to come in contact with pan. Cook 2 minutes or until egg mixture is almost set. Sprinkle with cheese.
4. Bake at 400° for 8 minutes or until center is set. Transfer frittata to a serving platter immediately; cut into 6 wedges. Serves 6 (serving size: 1 wedge)

CALORIES 185; FAT 12.2g (sat 4.8g, mono 3.9g, poly 2g); PROTEIN 13g; CARB 6.6g; FIBER 1.4g; CHOL 295mg; IRON 1.9mg; SODIUM 246mg; CALC 168mg

"These are my favorite because my mom lets me choose what to put in mine." —Jack, age 8

Inken Chrisman, my right-hand woman, came up with this idea. These cute little crustless quiches are ideal for families on the go. Whip up a batch (or two) on Sunday evening, and you have an easy go-to breakfast for busy weekday mornings. They're also quite versatile—this version features spinach and mozzarella, but cooked broccoli and cheddar or crispy bacon are yummy substitutes or additions. They freeze well, too.

BREAKFAST QUICHE BITES

HANDS-ON TIME: 14 MINUTES | TOTAL TIME: 34 MINUTES

Cooking spray
1 tablespoon olive oil
¼ cup diced onion
1 cup baby spinach leaves, coarsely chopped
2 ounces shredded part-skim mozzarella cheese (about ½ cup)
¼ cup 2% reduced-fat milk
½ teaspoon kosher salt
¼ teaspoon freshly ground black pepper
4 large eggs

1. Preheat oven to 350°.
2. Coat 6 muffin cups with cooking spray. Heat a medium nonstick skillet over medium-high heat. Add oil; swirl to coat. Add onion; sauté 3 minutes or until almost tender. Add spinach; sauté 2 minutes or just until spinach begins to wilt, stirring constantly. Transfer spinach mixture to a small bowl; cool 3 minutes. Stir in cheese.
3. Combine milk and remaining ingredients, stirring with a whisk until blended. Stir in cheese mixture. Divide mixture evenly among prepared muffin cups. Bake at 350° for 20 minutes or until puffed and set. (Quiches will deflate slightly as they cool.) Serve warm. Serves 6 (serving size: 1 quiche)

CALORIES 108; FAT 8g (sat 2.7g, mono 3.5g, poly 0.8g); PROTEIN 7.2g; CARB 2.2g; FIBER 0.3g; CHOL 147mg; IRON 0.8mg; SODIUM 268mg; CALC 103mg

When I was nine, my mom took us to France on an exchange program. I fell in love with the food. I lived on quiche Lorraine, chocolate croissants, and chocolate mousse. A year ago, I got a wild hair and tried to re-create the quiche. I got it right on the first try. It was fluffy, salty, cheesy, and took me right back to that first trip to France. I even used a gluten-free pie shell with outstanding results. Serve this for breakfast or for brunch with a mixed greens salad.

QUICHE LORRAINE

HANDS-ON TIME: 15 MINUTES | TOTAL TIME: 1 HOUR AND 5 MINUTES

1 unbaked frozen 9-inch deep-dish pastry shell
1 teaspoon olive oil
1 cup halved and thinly sliced onion
4 center-cut bacon slices, cooked and crumbled
3 ounces grated Gruyère cheese (about ³⁄₄ cup)
3 large eggs, lightly beaten
3 large egg whites, lightly beaten
1¹⁄₂ cups 2% reduced-fat milk
¹⁄₄ teaspoon ground nutmeg
¹⁄₂ teaspoon salt
¹⁄₄ teaspoon freshly ground black pepper

1. Preheat oven to 375°.
2. Pierce bottom and sides of pastry shell with a fork. Bake at 375° for 15 minutes. Let cool on a wire rack. Increase oven temperature to 450°.
3. Heat a large nonstick skillet over medium-high heat. Add oil; swirl to coat. Add onion; sauté 8 minutes or until tender, stirring occasionally. Remove from pan; let cool.
4. Sprinkle onion, bacon, and cheese into pastry shell. Combine eggs and egg whites in a bowl, beating with a whisk. Add milk and remaining ingredients, beating with a whisk.
5. Pour milk mixture over cheese mixture in pastry shell. Place quiche on a baking sheet. Bake at 450° for 10 minutes. Reduce oven temperature to 350°. Bake at 350° for 40 minutes, shielding edges after 15 minutes, if necessary, to prevent excess browning. Let cool on wire rack 15 minutes. Cut into wedges, and serve immediately. Serves 6 (serving size: 1 wedge)

CALORIES 292; FAT 17.3g (sat 7.1g, mono 6.8g, poly 1.6g); PROTEIN 14.4g; CARB 20g; FIBER 1.2g; CHOL 130mg; IRON 1.3mg; SODIUM 510mg; CALC 239mg

Think of this granola as a topping rather than a cereal. Instead of getting your kids all hopped-up on a full bowl (it's loaded with delicious maple syrup), sprinkle it over yogurt with fresh blueberries or raspberries on top. You'll still get the wonderful taste of the granola and the health benefits of the oats without too much sugar. If you're gluten intolerant, just look for gluten-free oats. Bob's Red Mill sells them in large bags at many grocers. The granola keeps well in an airtight container for up to two weeks.

CRUNCHY MAPLE GRANOLA

HANDS-ON TIME: 13 MINUTES | TOTAL TIME: 39 MINUTES

3 cups old-fashioned rolled oats
1 cup whole natural almonds,
    coarsely chopped
Cooking spray
¼ cup unsalted butter
¼ cup maple syrup
½ cup sweetened dried cranberries
¼ cup sunflower seed kernels

1. Preheat oven to 350°.
2. Place oats and almonds in a 13 x 9-inch metal baking pan coated with cooking spray. Combine butter and syrup in a small saucepan over low heat; cook 5 minutes or until butter melts, stirring to combine. Pour butter mixture over oat mixture; toss to coat.
3. Bake at 350° for 10 minutes; stir. Bake an additional 10 minutes. Add cranberries; bake an additional 6 minutes or until golden brown. Cool completely in pan. Stir in sunflower seed kernels. Transfer granola to an airtight container. Store up to two weeks. Serves 19 (serving size: ¼ cup)

CALORIES 143; **FAT** 8.1g (sat 2.1g, mono 3.6g, poly 1.8g); **PROTEIN** 3.6g; **CARB** 16g; **FIBER** 2.5g; **CHOL** 6mg; **IRON** 1mg; **SODIUM** 1mg; **CALC** 25mg

Kids love having some control over what they're eating. You just need to make sure you give them smart ingredients to choose from. Any of these are good choices.

BUILD YOUR OWN BAGEL

HANDS-ON TIME: 4 MINUTES PER VARIATION | TOTAL TIME: 15 MINUTES

2 tablespoons ⅓-less-fat
    cream cheese, softened
1 teaspoon chopped fresh dill
½ teaspoon grated lemon rind
1 (4-ounce) bagel, split and toasted
4 ounces cold-smoked salmon

Cream Cheese and Smoked Salmon Bagel
1. Combine first 3 ingredients in a small bowl. Spread half of cream cheese mixture over cut side of each bagel half; top each half with 2 ounces salmon. Serves 2 (serving size: 1 bagel half)

CALORIES 260; FAT 6.5g (sat 1.5g, mono 0.7g, poly 0.5g); PROTEIN 20g; CARB 29.3g; FIBER 1.3g; CHOL 8mg; IRON 1.8mg; SODIUM 351mg; CALC 67mg

2 tablespoons creamy peanut butter
1 (4-ounce) bagel, split and toasted
2 teaspoons honey
1 tablespoon raisins

Peanut Butter, Honey, and Raisin Bagel
1. Spread 1 tablespoon peanut butter over cut side of each bagel half. Drizzle each half with 1 teaspoon honey, and top with 1½ teaspoons raisins. Serves 2 (serving size: 1 bagel half)

CALORIES 276; FAT 8.9g (sat 1.6g, mono 0.1g, poly 0.4g); PROTEIN 9.7g; CARB 41.4g; FIBER 2.4g; CHOL 0mg; IRON 1.2mg; SODIUM 356mg; CALC 12mg

2 (0.75-ounce) slices reduced-fat
    sharp cheddar cheese
1 (4-ounce) bagel, split and toasted
1 large egg
Dash of salt
Dash of freshly ground black pepper
1 teaspoon butter

Scrambled Egg and Cheese Bagel
1. Place 1 cheese slice on cut side of each bagel half. Combine egg, salt, and pepper in a bowl, stirring with a whisk. Melt butter in a small nonstick skillet over medium heat. Add egg mixture; cook, without stirring, until mixture sets on bottom. Draw a spatula across bottom of pan to form curds. Continue cooking, stirring occasionally, until egg mixture is thickened but still moist. Immediately spoon half of egg over cheese on each bagel half. Serves 2 (serving size: 1 bagel half)

CALORIES 281; FAT 11g (sat 5.5g, mono 2g, poly 1.1g); PROTEIN 14.2g; CARB 29.5g; FIBER 1.2g; CHOL 128mg; IRON 1.1mg; SODIUM 635mg; CALC 184mg

2 tablespoons ⅓-less-fat cream cheese
1 (4-ounce) bagel, split and toasted
2 tomato slices
1 (⅛-inch-thick) red onion slice, halved
½ avocado, peeled and sliced
⅛ teaspoon freshly ground black
    pepper

Cream Cheese, Tomato, Red Onion, and Avocado Bagel
1. Spread 1 tablespoon cream cheese over cut side of each bagel half. Top each half with 1 tomato slice, half of onion slice, and half of avocado slices. Sprinkle evenly with pepper. Serves 2 (serving size: 1 bagel half)

CALORIES 261; FAT 10.5g (sat 2.6g, mono 5.6g, poly 1.4g); PROTEIN 7.9g; CARB 34.9g; FIBER 4.9g; CHOL 8mg; IRON 1.1mg; SODIUM 355mg; CALC 41mg

Have you ever read the nutritional content on a smoothie? It's packed with sugar. Here's one that's better. Put frozen fruit straight into the blender. It acts like ice. Serve with Build Your Own Bagel (page 65) for a filling breakfast.

ICY TROPICAL SMOOTHIES

HANDS-ON TIME: 5 MINUTES | TOTAL TIME: 5 MINUTES

2 cups orange juice
2 cups frozen unsweetened whole organic strawberries
1 cup frozen organic pineapple chunks
1 cup frozen organic mango

1. Place all ingredients in a blender; process until smooth. Serve immediately. Serves 4 (serving size: 1 cup)

CALORIES 137; **FAT** 0.1g (sat 0g, mono 0g, poly 0.1g); **PROTEIN** 0.9g; **CARB** 34.7g; **FIBER** 3.1g; **CHOL** 0mg; **IRON** 0.7mg; **SODIUM** 2mg; **CALC** 17mg

Let your kids measure out the juice and the fruit for you.

Hash browns are delicious, but they're too much work to make at home. Here's an easier method using fingerling potatoes that's equally as good and makes the perfect accompaniment to fried eggs. Your kids might even think the potatoes are better than French fries.

POTATO COINS WITH FRIED EGGS

HANDS-ON TIME: 8 MINUTES | TOTAL TIME: 24 MINUTES

2 tablespoons olive oil, divided
1 pound fingerling potatoes,
    cut into ¼-inch-thick slices
    (3½ cups)
1 cup (¼-inch) vertically sliced onion
¼ teaspoon kosher salt
1 garlic clove, minced
1 tablespoon chopped fresh thyme
1 tablespoon chopped fresh parsley
1 tablespoon chopped fresh rosemary
½ teaspoon freshly ground black
    pepper
4 large eggs

1. Heat a large nonstick skillet over medium-high heat. Add 1 tablespoon oil; swirl to coat. Add potato slices, onion, and salt; sauté 6 minutes, stirring after 3 minutes. Sauté 6 additional minutes or until potato is tender, stirring occasionally, adding garlic during last 1 minute of cooking time. Remove from heat; stir in thyme and next 3 ingredients (through pepper). Remove potato mixture from pan; keep warm. Heat pan over medium-low heat. Add remaining 1 tablespoon oil; swirl to coat. Add eggs to pan; cook 1 minute or until whites are just set around edges. Carefully turn eggs over; cook 1 minute or until whites are set. Serve immediately with potatoes. Serves 4 (serving size: 1 egg and ½ cup potatoes)

CALORIES 236; FAT 11.9g (sat 2.5g, mono 6.9g, poly 1.5g); PROTEIN 9.2g; CARB 24.3g; FIBER 2.2g; CHOL 212mg; IRON 2.2mg; SODIUM 198mg; CALC 56mg

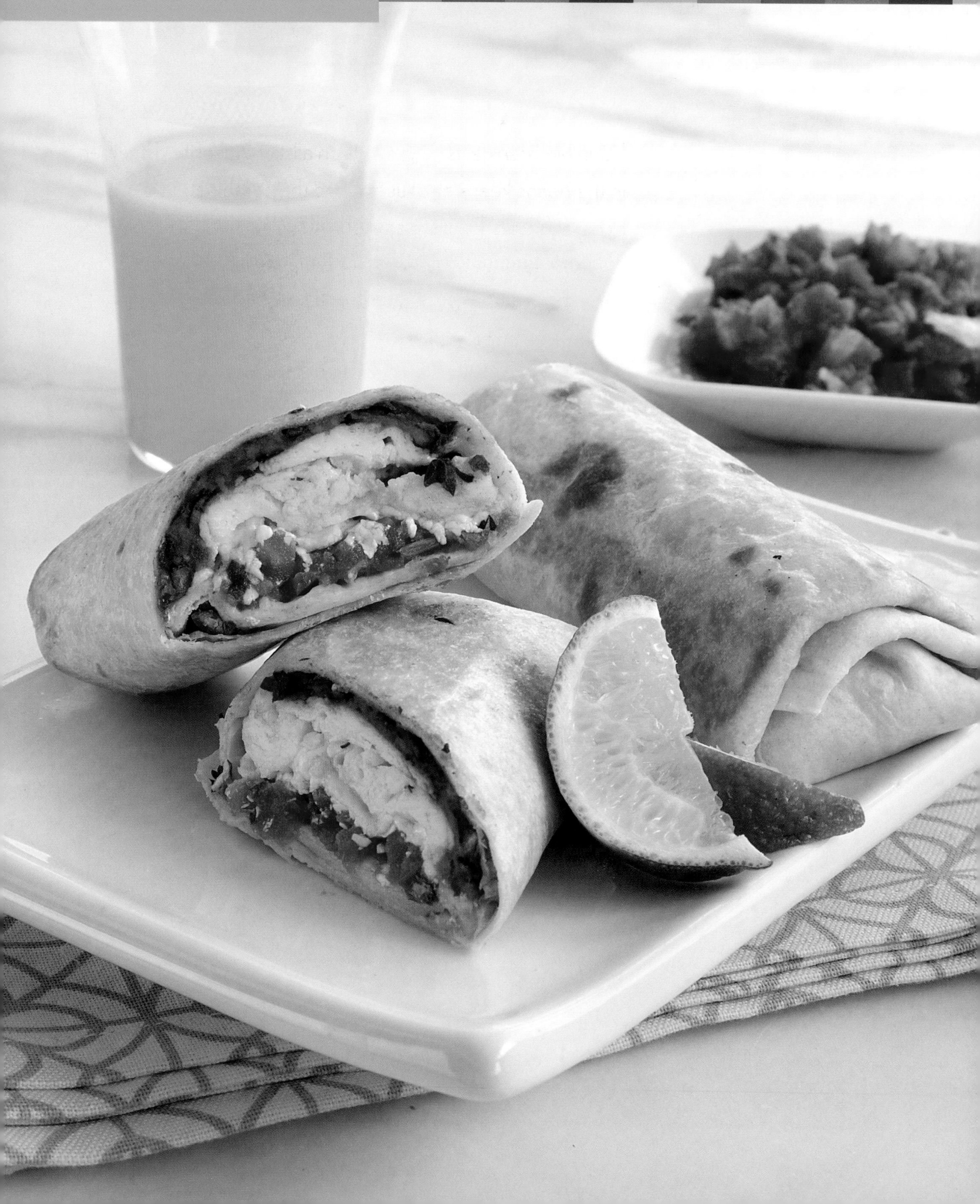

I love big breakfasts. This one is an all-time favorite. The fiber in the beans keeps all of us full, and the combination is out of this world. If you have any leftover pulled pork from the Citrus-Marinated Pork Tacos (page 225), consider adding a little for a weekend treat. For a gluten-free burrito, use gluten-free corn tortillas.

MEXICAN BREAKFAST BURRITOS

HANDS-ON TIME: 17 MINUTES | TOTAL TIME: 17 MINUTES

1 (15-ounce) can no-salt-added
   black beans, drained
2 teaspoons fresh lime juice
Cooking spray
6 large eggs, lightly beaten
8 (8-inch) flour tortillas
1 cup Fresh Salsa (page 41)
2 ounces crumbled Cotija
   cheese (about ½ cup)
Lime wedges (optional)

1. Place beans and lime juice in a small bowl; mash with the back of a spoon until almost smooth.
2. Heat a large skillet over medium-high heat. Coat pan with cooking spray. Add eggs to pan. Cook, without stirring, until mixture sets on bottom. Draw a spatula across bottom of pan to form curds. Continue cooking, stirring occasionally, until egg is thickened but still moist. Remove from pan immediately.
3. Heat skillet over medium heat. Coat pan with cooking spray. Add 1 tortilla to pan. Heat 20 seconds on each side or just until soft. Remove from pan, and keep warm. Repeat procedure with remaining tortillas.
4. Spoon 2 tablespoons bean mixture, 2½ tablespoons egg, 2 tablespoons Fresh Salsa, and 1 tablespoon cheese down center of each tortilla. Roll up. Recoat skillet with cooking spray. Place burritos in pan, and cook over medium heat 4 minutes or until lightly browned, turning occasionally. Garnish with lime wedges, if desired. Serves 8 (serving size: 1 burrito)

CALORIES 243; FAT 9.6g (sat 3.7g, mono 2.1g, poly 0.6g); PROTEIN 11.7g; CARB 25.7g; FIBER 3.4g; CHOL 167mg; IRON 1.3mg; SODIUM 537mg; CALC 100mg

"I didn't know I liked curry until my mom made up this recipe."
–Connor, age 9

I just love it when magic happens in the kitchen! After reading about the potential health benefits of curry powder (when turmeric is combined with black pepper, it becomes an amazing anti-inflammatory agent!), I found myself trying to experiment with it. I came up with this tasty little wrap that we couldn't stop eating. To save time, I use store-bought naan as the base. If you're looking for another great use for curry powder, sprinkle it into a vinaigrette or over chicken salad.

CHICKEN WRAPS WITH MANGO CHUTNEY

HANDS-ON TIME: 30 MINUTES | TOTAL TIME: 30 MINUTES

2 (6-ounce) skinless, boneless chicken breast halves
1 tablespoon curry powder
¼ teaspoon kosher salt
½ teaspoon freshly ground black pepper, divided
1 tablespoon olive oil
½ cup 2% reduced-fat Greek yogurt
¼ cup mango chutney
3 tablespoons sliced green onions
1 (8.8-ounce) package white naan bread
2 cups mixed spring greens

1. Place chicken between 2 sheets of plastic wrap; pound to ½-inch thickness using a meat mallet or small heavy skillet. Cut each chicken breast half in half crosswise.
2. Combine curry powder, salt, and ¼ teaspoon pepper. Sprinkle curry mixture over both sides of chicken. Heat a large nonstick skillet over medium-high heat. Add oil; swirl to coat. Add chicken to pan. Cook 3 minutes on each side or until done. Remove from pan; let stand 5 minutes.
3. While chicken stands, combine yogurt, chutney, green onions, and remaining ¼ teaspoon pepper in a small bowl.
4. Warm naan according to package directions; cut in half crosswise. Cut chicken into ½-inch-thick slices. Spread yogurt mixture evenly over naan halves. Top evenly with greens and chicken; roll up. Serves 4 (serving size: 1 wrap)

CALORIES 405; FAT 10.2g (sat 2.7g, mono 2.8g, poly 0.6g); PROTEIN 27.6g; CARB 47.9g; FIBER 2.4g; CHOL 56mg; IRON 3.2mg; SODIUM 797mg; CALC 40mg

This is a convenient and quick weeknight or weekend meal. Set it up like a salad bar, and let everyone build their own.

TURKEY CLUB WRAPS

HANDS-ON TIME: 21 MINUTES | TOTAL TIME: 21 MINUTES

$\frac{1}{2}$ **ripe avocado, seeded**
1 teaspoon fresh lemon juice
Dash of ground red pepper
1 small garlic clove, minced
2 (2-ounce) low-carb, low-fat sandwich wraps (such as California Lavash)
4 ounces organic lower-sodium deli turkey
4 ($\frac{1}{4}$-inch) slices tomato
$\frac{1}{2}$ **cup thinly vertically sliced red onion**
1 cup shredded romaine lettuce
4 center-cut bacon slices, cooked

1. Scoop pulp from avocado; place in a bowl. Add lemon juice, pepper, and garlic; mash with a fork to desired consistency.

2. Spread avocado mixture evenly over wraps. Layer 2 ounces turkey, 2 tomato slices, $\frac{1}{4}$ cup onion, $\frac{1}{2}$ cup lettuce, and 2 bacon slices on each wrap; roll up. Cut wraps in half. Secure with wooden picks. Serve immediately. Serves 4 (serving size: $\frac{1}{2}$ wrap)

CALORIES 178; **FAT** 7.5g (sat 1.8g, mono 2.5g, poly 0.5g); **PROTEIN** 15.6g; **CARB** 12.5g; **FIBER** 6.4g; **CHOL** 18mg; **IRON** 1.3mg; **SODIUM** 592mg; **CALC** 114mg

Tip: Avocados are loaded with vitamins B6, C, K, and folate, and are also a great source of fiber and potassium. Many kids gravitate toward them, so they're a wonderful food to add to salads, sandwiches, dips, and more.

This little gem of a recipe was born from leftover veggies. It is beautiful, tasty, and nutritious and has quickly become one of my favorite things to make for lunch, dinner, and even breakfast. For a vegetarian option, substitute tofu or edamame for the chicken.

CHICKEN FRIED RICE

HANDS-ON TIME: 20 MINUTES | TOTAL TIME: 30 MINUTES

2 tablespoons dark sesame oil
1 tablespoon canola oil
1 cup chopped carrot
1 cup coarsely chopped broccoli
 florets
1 cup diced skinless, boneless
 rotisserie chicken breast
1 cup frozen petite green peas
2/3 cup sliced green onions
 (4 green onions), divided
2 garlic cloves, minced
1 teaspoon grated peeled fresh ginger
3 cups cooked long-grain brown rice,
 chilled
2 large eggs, lightly beaten
2 tablespoons lower-sodium
 soy sauce
1/2 teaspoon kosher salt
1/4 teaspoon freshly ground
 black pepper

1. Heat a large nonstick skillet over medium-high heat. Add oils; swirl to coat. Add carrot and broccoli; stir-fry 3 minutes or until crisp-tender. Add chicken, peas, 1/2 cup onions, garlic, and ginger. Stir-fry 2 minutes or until onions are tender. Add rice; cook 3 minutes or until thoroughly heated, stirring occasionally. Reduce heat to medium.
2. Push rice mixture to 1 side of pan; add eggs to opposite side of pan. Cook, without stirring, for 10 seconds. Cook, stirring frequently, 2 additional minutes or until eggs are scrambled. Stir in soy sauce, salt, and pepper. Sprinkle with remaining onions. Serve immediately. Serves 4 (serving size: 1 1/2 cups)

CALORIES 407; FAT 15.7g (sat 2.7g, mono 6.8g, poly 5.1g); PROTEIN 21.5g; CARB 45.3g; FIBER 6.4g; CHOL 136mg; IRON 2.6mg; SODIUM 535mg; CALC 77mg

Revolution Foods is a San Francisco Bay Area company that is bringing nutritious lunches to more than 200,000 kids across the country each day. For the cost of a federal lunch reimbursement, chef Amy Klein is finding ways to serve kids whole-grain pastas, black beans, salads, and more. The best news? Kids love her food! A little advice from Klein: "Break the lunchroom routine and be a hero with this easy-to-make variation on a kid classic. Use whole-wheat waffles from the freezer aisle (gluten free, if desired) and real maple syrup. You can skip the added fat of butter, and the cheese is a rich accompaniment to the sweet syrup and the roast turkey slice. This sandwich strikes the perfect balance between sweet and savory!"

WAFFLE TURKEY-AND-CHEESE SAMI

HANDS-ON TIME: 15 MINUTES | TOTAL TIME: 15 MINUTES

2 tablespoons canola mayonnaise
1 tablespoon maple syrup
1½ teaspoons Dijon mustard
8 (1.6-ounce) frozen whole-wheat waffles, toasted
4 (½-ounce) slices Swiss cheese
4 green leaf lettuce leaves
8 ounces lower-sodium organic deli roast turkey slices

1. Combine first 3 ingredients in a small bowl. Spread mayonnaise mixture evenly over 1 side of each waffle. Layer 1 cheese slice, 1 lettuce leaf, and 2 ounces turkey on each of 4 waffles; top with remaining waffles. Serves 4 (serving size: 1 sandwich)

CALORIES 363; **FAT** 16g (sat 3.8g, mono 4.5g, poly 1.9g); **PROTEIN** 21.3g; **CARB** 33.2g; **FIBER** 3.3g; **CHOL** 36mg; **IRON** 4.3mg; **SODIUM** 889mg; **CALC** 224mg

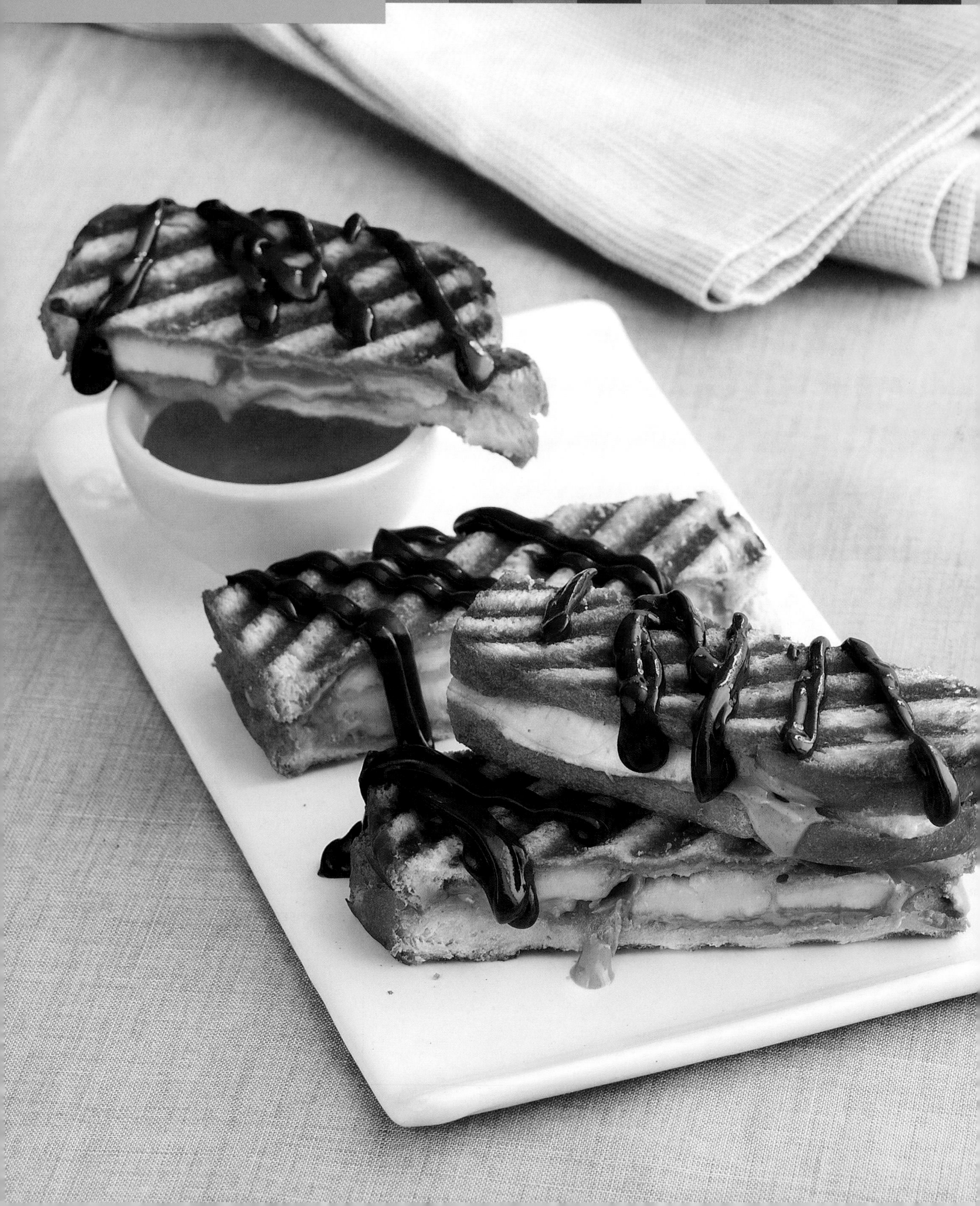

Why do sandwiches taste so good heated? I'm pretty sure my family would eat anything between two slices of bread if it has been grilled. Here's our favorite treat. Make this a complete meal by adding a cup of 1% low-fat milk per serving.

GRILLED PEANUT BUTTER–BANANA FINGERS

HANDS-ON TIME: 5 MINUTES | TOTAL TIME: 6 MINUTES

2 tablespoons creamy peanut butter
4 (0.8-ounce) slices white bread
1 small banana, halved crosswise
Cooking spray
1 tablespoon chocolate syrup
2 tablespoons honey

1. Preheat panini grill.
2. Spread peanut butter evenly over 2 bread slices. Cut each banana half lengthwise into 3 slices. Layer banana slices over peanut butter on bread slices. Top with remaining bread slices.
3. Coat outsides of sandwiches with cooking spray. Place sandwiches on panini grill; cook 1 minute or until golden. Cut each sandwich into 4 sticks. Drizzle sandwich sticks evenly with chocolate syrup. Serve with honey for dipping. Serves 4 (serving size: 2 sandwich sticks and 1½ teaspoons honey)

CALORIES 177; FAT 5.1g (sat 0.9g, mono 0.2g, poly 0.3g); PROTEIN 4.2g; CARB 30.7g; FIBER 1.7g; CHOL 0mg; IRON 1.2mg; SODIUM 196mg; CALC 36mg

Tip: If you don't have a panini grill, use a grill pan or skillet. Add your sandwiches, and then top them with another heavy skillet.

KIDS CAN HELP

Kids can spread the peanut butter on the bread, top it with the bananas, and place the bread on top. They can also drizzle the chocolate.

SNACK TIME & HAPPY HOUR

We love popcorn. The fiber sustains the boys through sports practice. I buy Whole Foods Market popcorn that has no added ingredients. Sprinkled with the cinnamon-sugar mixture on top, it's a yummy treat.

CINNAMON-SUGAR POPCORN

HANDS-ON TIME: 2 MINUTES | TOTAL TIME: 4 MINUTES

10 cups popcorn (popped without salt or fat)
2 tablespoons light brown sugar
1 teaspoon ground cinnamon
⅛ teaspoon salt
2 tablespoons butter, melted
Cooking spray

1. Place popcorn in a large bowl. Combine brown sugar, cinnamon, and salt in a small bowl.
2. Drizzle popcorn with butter; toss to coat. Coat popcorn generously with cooking spray. Sprinkle with sugar mixture; toss well. Serves 10 (serving size: 1 cup)

CALORIES 65; **FAT** 3g (sat 1.5g, mono 0.7g, poly 0.2g); **PROTEIN** 1.1g; **CARB** 9.2g; **FIBER** 1.3g; **CHOL** 6mg; **IRON** 0.3mg; **SODIUM** 47mg; **CALC** 6mg

KIDS CAN HELP

While the popcorn pops, kids can measure the cinnamon-sugar mixture and then toss it with the popcorn and butter.

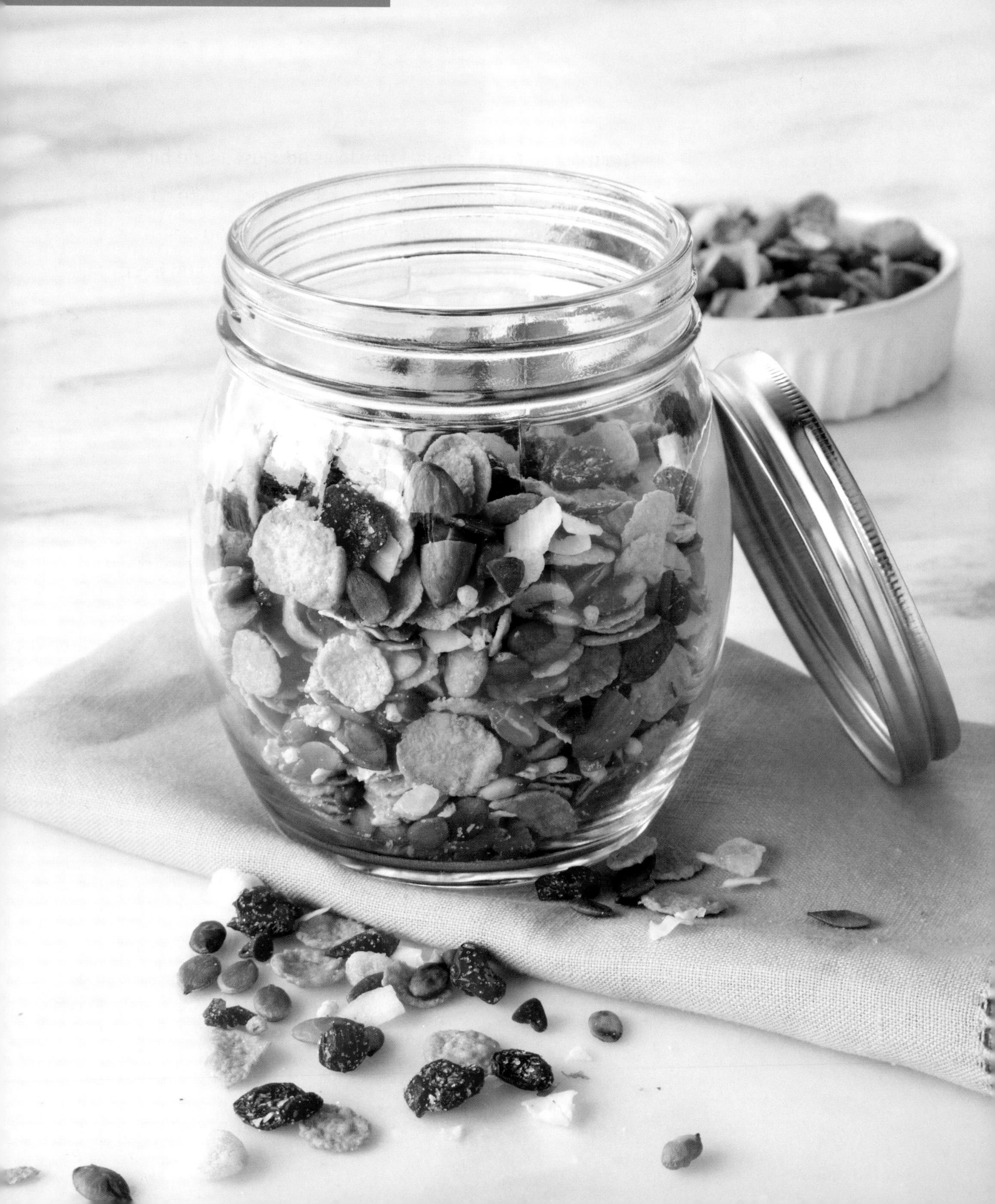

The trick to get kids to eat trail mix—add just a little bit of the sweet stuff to the nutritious stuff so it tastes like a treat! Pumpkinseeds are loaded with magnesium and zinc, and the cranberries are chock-full of vitamin C and fiber.

TRAIL MIX

HANDS-ON TIME: 2 MINUTES | TOTAL TIME: 48 MINUTES

1 cup unsalted pumpkinseed kernels
½ cup whole natural almonds,
coarsely chopped
1 teaspoon olive oil
1 teaspoon sugar
⅛ teaspoon kosher salt
2 cups wheat bran flakes cereal
with raisins and clusters
½ cup sweetened dried cranberries
¼ cup chopped crystallized ginger
¼ cup flaked unsweetened coconut
2 tablespoons semisweet chocolate
minichips

1. Preheat oven to 375°.
2. Place pumpkinseed kernels and almonds on a jelly-roll pan. Drizzle with olive oil. Sprinkle with sugar and salt; toss to coat.
3. Bake at 375° for 10 minutes. Let cool on pan 30 minutes.
4. Transfer pumpkinseed mixture to a large bowl; add cereal and remaining ingredients, tossing well. Serves 15 (serving size: ⅓ cup)

CALORIES 161; **FAT** 9.9g (sat 2.2g, mono 1.8g, poly 0.6g); **PROTEIN** 4.5g; **CARB** 15.4g; **FIBER** 2.9g; **CHOL** 0mg; **IRON** 2mg; **SODIUM** 54mg; **CALC** 30mg

Kids can measure all the ingredients, pour them into the bowl, and toss. Then they can measure individual portions into snack containers so they're ready to go for the week.

One day I was making hummus when I realized I didn't have one of the key ingredients—tahini. So I took a sharp left turn into my pantry and added a few secret ingredients. This is now my go-to party dip for adults and kids. Serve it with Baked Pita Chips (page 95) or fresh veggies like jicama or celery. You can even spread it on a chicken sandwich. Yum!

CREAMY GARBANZO DIP WITH SUN-DRIED TOMATOES

HANDS-ON TIME: 9 MINUTES | TOTAL TIME: 9 MINUTES

1 garlic clove, peeled
¼ cup olive oil
2 tablespoons water
2 tablespoons fresh lemon juice
1 teaspoon paprika
½ teaspoon ground cumin
½ teaspoon ground turmeric
½ teaspoon salt
1 (15-ounce) can chickpeas (garbanzo beans), rinsed and drained
1 tablespoon coarsely chopped sun-dried tomatoes, packed without oil
2 teaspoons chopped fresh flat-leaf parsley

1. Drop garlic through food chute with processor on; process until minced. Add oil and next 7 ingredients (through chickpeas). Process until smooth, scraping sides as necessary. Add tomatoes, and pulse 3 times or until blended and tomatoes are coarsely chopped. Spoon dip into a serving bowl, and sprinkle with parsley. Serves 12 (serving size: 2 tablespoons)

CALORIES 62; **FAT** 4.8g (sat 0.6g, mono 3.3g, poly 0.5g); **PROTEIN** 1.1g; **CARB** 3.9g; **FIBER** 0.9g; **CHOL** 0mg; **IRON** 0.4mg; **SODIUM** 108mg; **CALC** 6mg

For some reason, it seems like every kid I know will eat hummus! And we grown-ups like it, too. It's a quick snack to make before dinner. Throw all the ingredients into a food processor, give it a whirl, and presto—you've bought yourself an hour to make a meal. Healthy dippers include baby carrots, radishes, jicama, and sugar snap peas.

HAPPY-HOUR HUMMUS

HANDS-ON TIME: 5 MINUTES | TOTAL TIME: 5 MINUTES

5 tablespoons water
¼ cup fresh lemon juice
¼ cup tahini (roasted sesame seed paste)
3 tablespoons olive oil
½ teaspoon salt
2 (15-ounce) cans chickpeas (garbanzo beans), rinsed and drained
1 garlic clove, crushed
½ teaspoon paprika (optional)
Fresh chopped flat-leaf parsley (optional)
1 tablespoon pine nuts, toasted (optional)

1. Place first 7 ingredients in a food processor; process until smooth, scraping sides as necessary. Spoon hummus into a bowl. Sprinkle with paprika, parsley, and pine nuts, if desired. Serves 13 (serving size: ¼ cup)

CALORIES 91; FAT 6.1g (sat 0.8g, mono 3.2g, poly 1.4g); PROTEIN 2.6g; CARB 7.4g; FIBER 1.6g; CHOL 0mg; IRON 0.6mg; SODIUM 151mg; CALC 14mg

"These taste like green potato chips!"

—Laney, age 7

These chips are crispy, crunchy, salty, and so easy to make. Opt for them instead of potato chips next time you're craving a salty snack. For a different flavor, try sprinkling the kale with grated Parmesan, red pepper flakes, or sweet paprika before baking.

KALE CHIPS

HANDS-ON TIME: 8 MINUTES | TOTAL TIME: 23 MINUTES

10½ ounces trimmed curly kale, torn into 2-inch pieces (about 14 cups)
1 tablespoon olive oil
¼ teaspoon kosher salt

1. Preheat oven to 350°.
2. Rinse kale; drain well, and pat dry with paper towels. Place in a large bowl. Drizzle with olive oil, and sprinkle with salt. Toss well. Place kale in a single layer on 3 (16 x 13–inch) baking sheets.
3. Bake at 350° for 15 minutes. (Watch closely to prevent leaves from burning.) Cool completely. Store in an airtight container. Serves 4 (serving size: 1 cup)

CALORIES 67; FAT 4g (sat 0.5g, mono 2.5g, poly 0.6g); PROTEIN 2.5g; CARB 7.5g; FIBER 1.5g; CHOL 0mg; IRON 1.3mg; SODIUM 152mg; CALC 101mg

KIDS CAN HELP

Once you've rinsed the kale, kids can help dry it and then drizzle with olive oil and toss to coat.

"My mom always makes me eat dip with my chips. This one is my favorite." —Charlie, age 6

I am constantly trying to find snacks that are filling, free of refined ingredients, and nutritious. Bean dips are full of protein and fiber to help you get through the afternoon. Serve this dip with baked tortilla chips, Baked Pita Chips (page 95), over scrambled eggs with salsa, or on quesadillas for a fun twist.

BLACK BEAN DIP

HANDS-ON TIME: 16 MINUTES | TOTAL TIME: 16 MINUTES

1 tablespoon olive oil
1½ cups diced onion
2 teaspoons chili powder
1 teaspoon ground cumin
2 tablespoons fresh lime juice
1 tablespoon water
1 teaspoon chopped fresh oregano
½ teaspoon chopped chipotle chile, canned in adobo sauce
¼ teaspoon salt
2 (15-ounce) cans black beans, rinsed and drained
2 tablespoons crumbled queso fresco
1 tablespoon minced red onion
Chopped fresh cilantro (optional)
60 corn chips

1. Heat a large nonstick skillet over medium-high heat. Add oil; swirl to coat. Add onion; sauté 5 minutes or until tender, stirring occasionally. Add chili powder and cumin; sauté 1 minute. Place onion mixture, lime juice, and next 5 ingredients (through black beans) in a food processor; process until smooth. Spoon mixture into a serving bowl; top with queso fresco, red onion, and if desired, chopped cilantro. Serve with corn chips. Serves 12 (serving size: ¼ cup dip and 5 chips)

CALORIES 103; FAT 3.3g (sat 0.5g, mono 0.1g, poly 1.2g); PROTEIN 4.2g; CARB 14g; FIBER 3.3g; CHOL 1mg; IRON 1mg; SODIUM 227mg; CALC 39mg

technique: how to prep beans

Canned beans are more convenient than dried beans. For the best results, rinse thoroughly with tap water before using, and drain in a colander. Draining and rinsing canned beans gets rid of the thick liquid in the can and reduces the sodium by 40 percent.

I love doubling or tripling this recipe so I can put the chips in lunchboxes all week long for dipping. Serve them with Creamy Garbanzo Dip with Sun-Dried Tomatoes (page 87), Happy-Hour Hummus (page 89), or Black Bean Dip (page 93).

BAKED PITA CHIPS

HANDS-ON TIME: 7 MINUTES | TOTAL TIME: 34 MINUTES

4 (6-inch) pitas
2 tablespoons olive oil
¼ teaspoon kosher salt
1 teaspoon ground cumin
1 teaspoon ancho chile powder

1. Preheat oven to 350°.
2. Split pitas; cut each into 6 wedges. Place wedges in a large bowl. Drizzle with oil; toss to coat.
3. Combine salt, cumin, and chile powder in a small bowl. Gradually sprinkle spice mixture over wedges, tossing to coat. Spread wedges in a single layer on 2 large baking sheets.
4. Bake at 350° for 12 minutes or until crisp and golden. Let cool completely on pans. Store in an airtight container. Serves 6 (serving size: 8 pita chips)

CALORIES 148; **FAT** 4.6g (sat 0.6g, mono 3.3g, poly 0.5g); **PROTEIN** 4.7g; **CARB** 22.1g; **FIBER** 0.8g; **CHOL** 0mg; **IRON** 1.9mg; **SODIUM** 201mg; **CALC** 29mg

KIDS CAN HELP

Using a plastic knife, kids can cut the pitas with your help. It's OK if the chips don't look perfect. The kids will feel like they're mastering a skill.

I love any food that allows kids to add their own personality, and smoothies are the perfect base for letting them get creative. This is my son Charlie's favorite (I think it's because it's pink!). The yogurt gives it a dose of calcium. Be sure to use frozen fruit—it eliminates the need for ice.

HOT-PINK SMOOTHIES

HANDS-ON TIME: 5 MINUTES | TOTAL TIME: 5 MINUTES

1 cup frozen unsweetened
   raspberries
1 cup frozen unsweetened
   strawberries
1 cup orange juice
$\frac{1}{2}$ cup plain 2% reduced-fat
   Greek yogurt
2 tablespoons agave syrup

1. Place all ingredients in a blender; process until smooth. Serves 2 (serving size: 1¼ cups)

CALORIES 208; FAT 1.2g (sat 0.8g, mono 0g, poly 0g); PROTEIN 6g; CARB 45.9g; FIBER 4g; CHOL 4mg; IRON 1mg; SODIUM 33mg; CALC 67mg

KIDS CAN HELP

To get your kids excited about fruit, let them pick which types to put in these smoothies.

"This tastes
like a milk
shake!"

—Ella, age 11

This classic combination of peanut butter, banana, and chocolate is an easy sell with most kids. Parents will love that these are full of potassium, fiber, and protein.

PEANUT BUTTER, BANANA, AND CHOCOLATE SMOOTHIES

HANDS-ON TIME: 5 MINUTES | TOTAL TIME: 5 MINUTES

1 cup unsweetened almond milk
½ cup vanilla low-fat Greek yogurt
1 tablespoon ground flaxseed
1 tablespoon unsweetened cocoa
2 tablespoons creamy peanut butter
½ teaspoon vanilla extract
2 bananas, broken into pieces
    and frozen
Whipped cream (optional)
Cocoa (optional)

1. Place all ingredients in a blender; process until smooth. Garnish with whipped cream and cocoa, if desired. Serves 3 (serving size: about 1 cup)

CALORIES 209; FAT 8.2g (sat 1.4g, mono 0.2g, poly 0.8g); PROTEIN 7.5g; CARB 30.3g; FIBER 3.8g; CHOL 4mg; IRON 1mg; SODIUM 127mg; CALC 125mg

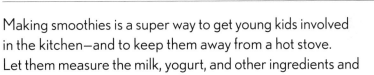

Making smoothies is a super way to get young kids involved in the kitchen—and to keep them away from a hot stove. Let them measure the milk, yogurt, and other ingredients and place them directly into the blender for you.

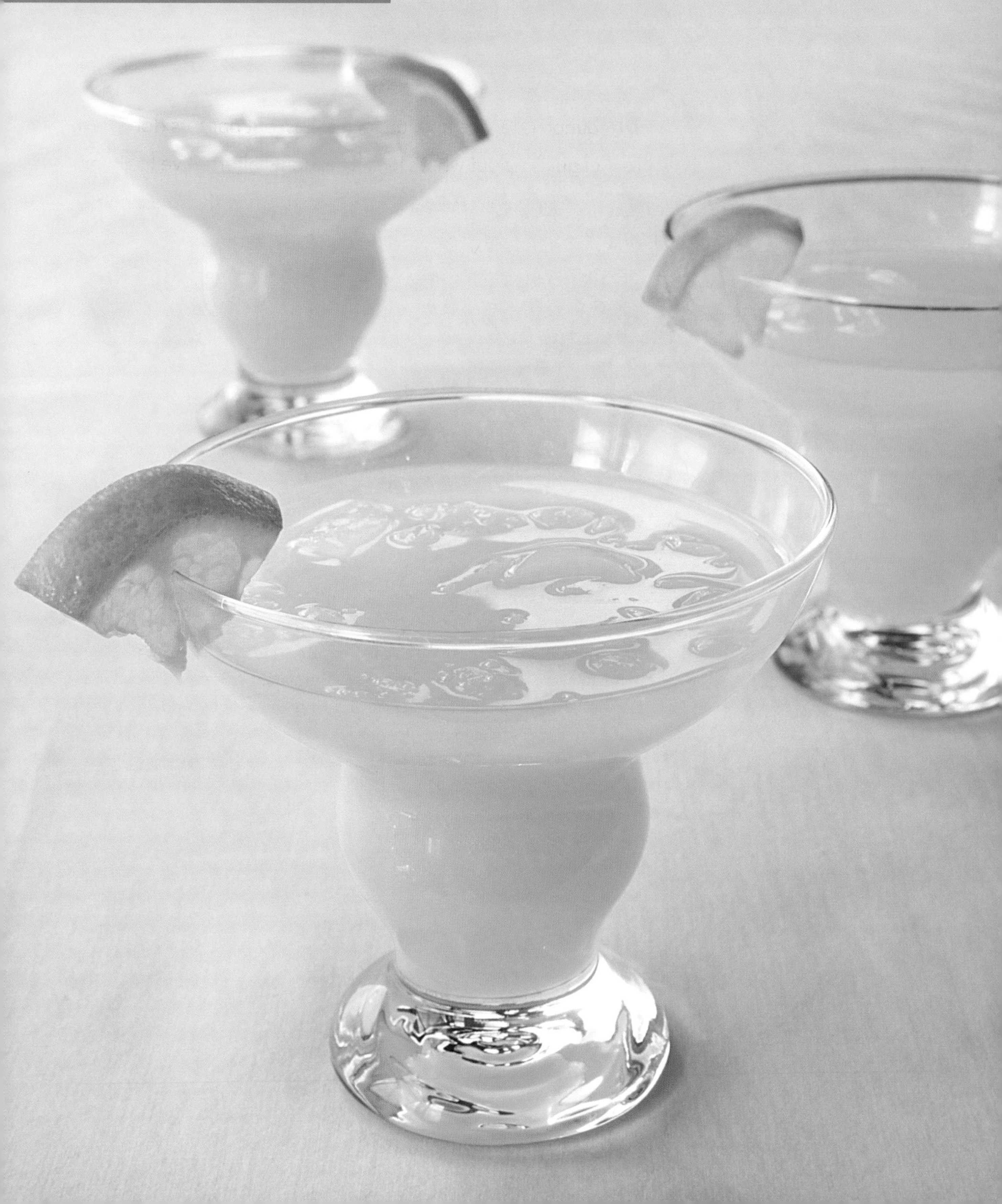

This punch is festive and fun for parties, but parents don't have to feel guilty about what's in it. It's an ideal alternative to other punch recipes. You can also make ice pops with the orange and pineapple juice for a refreshing frozen snack.

TROPICAL FRUIT PUNCH

HANDS-ON TIME: 3 MINUTES | TOTAL TIME: 3 MINUTES

4 cups orange juice, chilled
4 cups pineapple juice, chilled
2 cups club soda, chilled
Ice cubes
10 orange slices (optional)

1. Combine orange juice and pineapple juice in a pitcher. Stir in club soda just before serving. Serve over ice cubes. Garnish each serving with 1 orange slice, if desired. Serves 10 (serving size: 1 cup)

CALORIES 100; **FAT** 0g; **PROTEIN** 0.4g; **CARB** 24g; **FIBER** 0g; **CHOL** 0mg; **IRON** 0.2mg; **SODIUM** 22mg; **CALC** 26mg

KIDS CAN HELP

For extra fun, kids can place cubes of pineapple in an ice-cube tray, and then parents can pour juice over them. Freeze, and then add them to the punch.

"I love when Mrs. Haas makes these drinks. They're my favorite with her tacos." –Bianca, age 5

How often do you go to a child's party where they offer up sugary juice box after juice box? This agua fresca is still yummy and sweet, but has a lot less sugar. Plus, you can control the amount of juice kids are having by pouring servings in 4-ounce cups. The strawberries are so delicious in this drink, but watermelon and pineapple are also good stand-ins. For a real happy hour, stir in some rum for an adult cocktail.

STRAWBERRY-LIME AGUA FRESCA

HANDS-ON TIME: 10 MINUTES | TOTAL TIME: 10 MINUTES

5 cups hulled strawberries, divided
3 cups water, divided
½ cup sugar
⅓ cup fresh lime juice
Lime wedges (optional)
Mint sprigs (optional)
1½ cups rum (optional)

1. Place 2½ cups strawberries and 1½ cups water in a blender; process until smooth. Strain strawberry mixture through a sieve into a pitcher. Repeat procedure with remaining strawberries and water. Add sugar and lime juice to pitcher, stirring until sugar dissolves. Serve with lime wedges, mint, and 2 tablespoons rum per serving (for adults only), if desired. Serves 12 (serving size: ½ cup)

CALORIES 53; **FAT** 0.2g (sat 0g, mono 0g, poly 0.1g); **PROTEIN** 0.4g; **CARB** 13.6g; **FIBER** 1.2g; **CHOL** 0mg; **IRON** 0.3mg; **SODIUM** 3mg; **CALC** 12mg

My friend Denise is an amazing hostess and cook. She always greets us with a cocktail, and these margaritas are a favorite. It's definitely worth taking the time to squeeze the limes. If you microwave them for 20 to 30 seconds beforehand, they will release even more juice.

CLASSIC MARGARITAS

HANDS-ON TIME: 15 MINUTES | TOTAL TIME: 25 MINUTES

1³/₄ cups water
³/₄ cup sugar
1³/₄ cups tequila
1 cup fresh lime juice
(about 5 limes)
¹/₂ cup orange-flavored liqueur
Lime wedges (optional)
Coarse salt (optional)
6 cups crushed ice

1. Combine water and sugar in a small saucepan. Bring to a boil; boil 3 minutes, stirring until sugar dissolves. Remove from heat. Place pan in a large ice-filled bowl until syrup cools to room temperature (about 10 minutes), stirring occasionally.

2. Combine syrup, tequila, lime juice, and liqueur in a pitcher. If desired, rub a lime wedge around rims of 12 margarita glasses, and dip rims in salt. Place ¹/₂ cup crushed ice in each glass. Pour margarita mixture evenly over ice. Garnish with lime wedges, if desired. Serves 12 (serving size: about ¹/₂ cup)

CALORIES 173; **FAT** 0.1g; **PROTEIN** 0.2g; **CARB** 19.7g; **FIBER** 0.1g; **CHOL** 0mg; **IRON** 0.1mg; **SODIUM** 2mg; **CALC** 6mg

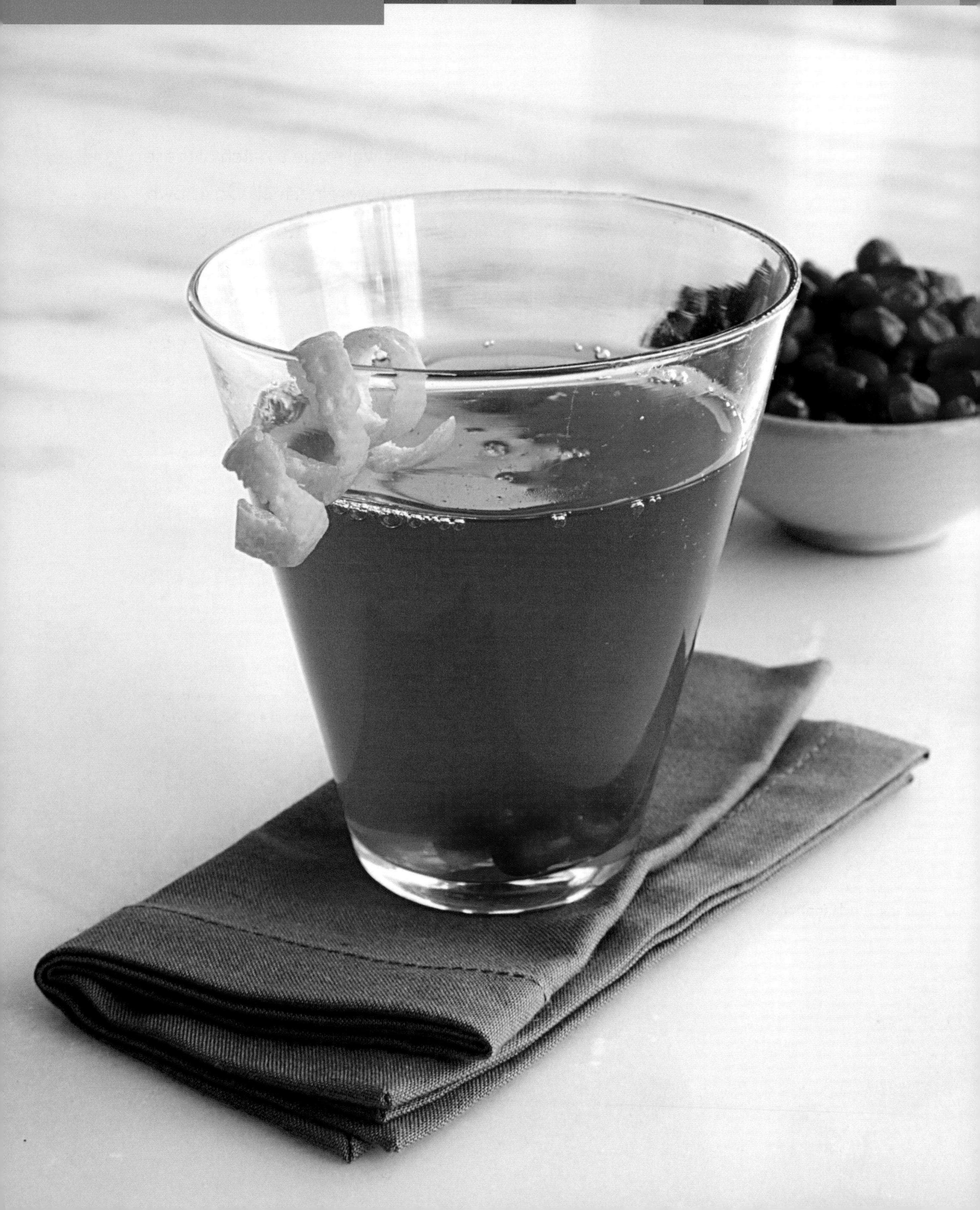

Our dear friends Dave and Val made a batch of these for a holiday party, and they were perfect! On its own, I don't love the taste of pomegranate, but the addition of the cranberry and orange flavors sweetens the taste. If you really want to enjoy your own party, just make a big batch of these, chill it in the fridge, and then pour individual servings into the cocktail shaker when you're ready—so much easier! For extra sparkle, run an orange slice around the rim of each martini glass, and then dip it in superfine sugar. Beautiful!

POMEGRANATE-ORANGE MARTINIS

HANDS-ON TIME: 5 MINUTES | TOTAL TIME: 5 MINUTES

6 tablespoons pomegranate juice, divided

6 tablespoons cranberry juice cocktail, divided

2 tablespoons orange-flavored liqueur, divided

¼ cup raspberry-flavored or plain vodka, divided

Crushed ice

Pomegranate seeds (optional)

Orange curls (optional)

1. Combine 3 tablespoons pomegranate juice, 3 tablespoons cranberry juice cocktail, 1 tablespoon liqueur, and 2 tablespoons vodka in a cocktail shaker; fill shaker with crushed ice. Shake for 15 seconds; strain into a martini glass. Repeat procedure with remaining pomegranate juice, cranberry juice cocktail, liqueur, and vodka. Garnish with pomegranate seeds and an orange curl, if desired. Serves 2 (serving size: about ⅔ cup)

CALORIES 169; **FAT** 0.1g; **PROTEIN** 0.2g; **CARB** 17.8g; **FIBER** 0g; **CHOL** 0mg; **IRON** 0.1mg; **SODIUM** 7mg; **CALC** 9mg

Tip: This cocktail can be made gluten free by using potato vodka instead of regular vodka.

Spiced apple cider is a fun drink to make for your family for a holiday meal or celebration. It's also an amazing pick-me-up on a cold Sunday afternoon while hanging out watching football. If you're serving it at a holiday party for adults, add a shot of spiced rum to each mug. Delicious!

SPICED APPLE CIDER

HANDS-ON TIME: 2 MINUTES | TOTAL TIME: 25 MINUTES

6 cups organic apple cider
4 whole cloves
1 (3-inch) cinnamon stick
1 star anise
5 tablespoons whipped cream
  (optional)
10 cinnamon sticks (optional)

1. Combine first 4 ingredients in a Dutch oven. Bring to a simmer; reduce heat to low, and cook 15 minutes.
2. Ladle cider into small cups. Garnish each serving with 1½ teaspoons whipped cream and 1 cinnamon stick, if desired. Serves 10 (serving size: ½ cup)

CALORIES 86; **FAT** 1.4g (sat 0.9g, mono 0.4g, poly 0.1g); **PROTEIN** 0.1g; **CARB** 18.2g; **FIBER** 0.1g; **CHOL** 5mg; **IRON** 0mg; **SODIUM** 17mg; **CALC** 4mg

SALADS & SIDE DISHES

Don't tell—adding fruit to salads is how I convince kids to eat them. Cool and crisp, this is the perfect salad for summer. Tangy feta and the clean flavors of mint and lime balance the sweet watermelon. A delicious alternative to traditional lemon versions, the vinaigrette would be yummy with grilled shrimp or chicken, too. If stone fruits are in season, try using peaches or nectarines instead of watermelon. A-maz-ing!

WATERMELON AND FENNEL SALAD WITH HONEY-LIME VINAIGRETTE

HANDS-ON TIME: 10 MINUTES | TOTAL TIME: 10 MINUTES

3 tablespoons fresh lime juice
2 tablespoons olive oil
1 tablespoon honey
1/4 teaspoon kosher salt
1/4 teaspoon freshly ground
   black pepper
1 tablespoon finely minced shallots
3 1/4 cups thinly sliced fennel bulb
3 cups cubed watermelon
1/4 cup chopped fresh mint
2 ounces crumbled feta cheese
   (about 1/2 cup)

1. Combine first 5 ingredients, stirring with a whisk. Stir in shallots. Combine fennel and watermelon in a large bowl. Drizzle dressing over watermelon mixture; toss gently. Sprinkle with mint and cheese. Serves 8 (serving size: about 3/4 cup)

CALORIES 88; FAT 5g (sat 1.5g, mono 2.8g, poly 0.4g); PROTEIN 1.9g; CARB 10.2g; FIBER 1.4g; CHOL 6mg; IRON 0.5mg; SODIUM 159mg; CALC 60mg

KIDS CAN HELP

Using a plastic or child-safe knife, kids can cube the watermelon. They can also make the vinaigrette.

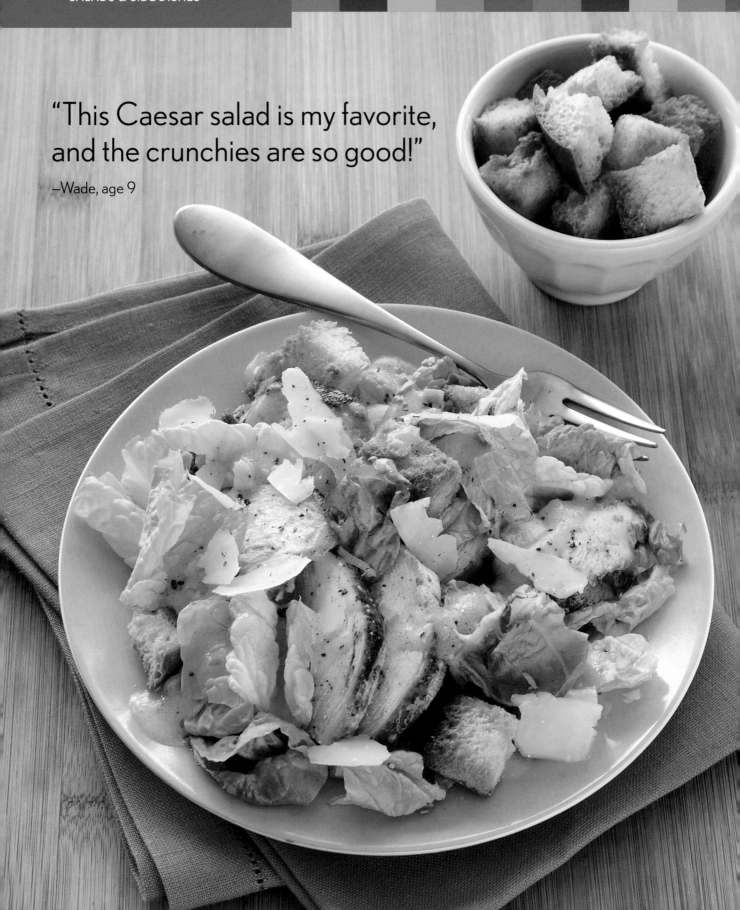

"This Caesar salad is my favorite, and the crunchies are so good!"

—Wade, age 9

Once you make this salad for the first time, you'll never feel the need to make a real Caesar again. The lemon juice and olive oil add such fresh flavors. Let your kids choose chicken, fish, or steak to eat with it. Make this a gluten-free salad by replacing the French bread with a gluten-free option.

LEMON CAESAR SALAD

HANDS-ON TIME: 20 MINUTES | TOTAL TIME: 37 MINUTES

1 teaspoon grated lemon rind

2¹/₂ tablespoons fresh
    lemon juice

1 teaspoon Dijon mustard

1 garlic clove, minced

⁵/₈ teaspoon kosher salt, divided

³/₄ teaspoon freshly ground
    black pepper, divided

5 tablespoons olive oil, divided

1¹/₃ cups (³/₄-inch) cubed
    French bread

1 pound skinless, boneless chicken
    breast halves

7 cups coarsely chopped
    hearts of romaine lettuce
    (about 2 hearts)

¹/₃ cup shaved fresh Parmesan
    cheese

1. Combine first 4 ingredients, ¹/₄ teaspoon salt, and ¹/₂ teaspoon pepper in a small bowl, stirring with a whisk. Gradually add 3¹/₂ tablespoons oil, stirring with a whisk.
2. Heat a large nonstick skillet over medium-high heat. Add 1 tablespoon oil; swirl to coat. Add bread cubes to pan; sprinkle with ¹/₈ teaspoon salt. Cook 4 to 5 minutes or until crunchy and golden, stirring occasionally. Remove from heat.
3. Preheat grill to medium-high heat.
4. Brush chicken with remaining 1¹/₂ teaspoons oil; sprinkle with remaining ¹/₄ teaspoon salt and remaining ¹/₄ teaspoon pepper. Place chicken on grill rack; grill 6 minutes on each side or until done. Let stand 5 minutes; cut into thin slices.
5. Place lettuce in a large bowl; drizzle with dressing. Sprinkle with cheese; toss to coat. Place about 1³/₄ cups lettuce mixture on each of 4 plates; top each with ¹/₃ cup croutons and 3 ounces chicken. Serves 4 (serving size: 1 salad)

CALORIES 393; **FAT** 21.5g (sat 4.2g, mono 13.5g, poly 3.2g); **PROTEIN** 32.7g; **CARB** 18.2g; **FIBER** 2.5g; **CHOL** 72mg; **IRON** 2.6mg; **SODIUM** 668mg; **CALC** 128mg

Cobb salad is normally so high in calories that it defeats the purpose of ordering a salad. So here's a little twist on the usual. Instead of a creamy dressing, this recipe uses a vinaigrette. For a gluten-free version, substitute a good gluten-free bread for the French bread.

CHOPPED COBB SALAD

HANDS-ON TIME: 11 MINUTES | TOTAL TIME: 28 MINUTES

1½ cups (¾-inch) cubed French bread

Cooking spray

6 cups chopped hearts of romaine lettuce (about 2 hearts)

1 cup chopped seeded plum tomato

½ cup sliced green onions

2 ounces crumbled blue cheese (about ½ cup)

4 bacon slices, cooked and crumbled

2 hard-cooked large eggs, chopped

2 tablespoons white wine vinegar

2 teaspoons Dijon mustard

¼ teaspoon freshly ground black pepper

⅛ teaspoon kosher salt

3 tablespoons olive oil

2 tablespoons finely minced shallots

1. Preheat oven to 400°.

2. Place bread cubes on a large rimmed baking sheet. Coat bread generously with cooking spray; toss. Bake at 400° for 10 minutes or until crisp and golden, stirring after 5 minutes. Cool completely.

3. Place lettuce and next 5 ingredients (through eggs) in a large bowl. Cover and chill, if desired.

4. Combine vinegar and next 3 ingredients (through salt) in a medium bowl, stirring with a whisk. Gradually add oil, stirring with a whisk. Stir in shallots. Pour dressing over salad mixture; toss gently. Top with croutons, and serve immediately. Serves 4 (serving size: 1¾ cups)

CALORIES 294; FAT 21.2g (sat 6.1g, mono 11.1g, poly 2.2g); PROTEIN 12g; CARB 14.4g; FIBER 2.9g; CHOL 125mg; IRON 2mg; SODIUM 630mg; CALC 134mg

Tip: Make it easy on yourself and hard-cook the eggs, cook the bacon, and make the vinaigrette ahead, so all you have to do before dinner is assemble!

"This is how my mom got me to eat salad. It is so good that my brothers and I don't even complain about eating our salad anymore!" —Lindsey, age 8

Joey Altman is a friend, phenomenal chef, and cookbook author. And his salads all rock! I made a version of this salad with him at an event in the wine country and fell in love with the grilled fruit. Grilling caramelizes the sugars and brings out the amazing flavors of practically any fruit. So if your kids don't like salad, give this one a try.

GRILLED STONE FRUIT SALAD WITH GOAT CHEESE AND ALMONDS

HANDS-ON TIME: 17 MINUTES | TOTAL TIME: 21 MINUTES

4 medium peaches, nectarines, or plums, halved and pitted
Cooking spray
³/₈ teaspoon kosher salt, divided
³/₈ teaspoon freshly ground black pepper, divided
¹/₄ cup balsamic or sherry vinegar
3¹/₂ tablespoons extra-virgin olive oil
2 tablespoons minced shallots
6 cups arugula, baby spinach, or mixed greens
2 ounces crumbled goat cheese (about ¹/₂ cup)
¹/₄ cup whole blanched almonds, toasted

1. Preheat grill to medium-high heat.
2. Place fruit halves in a large bowl. Coat with cooking spray, and sprinkle with ¹/₈ teaspoon salt and ¹/₈ teaspoon pepper. Toss gently to coat.
3. Place fruit halves, cut sides down, on grill rack coated with cooking spray. Grill 2 minutes; turn halves over, and grill 2 minutes or until fruit begins to soften and peel loosens. Transfer to a bowl, and cool slightly. Remove peel. Chop each half into wedges.
4. Combine vinegar, oil, shallots, remaining ¹/₄ teaspoon salt, and remaining ¹/₄ teaspoon pepper in a small bowl, stirring with a whisk.
5. Place 1¹/₂ cups greens on each of 4 plates. Drizzle each with 2 tablespoons dressing. Sprinkle each with 2 tablespoons cheese and about 1 tablespoon almonds. Top each salad with 8 fruit wedges. Serves 4 (serving size: 1 salad)

CALORIES 286; FAT 21.3g (sat 4.9g, mono 13.3g, poly 2.3g); PROTEIN 7.1g; CARB 18.9g; FIBER 4.7g; CHOL 11mg; IRON 1.8mg; SODIUM 319mg; CALC 90mg

Tip: If you grill in the fall, pears are a wonderful substitute for the stone fruit.

Kids will go for chopped salads with lots of color, such as this one with edamame, chopped apple, and candied nuts. Most kids like the crunch of romaine lettuce, and letting them toss the ingredients in the bowl helps, too. The best part? Dinner is ready in 10 minutes.

CHOPPED SALAD

HANDS-ON TIME: 10 MINUTES | TOTAL TIME: 10 MINUTES

8 cups finely chopped
  hearts of romaine lettuce
  (about 2 hearts)
1¹/₃ cups chopped apple
  (1 large)
1 cup diced cooked chicken
  or turkey breast
³/₄ cup chopped carrot
¹/₂ cup sliced green onions
¹/₂ cup frozen shelled edamame
  (green soybeans), thawed
¹/₂ cup Apple Cider Vinaigrette
  (page 19)
¹/₂ cup candied pecans, chopped
4 ounces crumbled goat cheese
  (about 1 cup)

1. Combine first 6 ingredients in a large bowl. Drizzle with Apple Cider Vinaigrette; toss well. Sprinkle with pecans and goat cheese. Serves 4 (serving size: 2³/₄ cups)

CALORIES 411; FAT 24.7g (sat 5.9g, mono 8.9g, poly 3.8g); PROTEIN 20.9g; CARB 29.8g; FIBER 5.2g; CHOL 43mg; IRON 3mg; SODIUM 274mg; CALC 106mg

KIDS CAN HELP

Kids can help with a number of things in this salad, from chopping the lettuce to cutting the chicken or turkey to making the vinaigrette.

"Chinese Chicken Salad is the best salad ever!" —Connor, age 8

CRUNCHY CHINESE CHICKEN SALAD WITH WONTON CHIPS

HANDS-ON TIME: 35 MINUTES | TOTAL TIME: 1 HOUR

DRESSING:
1/4 cup canola oil
1/4 cup fresh lime juice
3 tablespoons dark sesame oil
2 tablespoons creamy peanut butter
2 tablespoons brown sugar
1/2 teaspoon kosher salt
2 green onions, cut into 2-inch pieces
1 garlic clove, peeled

CHICKEN:
2 (6-ounce) skinless, boneless
  chicken breast halves
1/4 teaspoon kosher salt
1/4 teaspoon freshly ground
  black pepper
1 tablespoon grated peeled
  fresh ginger
2 garlic cloves, minced
1/4 cup finely chopped
  green onions (about 2 onions)
Cooking spray

CHIPS:
6 wonton wrappers
1/4 teaspoon kosher salt

REMAINING INGREDIENTS:
2 cups thinly sliced napa
  (Chinese) cabbage
1 cup thinly sliced red cabbage
2 cups thinly sliced romaine lettuce
1 cup matchstick-cut carrots
1/2 cup coarsely chopped whole
  natural almonds, toasted
1/3 cup thinly sliced green onions
  (about 3 onions)

1. To prepare dressing, place first 8 ingredients in a blender; process until smooth. Cover and chill up to 3 days.
2. Preheat oven to 350°.
3. To prepare chicken, sprinkle with salt and pepper; rub ginger, garlic, and 1/4 cup green onions over chicken. Place in an 11 x 7-inch baking dish coated with cooking spray. Bake at 350° for 26 to 28 minutes or until chicken is done. Cool slightly, and cut crosswise into 1/4-inch slices.
4. Preheat broiler.
5. To prepare chips, stack wonton wrappers. Cut wrappers diagonally into quarters to form triangles; place in a single layer on a large baking sheet. Coat quarters with cooking spray, and sprinkle evenly with 1/4 teaspoon salt. Broil 30 seconds to 1 minute or until browned. (Watch closely to prevent burning.)
6. Place chicken, cabbages, and remaining ingredients in a large bowl. Drizzle with dressing; toss gently. Divide salad evenly among 6 plates. Serve with chips. Serves 6 (serving size: 1 1/2 cups salad and 4 chips)

CALORIES 381; **FAT** 26g (sat 2.7g, mono 12.8g, poly 7.4g); **PROTEIN** 19g; **CARB** 20.3g; **FIBER** 4g; **CHOL** 34mg; **IRON** 1.9mg; **SODIUM** 450mg; **CALC** 101mg

Tips: For quick and easy prep, place the cabbage and veggies in a bowl and make the dressing in the morning. Then, cook the chicken and chips right before dinner. If you're in a pinch, you can use leftover shredded chicken from Simplest Roast Chicken Ever (page 235). If you'd like to make this salad completely gluten free, simply omit the wonton chips.

Kids can help measure out the ingredients for the dressing, chicken, and salad. Then they can put it all in a bowl, and toss the salad, too.

My family always begs for Broccoli Crunch Salad from Whole Foods Market. One day I realized I could make it myself. The results were stellar!

BROCCOLI CRUNCH SALAD WITH BACON AND CURRANTS

HANDS-ON TIME: 6 MINUTES | TOTAL TIME: 8 MINUTES

5 cups broccoli florets
6 tablespoons canola mayonnaise
1 tablespoon apple cider vinegar
1 tablespoon agave syrup
¼ teaspoon freshly ground black pepper
⅓ cup currants
¼ cup finely diced red onion
3 center-cut bacon slices, cooked and crumbled

1. Steam broccoli, covered, 2 minutes. Plunge broccoli into ice water to stop the cooking process; drain and pat dry.
2. Combine mayonnaise and next 3 ingredients (through pepper) in a large bowl. Add broccoli, currants, onion, and bacon; toss well. Serves 6 (serving size: ⅔ cup)

CALORIES 170; **FAT** 12.3g (sat 1.6g, mono 6g, poly 3.1g); **PROTEIN** 2.7g; **CARB** 13.9g; **FIBER** 2.5g; **CHOL** 9mg; **IRON** 0.7mg; **SODIUM** 192mg; **CALC** 34mg

Tip: To avoid watery eyes while dicing an onion, peel it first, and chill it in the refrigerator before dicing.

technique: how to dice an onion

1. Trim the stem and root ends; discard. Remove the papery outer skins.

2. Stand the onion upright on a cutting board; cut a thin slice off one side. Make vertical slices through the onion to within ¼ inch of bottom.

3. Rotate onion 90° on cutting board. Repeat step 2.

4. Turn onion so cut side is flat on board. Cut vertically through onion.

I love coleslaw, but I wasn't sure if my kids would like it. I used a combo of red and green cabbage, hoping the color would win them over. The result? One son really liked it, and the other "kinda liked it." We, the parents, thought it rocked!

CRUNCHY, CREAMY COLESLAW

HANDS-ON TIME: 15 MINUTES | TOTAL TIME: 1 HOUR AND 15 MINUTES

3/4 cup reduced-fat mayonnaise
2 tablespoons sugar
2 tablespoons white wine vinegar
2 tablespoons reduced-fat
    sour cream
1 teaspoon dry mustard
1/2 teaspoon freshly ground
    black pepper
1/8 teaspoon salt
3 cups thinly sliced green cabbage
2 cups thinly sliced red cabbage
1 cup shredded carrot
    (about 2 medium)
1/2 cup thinly sliced celery

1. Combine first 7 ingredients in a large bowl, stirring with a whisk until smooth. Add cabbages, carrot, and celery; toss to coat. Cover and chill 1 hour. Serves 8 (serving size: 3/4 cup)

CALORIES 77; FAT 3.7g (sat 1.1g, mono 0g, poly 0g); PROTEIN 1.1g; CARB 10.9g; FIBER 1.6g; CHOL 2mg; IRON 0.4mg; SODIUM 258mg; CALC 33mg

Tip: The cabbage is thinly sliced, but you can also shred it, if you prefer. Use a box grater or the shredding disc on a food processor. Serve with pulled pork, chicken, or Fish Tacos with Lime Crema and Mango Salsa (page 171).

technique: how to prepare cabbage

Start by removing and discarding the tough outer leaves from the head of cabbage. Unlike its loose-leafed cousins mustard and kale, cabbage is tightly wound, so it doesn't pick up grit from the garden. Rinse under running water to clean it sufficiently, and then slice or chop it depending on the needs of the recipe.

Who said kids won't eat broccoli? I can get almost any kid to eat this dish. Roasting leaves it tasting its absolute best. Once you master the roasting technique, play around with flavor options. You can zest a lemon or grate Parmigiano-Reggiano cheese over the top after roasting, or mix in some currants at the end. Yum.

KID-APPROVED ROASTED BROCCOLI

HANDS-ON TIME: 6 MINUTES | TOTAL TIME: 18 MINUTES

1 pound broccoli florets,
    cut into 1-inch pieces
1 teaspoon olive oil
2 tablespoons grated fresh
    Parmigiano-Reggiano cheese
2 tablespoons dried currants
2 teaspoons grated lemon rind
1/4 teaspoon kosher salt
1/4 teaspoon freshly ground
    black pepper

1. Place a large cast-iron skillet in the oven.
2. Preheat oven to 500°.
3. Remove preheated skillet from oven. Add broccoli and oil; stir well. Bake at 500° for 8 minutes, stirring after 6 minutes.
4. Combine broccoli, cheese, and remaining ingredients in a bowl; toss gently. Serve immediately. Serves 6 (serving size: 1/2 cup)

CALORIES 43; **FAT** 1.5g (sat 0.5g, mono 0.6g, poly 0.2g); **PROTEIN** 3g; **CARB** 6.4g; **FIBER** 2.5g; **CHOL** 1mg; **IRON** 0.8mg; **SODIUM** 110mg; **CALC** 65mg

Tip: If you're buying whole heads of broccoli, cut off the florets, and then cut the top half of the stems into 1/3-inch coins. Toss them in with the florets to roast. They're delicious!

This is another example of how roasting the simplest veggies makes them taste amazing. My friends at my favorite restaurant, A16, came up with this wonderful springtime combination, but carrots with cauliflower is a great option, too. Tossing in the mint at the end turns this recipe from simple kid food into sophisticated family food—and basil works just as well.

ROASTED CARROTS AND SNAP PEAS

HANDS-ON TIME: 7 MINUTES | TOTAL TIME: 27 MINUTES

4 cups (¼-inch) diagonally
    sliced carrot (6 large)
2 tablespoons olive oil, divided
1 teaspoon freshly ground
    black pepper, divided
½ teaspoon kosher salt, divided
1 pound sugar snap peas, trimmed
1 tablespoon chopped fresh mint

1. Preheat oven to 450°.
2. Place carrot in a large bowl. Drizzle with 1 tablespoon olive oil, and sprinkle with ½ teaspoon pepper and ¼ teaspoon salt; toss well. Spread in a single layer on a large baking sheet. Bake at 450° for 15 minutes.
3. While carrot cooks, place peas in bowl; drizzle with remaining 1 tablespoon olive oil, and sprinkle with remaining ½ teaspoon pepper and remaining ¼ teaspoon salt; toss well. Stir pea mixture into carrot. Bake an additional 5 minutes. Transfer vegetables to a large serving bowl; sprinkle with mint, and toss gently. Serve immediately. Serves 6 (serving size: 1 cup)

CALORIES 106; **FAT** 4.7g (sat 0.7g, mono 3.3g, poly 0.6g); **PROTEIN** 2.5g; **CARB** 13.4g; **FIBER** 3.9g; **CHOL** 0mg; **IRON** 1.2mg; **SODIUM** 219mg; **CALC** 79mg

KIDS CAN HELP

Let your little ones add the oil, salt, and pepper to the carrots, and stir. Then let them help spread them out evenly on the baking sheet. They can also string the peas.

It's funny how we are all raised with food prejudices. My parents told me Brussels sprouts were awful, so I assumed they were! Then I had them for the first time prepared like this, and I was in heaven. And guess what? So were my kids. Loaded with bits of crispy bacon and shallots, they're sweet and caramelized and everything you could ask for in a side dish. Give this under-rated vegetable a try—you just might change your mind, too.

BRUSSELS SPROUTS WITH CRISPY BACON AND SHALLOTS

HANDS-ON TIME: 28 MINUTES | TOTAL TIME: 28 MINUTES

2 center-cut bacon slices, diced
1/3 cup finely chopped shallots
    (1 large shallot)
1 tablespoon butter
1 pound Brussels sprouts, trimmed,
    halved, and thinly sliced (5 cups)
1/4 cup fat-free, lower-sodium
    chicken broth
1 tablespoon red wine vinegar
1/2 teaspoon freshly ground
    black pepper

1. Cook bacon in a large nonstick skillet over medium heat 3 minutes, stirring often. Using a slotted spoon, remove bacon, reserving drippings in pan; drain bacon. Add shallots to drippings in pan; sauté 1 to 2 minutes or until lightly browned. Add butter and Brussels sprouts; sauté 3 minutes. Add broth; sauté 2 minutes. Stir in vinegar.
2. Remove pan from heat; stir in pepper, and sprinkle with bacon. Serves 7 (serving size: 1/2 cup)

CALORIES 70; FAT 4.2g (sat 2.1g, mono 1.3g, poly 0.4g); PROTEIN 2.8g; CARB 6.6g; FIBER 2.3g; CHOL 8mg; IRON 0.9mg; SODIUM 85mg; CALC 28mg

technique: how to trim Brussels sprouts

Thoroughly wash Brussels sprouts before trimming. Pull off any limp outer leaves, and closely trim the stem end—don't cut too much off or the Brussels sprouts may fall apart.

"I always eat these when Mrs. Haas brings them to my house!"

—Bennet, age 7

Unless I'm making my grandma's green bean casserole, we like 'em simple around here. The key is finding fresh, crisp beans.

GREEN BEANS WITH TOASTED ALMONDS AND LEMON

HANDS-ON TIME: 22 MINUTES | TOTAL TIME: 22 MINUTES

1 tablespoon olive oil
1 pound green beans, trimmed
1 shallot, thinly sliced
1/2 cup water
2 teaspoons unsalted butter
2 tablespoons sliced almonds
1 tablespoon fresh lemon juice
1/4 teaspoon kosher salt
1/4 teaspoon freshly ground
   black pepper

1. Heat a large skillet over medium heat. Add oil; swirl to coat. Add beans and shallots; cook 5 minutes, stirring frequently. Add 1/2 cup water; cover and cook 5 minutes or until beans are crisp-tender.
2. Melt butter in a small skillet over medium heat. Add almonds; cook 5 minutes or until browned, stirring frequently.
3. Add almond mixture, lemon juice, and remaining ingredients to bean mixture; toss well. Serves 4

CALORIES 105; **FAT** 6.9g (sat 1.8g, mono 3.9g, poly 0.8g); **PROTEIN** 2.9g; **CARB** 10.3g; **FIBER** 4.3g; **CHOL** 5mg; **IRON** 1.4mg; **SODIUM** 128mg; **CALC** 54mg

KIDS CAN HELP

For older kids who have practiced their cutting skills, let them trim the ends off the green beans with a child-safe knife. For the younger ones, teach them how to snap off the ends with their fingers.

"This is the best vegetable my mom makes—today."

—Charlie, age 6

Cauliflower gets as bad a rap as Brussels sprouts. But kids will adore this oven-roasted version, which caramelizes the sugars, leaving it incredibly sweet.

ROASTED CAULIFLOWER WITH SAGE

HANDS-ON TIME: 7 MINUTES | TOTAL TIME: 18 MINUTES

1 (1³/₄-pound) head cauliflower, trimmed and cut into 1¹/₂-inch florets
1 tablespoon olive oil
¹/₂ teaspoon freshly ground black pepper
¹/₄ teaspoon salt
2 tablespoons fresh sage leaves
2 teaspoons grated lemon rind

1. Preheat oven to 500°.
2. Place a large baking sheet in oven. Heat 5 minutes.
3. While pan heats, place cauliflower in a large bowl. Drizzle cauliflower with oil; toss until coated. Sprinkle with pepper and salt; toss well. Spread cauliflower in a single layer on hot pan.
4. Bake at 500° for 12 minutes or until browned and tender. Transfer cauliflower to a bowl. Add sage and lemon rind; toss well. Serve immediately. Serves 6 (serving size: ³/₄ cup)

CALORIES 55; **FAT** 2.4g (sat 0.3g, mono 1.7g, poly 0.3g); **PROTEIN** 2.7g; **CARB** 7.3g; **FIBER** 3.4g; **CHOL** 0mg; **IRON** 0.6g; **SODIUM** 138mg; **CALC** 35mg

This is one of the few recipes that belongs to my husband, Kyle. Every time we take it to a party, everyone raves. For an added layer of kid appeal, I mix in diced mango and crumbled Cotija cheese.

BLACK BEAN AND CORN SALAD WITH MANGO

HANDS-ON TIME: 10 MINUTES | TOTAL TIME: 10 MINUTES, PLUS 24 HOURS FOR MARINATING, IF DESIRED

1. Combine first 5 ingredients in a large bowl, stirring with a whisk. Add corn and next 7 ingredients (through bell pepper); toss gently. Cover and refrigerate overnight, if desired.

2. Add avocado and cheese; toss gently. Serve immediately. Serves 12 (serving size: about ³/₄ cup)

CALORIES 155; **FAT** 8.3g (sat 1.8g, mono 3.8g, poly 0.7g); **PROTEIN** 4.7g; **CARB** 17.1g; **FIBER** 3.9g; **CHOL** 5mg; **IRON** 1.1mg; **SODIUM** 200mg; **CALC** 59mg

Tip: Serve it with Pan-Fried Beef Tenderloin (page 195), grilled shrimp, or Cilantro-Lime Rice (page 145).

¹/₃ cup fresh lime juice
¹/₄ cup olive oil
¹/₂ teaspoon freshly ground
    black pepper
¹/₄ teaspoon salt
1 garlic clove, minced
1¹/₂ cups fresh corn kernels
    (about 3 ears)
1¹/₄ cups diced peeled mango
³/₄ cup minced green onions
    (about 6 onions)
¹/₂ cup chopped fresh cilantro
2 tablespoons minced seeded
    jalapeño pepper
2 (15-ounce) cans black beans,
    rinsed and drained
2 medium tomatoes, seeded
    and cut into ¹/₂-inch pieces
1 red bell pepper, cut into
    ¹/₂-inch pieces
³/₄ cup diced peeled avocado
    (about 1 large)
2 ounces crumbled Cotija cheese
    (about ¹/₂ cup)

KIDS CAN HELP

Kids can make the entire vinaigrette themselves and chop the tomatoes and red bell pepper with a plastic knife.

What's not to love about this salad? It's sweet, savory, crunchy, and full of bright herbs and lemon juice. You can make it ahead, cover it, and leave it at room temperature up to four hours before serving. Resist the urge to refrigerate it, though—the couscous will dry out quickly. If you're looking for a gluten-free option, try quinoa.

CRUNCHY COUSCOUS SALAD WITH CURRANTS AND MINT

HANDS-ON TIME: 12 MINUTES | TOTAL TIME: 12 MINUTES

1 cup water
1 cup uncooked couscous
1/4 cup fresh lemon juice
1 teaspoon Dijon mustard
1/2 teaspoon kosher salt
1/4 teaspoon freshly ground black pepper
1/4 cup canola oil
1/4 cup currants
1/2 cup diced carrot
1/3 cup pine nuts, toasted
1/3 cup sliced green onions
3 tablespoons chopped fresh mint

1. Bring 1 cup water to a boil in a medium saucepan. While water comes to a boil, place couscous in a large skillet. Cook, stirring constantly, over medium-high heat 3 minutes or until lightly toasted and fragrant. Stir couscous into boiling water. Cover and let stand 5 minutes; fluff with a fork.

2. While couscous stands, combine lemon juice and next 3 ingredients (through pepper) in a large bowl, stirring with a whisk. Gradually add oil, stirring constantly with a whisk. Add couscous, currants, and remaining ingredients; fluff with a fork. Serve warm, or cover and cool to room temperature. Serves 6 (serving size: about 1/3 cup)

CALORIES 269; **FAT** 14.7g (sat 1.1g, mono 7.3g, poly 5.3g); **PROTEIN** 5.1g; **CARB** 30.5g; **FIBER** 2.7g; **CHOL** 0mg; **IRON** 1.1mg; **SODIUM** 193mg; **CALC** 26mg

Oh. My. Quinoa! I had read about the health benefits of this gluten-free ancient grain but never had much luck making it at home until this. Red quinoa makes a beautiful main-dish salad, but you can use whichever color you'd like.

RED QUINOA SALAD

HANDS-ON TIME: 10 MINUTES | TOTAL TIME: 1 HOUR AND 20 MINUTES

1 cup uncooked red quinoa
¹/₃ cup olive oil
2 tablespoons red wine vinegar
1¹/₂ teaspoons finely minced shallots
¹/₄ teaspoon kosher salt
¹/₄ teaspoon freshly ground
   black pepper
2 cups (¹/₂-inch) diced seeded
   tomato
¹/₂ cup (¹/₂-inch) diced seeded
   cucumber
3 tablespoons chopped fresh mint
1 tablespoon chopped fresh oregano
1 (15-ounce) can chickpeas
   (garbanzo beans), rinsed
   and drained
2 ounces crumbled feta cheese
   (about ¹/₂ cup)
4 lemon wedges

1. Cook quinoa according to package directions, omitting salt and fat. Drain and place in a large bowl. Let cool 1 hour.
2. While quinoa cools, combine oil and next 4 ingredients (through pepper) in a small bowl, stirring with a whisk. Let stand 20 minutes.
3. Add dressing, tomato, and next 4 ingredients (through chickpeas) to quinoa; toss well. Add cheese, and toss gently. Serve with lemon wedges. Serves 4 (serving size: about 1³/₄ cups salad and 1 lemon wedge)

CALORIES 460; **FAT** 24.7g (sat 5g, mono 14.7g, poly 3.8g); **PROTEIN** 12.5g; **CARB** 48.4g; **FIBER** 7.4g; **CHOL** 13mg; **IRON** 3.5mg; **SODIUM** 499mg; **CALC** 133mg

KIDS CAN HELP

With a child-safe knife, kids can chop the tomatoes and cucumbers, and then crumble the feta.

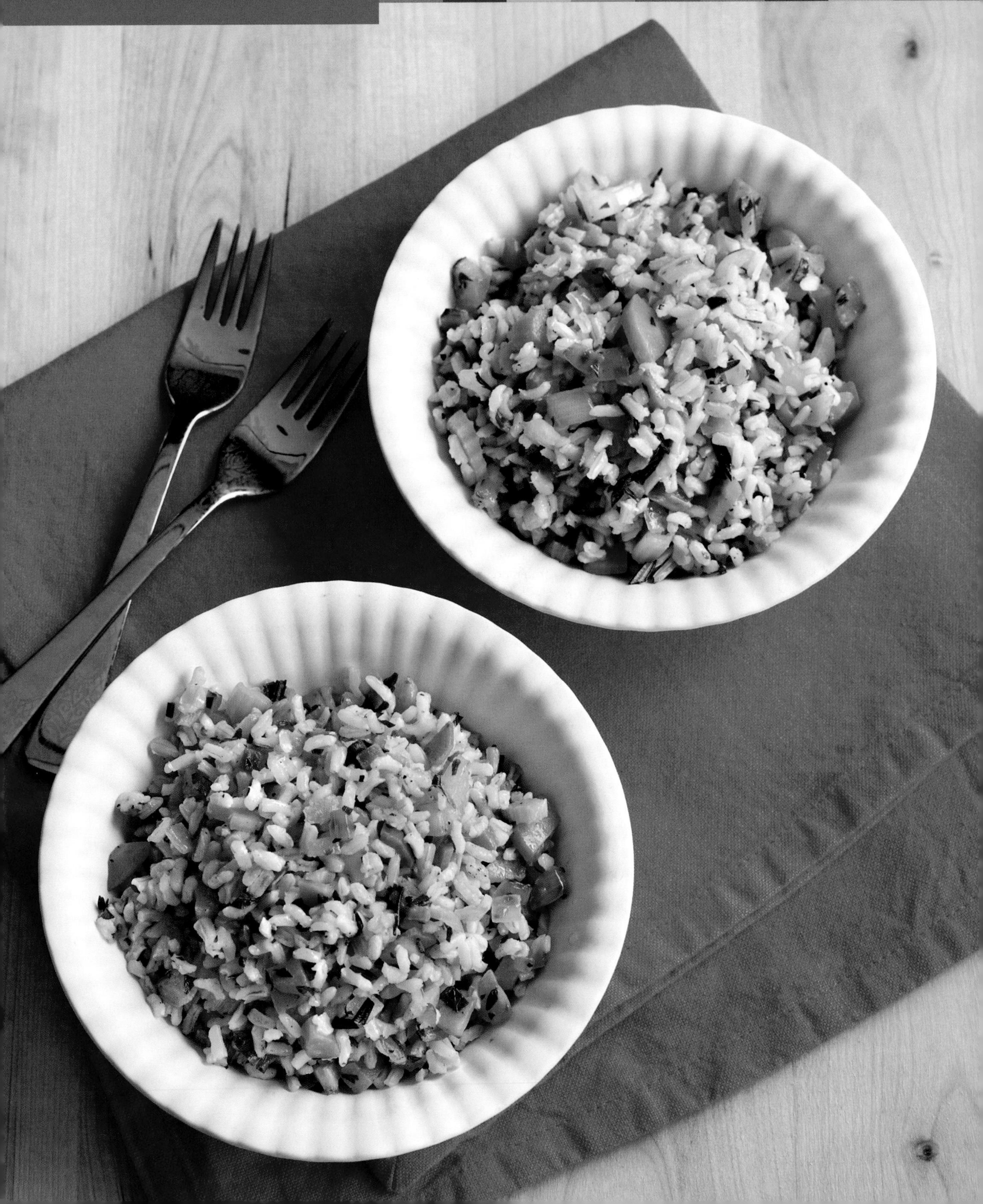

This is comfort food at its finest. My mom used to make this side all the time with a simple roast chicken, and it was one of the first things I started to cook on my own. For a little crunch, add some toasted almonds or pine nuts. Serve with Simplest Roast Chicken Ever (page 235).

HERBED BROWN RICE PILAF

HANDS-ON TIME: 17 MINUTES | TOTAL TIME: 57 MINUTES

½ cup uncooked brown rice
2 teaspoons olive oil
⅔ cup chopped onion
½ cup chopped celery
¼ cup chopped carrot
1 tablespoon chopped fresh
   flat-leaf parsley
½ teaspoon minced fresh rosemary
¾ teaspoon chopped fresh thyme
¼ teaspoon salt
⅛ teaspoon freshly ground
   black pepper

1. Cook rice according to package directions, omitting salt and fat.
2. While rice cooks, heat a medium skillet over medium-high heat. Add oil; swirl to coat. Add onion, celery, and carrot; sauté 5 minutes or until tender. Remove from heat; stir in parsley and remaining ingredients. Add vegetable mixture to cooked rice; fluff with a fork. Serve immediately. Serves 4 (serving size: ½ cup)

CALORIES 122; FAT 3g (sat 0.5g, mono 1.9g, poly 0.5g); PROTEIN 2.3g; CARB 21.7g; FIBER 1.7g; CHOL 0mg; IRON 0.6mg; SODIUM 164mg; CALC 22mg

Tip: Chop all your vegetables and herbs in the morning so when you come home from work, the recipe is a cinch to complete.

RED COCONUT RICE

CILANTRO-LIME RICE

Red Coconut Rice is the perfect balance of sweet coconut and pungent spice. Kids love the color and taste, and adults love the layer of flavor you get from the curry paste. Serve this with your favorite stir-fry as a great alternative to plain rice. The Cilantro-Lime Rice is my family's favorite! I serve it with practically everything, from fish tacos to Skirt Steak with Chimichurri Sauce (page 243).

RED COCONUT RICE

HANDS-ON TIME: 3 MINUTES | TOTAL TIME: 33 MINUTES

1 teaspoon canola oil
2 garlic cloves, minced
1 tablespoon red curry paste
1/2 teaspoon grated peeled fresh ginger
1/2 cup water
1/2 teaspoon salt
1 (13.5-ounce) can light coconut milk
1 cup jasmine rice
1/4 cup organic dried coconut flakes (optional)

1. Heat a large saucepan over medium-low heat. Add oil; swirl to coat. Add garlic; sauté 30 seconds. Add curry paste and ginger; sauté 30 seconds. Add 1/2 cup water, salt, and coconut milk, stirring with a whisk. Bring to a boil; add rice. Cover, reduce heat, and simmer 20 minutes or until liquid is absorbed. Remove from heat, and let stand 5 minutes; fluff with a fork. Garnish with coconut, if desired. Serves 8 (serving size: 1/2 cup)

CALORIES 54; FAT 1.2g (sat 0.5g, mono 0.4g, poly 0.2g); PROTEIN 0.9g; CARB 9.8g; FIBER 0.1g; CHOL 0mg; IRON 0.1mg; SODIUM 183mg; CALC 1mg

CILANTRO-LIME RICE

HANDS-ON TIME: 3 MINUTES | TOTAL TIME: 27 MINUTES

1/2 teaspoon canola oil
1/2 cup chopped onion
1 cup jasmine rice
11/2 cups fat-free, lower-sodium chicken broth
2 tablespoons fresh lime juice, divided
1/4 cup coarsely chopped fresh cilantro

1. Heat a medium saucepan over medium heat. Add oil; swirl to coat. Add onion; cook 5 minutes or until tender, stirring frequently. Stir in rice, chicken broth, and 1 tablespoon lime juice.
2. Bring to a boil; reduce heat, cover, and simmer 15 minutes or until rice is tender and liquid is absorbed. Remove from heat. Add remaining 1 tablespoon lime juice and cilantro; fluff with a fork. Serves 7 (serving size: 1/2 cup)

CALORIES 55; FAT 0.4g (sat 0g, mono 0.2g, poly 0.1g); PROTEIN 1.2g; CARB 11.7g; FIBER 0.4g; CHOL 0mg; IRON 0.1mg; SODIUM 97mg; CALC 3mg

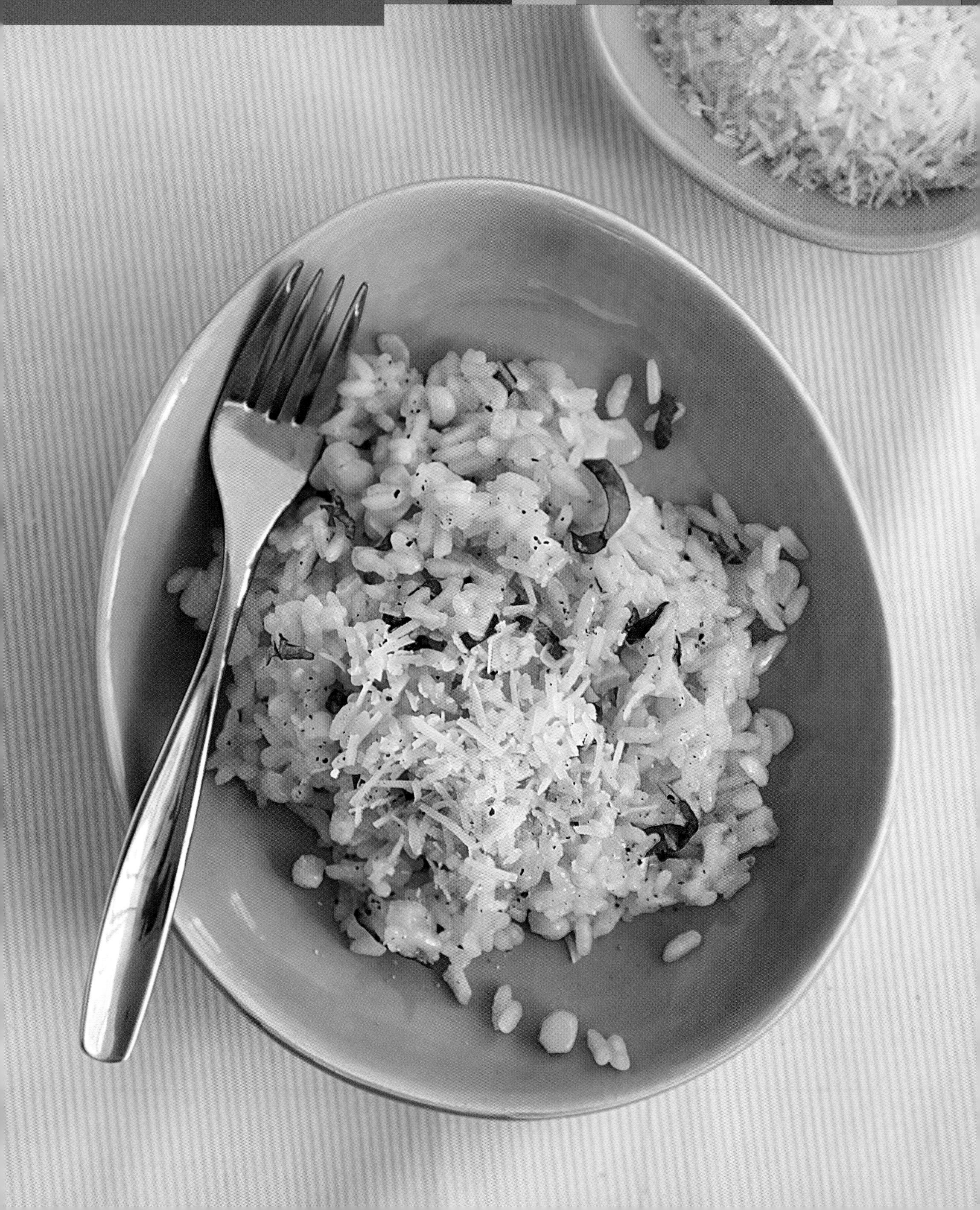

Risotto is great because you can add practically any ingredient to it and it will taste delicious. This is my favorite version for the summer.

RISOTTO WITH CORN AND BASIL

HANDS-ON TIME: 5 MINUTES | TOTAL TIME: 24 MINUTES

1 (32-ounce) container fat-free, lower-sodium chicken broth
1 tablespoon olive oil
1 tablespoon unsalted butter
3/4 cup chopped onion
1 cup uncooked Arborio rice
1/2 cup dry white wine
1 cup fresh corn kernels
3 tablespoons chopped fresh basil
1/4 teaspoon freshly ground black pepper
1/8 teaspoon kosher salt
2 ounces grated fresh Parmigiano-Reggiano cheese (about 1/2 cup), divided

1. Bring broth to a simmer in a 2-quart saucepan (do not boil). Keep warm over low heat.
2. Heat a Dutch oven over medium heat. Add olive oil and butter; cook until butter melts. Add onion; cook 2 minutes or until golden, stirring occasionally. Add rice; cook 1 minute, stirring constantly. Stir in wine; cook 1 to 2 minutes or until wine evaporates, stirring constantly. Add broth, 1 cup at a time, stirring constantly until each portion of broth is absorbed before adding the next (about 12 minutes total). Remove from heat.
3. Add corn, next 3 ingredients (through salt), and 1/3 cup cheese, stirring gently until cheese melts. Sprinkle with remaining cheese. Serve immediately. Serves 4 (serving size: about 1 cup)

CALORIES 132; FAT 3.5g (sat 1.3g, mono 1.5g, poly 0.3g); PROTEIN 3.4g; CARB 21.6g; FIBER 1.6g; CHOL 4mg; IRON 0.3mg; SODIUM 237mg; CALC 21mg

Tip: If you've never made risotto, there are a few tricks. Make sure your broth is warm. Also, you always want to keep a thin veil of liquid on the rice. When it starts to evaporate, you know it's time to add more. And keep stirring! It may seem like forever, but risotto only takes 12 to 15 minutes to cook once you've added the rice to the pan. Toward the end of cooking, make sure to keep tasting it. You want to pull it off the heat while it's still a bit al dente.

Thanks again to the fantastic cookbook *A16: Food + Wine*. When I tested the recipes for it, this became an instant family favorite. The beans are creamy, flavorful, and full of protein. Don't worry if you don't have the herbs. The garlic alone adds so much flavor to the beans. Serve them as an entrée on their own, or alongside braised meat or chicken.

CREAMY CANNELLINI BEANS WITH GARLIC AND OREGANO

HANDS-ON TIME: 16 MINUTES | TOTAL TIME: 11 HOURS AND 6 MINUTES

2 cups dried cannellini beans
1 gallon water
1¼ teaspoons kosher salt
¼ cup olive oil
¼ teaspoon dried oregano
2 garlic cloves, crushed
1 bay leaf
Freshly ground black pepper
   (optional)

1. Sort and wash beans; place in a 6-quart Dutch oven. Cover with water to 2 inches above beans; cover and let stand 8 hours.
2. Drain beans; return to pan. Add 1 gallon water. Bring to a boil; reduce heat, and simmer, uncovered, 2 hours or until tender. Drain beans, reserving ¾ cup cooking liquid. Place beans in a bowl; stir in reserved cooking liquid and salt. Let stand 30 minutes. Wash and dry pan.
3. Heat pan over medium heat. Add oil; swirl to coat. Add oregano, garlic, and bay leaf; sauté 2 minutes or until garlic is golden. Stir in bean mixture. Bring to a simmer; cook 4 minutes or until creamy, stirring frequently. Remove from heat; remove and discard garlic and bay leaf. Sprinkle with pepper, if desired. Serves 8 (serving size: ½ cup)

CALORIES 231; FAT 6.8g (sat 0.9g, mono 4.9g, poly 0.7g); PROTEIN 12.1g; CARB 30.3g; FIBER 8g; CHOL 0mg; IRON 5.5mg; SODIUM 310mg; CALC 102mg

"This is my favorite food from my Aunt Amanda. My mom [Amanda's sister] is a really good cook, so she makes me these to go with my favorite turkey burger." —Maddie, age 10

Sweet potatoes are so good for you. They're an excellent source of vitamin B₆, C, and D, and contain iron and magnesium. I'll let my kids order sweet potato fries at a local diner, but I don't fry them at home. And when I've tried to bake sweet potato fries, they're too soggy. So, what's a girl to do? Dice them up and bake them at a really high temperature. The results are awesome!

CHILI-ROASTED SWEET POTATO NUGGETS

HANDS-ON TIME: 10 MINUTES | TOTAL TIME: 38 MINUTES

2³/₄ pounds sweet potatoes,
    peeled and cut into 1-inch pieces
2 tablespoons olive oil
1 teaspoon light brown sugar
1 teaspoon chili powder
¹/₂ teaspoon kosher salt
¹/₄ teaspoon freshly ground
    black pepper

1. Preheat oven to 450°.
2. Place sweet potato on a 17 x 12–inch baking pan. Drizzle with oil; toss with a spatula until coated. Combine brown sugar and remaining ingredients in a small bowl. Sprinkle brown sugar mixture over potato, tossing to coat.
3. Bake at 450° for 20 minutes; turn with a spatula. Bake an additional 5 minutes or until tender. Serves 7 (serving size: ¹/₂ cup)

CALORIES 172; **FAT** 4.1g (sat 0.6g, mono 2.8g, poly 0.5g); **PROTEIN** 2.5g; **CARB** 32.3g; **FIBER** 4.5g; **CHOL** 0mg; **IRON** 1.3mg; **SODIUM** 197mg; **CALC** 49mg

These are hands down the easiest potatoes to make. They get all crispy and delicious in the oven. On busy nights, I'll simply add olive oil, salt, and pepper, and the boys gobble them up. When I have more time, I'll mix in a few cloves of minced garlic and chopped thyme or rosemary for extra flavor.

ROASTED FINGERLING FRIES

HANDS-ON TIME: 6 MINUTES | TOTAL TIME: 26 MINUTES

1 pound fingerling potatoes
2 tablespoons extra-virgin olive oil
1½ teaspoons chopped fresh thyme
1½ teaspoons chopped fresh rosemary
½ teaspoon kosher salt
½ teaspoon freshly ground black pepper
2 garlic cloves, minced

1. Preheat oven to 450°.
2. Scrub and rinse potatoes; pat dry with paper towels. Cut potatoes diagonally into ⅓-inch slices. Combine potato, oil, and next 4 ingredients (through pepper) in a large bowl; toss to coat. Spread potato mixture in a single layer on a large baking sheet. Bake at 450° for 10 minutes.
3. Sprinkle garlic over potato mixture; turn potato mixture with a spatula. Bake an additional 10 minutes or until crisp-tender. Serves 6 (serving size: ½ cup)

CALORIES 103; **FAT** 4.8g (sat 0.7g, mono 3.6g, poly 0.5g); **PROTEIN** 1.6g; **CARB** 13.7g; **FIBER** 1.8g; **CHOL** 0mg; **IRON** 0.7mg; **SODIUM** 165mg; **CALC** 13mg

KIDS CAN HELP

Once you've sliced the potatoes, kids can toss them with the olive oil and other ingredients, and then spread them out on the baking sheet. They can also pick the thyme and rosemary off the stems for you if they really want to learn!

These creamy, fluffy, kid-friendly mashed potatoes get their texture from butter, milk, and a touch of sour cream. If you're looking to try something just a little different, replace a few potatoes with celeriac (also known as celery root). Most kids love the sweet flavor, and celeriac is full of vitamins. For the fluffiest, lump-free potatoes, it's worth investing in a food mill or potato ricer. You won't be disappointed with the results.

CLASSIC MASHED POTATOES

HANDS-ON TIME: 15 MINUTES | TOTAL TIME: 43 MINUTES

4 pounds russet potatoes,
   peeled and cut into 1-inch cubes
6 tablespoons unsalted butter
½ cup 2% reduced-fat milk
½ cup reduced-fat sour cream
½ teaspoon kosher salt
½ teaspoon freshly ground
   black pepper

1. Place potatoes in a large saucepan; cover with water. Bring to a boil; cook 15 minutes or until tender. Drain.
2. Press potatoes through a food mill or potato ricer into a large bowl. Add butter, stirring until melted. Stir in milk and remaining ingredients. Serves 16 (serving size: ½ cup)

CALORIES 146; **FAT** 5.5g (sat 3.5g, mono 1.2g, poly 0.2g); **PROTEIN** 2.5g; **CARB** 22.2g; **FIBER** 1.9g; **CHOL** 16mg; **IRON** 0.3mg; **SODIUM** 74mg; **CALC** 31mg

Tip: If you want to make these mashed potatoes a few hours ahead of time, simply keep them warm over a double boiler on very low heat. Keep in mind that you may need to add a little milk before serving if the consistency becomes too thick.

Every year, Williams-Sonoma holds a competition among their corporate employees for the best Thanksgiving side dishes. This recipe is adapted from Rachel Thur's winning recipe. I enjoyed it so much that I served it at Thanksgiving the following week, and everyone asked for the recipe. It must be something about the contrast of smooth sweet potatoes, salty bacon, and crunchy pecans mixed with the right amount of brown sugar. I owe you one, Rachel!

TWICE-BAKED SWEET POTATO BOATS WITH BACON-PECAN TOPPING

HANDS-ON TIME: 20 MINUTES | TOTAL TIME: 1 HOUR AND 45 MINUTES

6 (8-ounce) sweet potatoes
2 teaspoons olive oil
¼ cup packed brown sugar
3 tablespoons all-purpose flour
1½ tablespoons butter, softened
¼ cup chopped pecans
4 bacon slices, cooked and crumbled
¼ cup granulated sugar
¼ cup 2% reduced-fat milk
½ teaspoon salt
½ teaspoon vanilla extract
1 large egg

1. Preheat oven to 400°.
2. Scrub potatoes; pat dry with paper towels. Rub potatoes with olive oil. Place on a foil-lined baking sheet. Bake at 400° for 1 hour and 5 minutes or until tender. Cool slightly on pan.
3. While potatoes cook, combine brown sugar and flour, stirring with a whisk. Cut in butter with a pastry blender or 2 knives until crumbly. Stir in pecans and bacon.
4. Cut potatoes in half lengthwise. Scoop out pulp, leaving a ¼-inch-thick shell. Place pulp in a food processor. Add granulated sugar and remaining ingredients; process until smooth. Spoon potato mixture evenly into shells; top evenly with brown sugar mixture. Bake at 400° for 20 minutes or until thoroughly heated. Serves 12 (serving size: 1 stuffed potato half)

CALORIES 188; FAT 5.5g (sat 1.7g, mono 2.5g, poly 0.8g); PROTEIN 3.9g; CARB 31.2g; FIBER 3.8g; CHOL 25mg; IRON 1mg; SODIUM 242mg; CALC 36mg

QUICK & EASY

This pesto is also delicious over seared chicken with a piece of fresh mozzarella melted over the top. Heavenly! If you'd like to use gluten-free pasta, purchase Bionaturae or Ancient Harvest pasta.

PESTO PASTA WITH CHICKEN AND TOMATOES

HANDS-ON TIME: 40 MINUTES | TOTAL TIME: 40 MINUTES

8 ounces uncooked fusilli or rotini (corkscrew pasta)
2 garlic cloves, peeled
3 cups fresh basil leaves
2 tablespoons pine nuts, toasted
1 tablespoon fresh lemon juice
1 teaspoon kosher salt
1 teaspoon freshly ground black pepper
1/4 cup extra-virgin olive oil
2 tablespoons balsamic vinegar, divided
1 medium onion, cut into 1/2-inch slices
3 (6-ounce) skinless, boneless chicken breast halves
4 cups cherry tomatoes
Cooking spray
1.3 ounces finely grated fresh Parmigiano-Reggiano cheese (about 1/3 cup), divided

1. Preheat grill to high heat.
2. Cook pasta according to package directions, omitting salt and fat; drain. Place in a large bowl, and keep warm.
3. Place garlic in food processor; process until minced. Add basil and next 4 ingredients (through pepper). With processor on, slowly pour oil through food chute; process until smooth.
4. Brush 1 tablespoon vinegar over onion slices; brush remaining 1 tablespoon vinegar over chicken. Place 2 cups tomatoes in center of each of 2 (24- x 12-inch) pieces of foil. Fold foil over tomatoes; tightly seal edges.
5. Place chicken, onion, and foil pouches on grill rack coated with cooking spray. Grill chicken, onion, and foil pouches 15 minutes or until onion is tender and tomatoes pop, turning all after 5 minutes. Remove onion and foil pouches from grill; turn chicken over, and cook an additional 5 minutes or until done. Let chicken stand 5 minutes. Chop onion; cut chicken into into 1/4-inch slices. Add pesto, tomatoes, chicken, and onion to pasta; toss well. Sprinkle with 1/4 cup cheese; toss gently. Sprinkle remaining cheese evenly over servings. Serve immediately. Serves 6 (serving size: 1 2/3 cups)

CALORIES 391; FAT 14.7g (sat 2.8g, mono 8g, poly 2.2g); PROTEIN 28.8g; CARB 36.4g; FIBER 3.3g; CHOL 53mg; IRON 3mg; SODIUM 412mg; CALC 137mg

Most kids are hooked on breaded chicken of some sort. So here's a pan-fried version that's much healthier than drive-through or frozen-food options. Using chicken breast tenders makes these look like fast food, but you'll feel so much better about feeding them to your kids. The crispy, crunchy panko breadcrumbs lend incredible texture. Serve with Kid-Approved Roasted Broccoli (page 127), Roasted Cauliflower with Sage (page 135), or Chili-Roasted Sweet Potato Nuggets (page 151). With a glass of wine, these appeal to grown-ups, too!

PARMESAN–PANKO CHICKEN TENDERS

HANDS-ON TIME: 19 MINUTES | TOTAL TIME: 31 MINUTES

1½ pounds chicken breast tenders (about 12 tenders)
½ teaspoon kosher salt
¼ teaspoon freshly ground black pepper
⅛ teaspoon garlic powder
2 large eggs, lightly beaten
1 cup panko (Japanese breadcrumbs)
1.3 ounces grated fresh Parmesan cheese (about ⅓ cup)
2 tablespoons canola oil, divided
2 tablespoons finely chopped fresh parsley (optional)
4 lemon quarters (optional)

1. Sprinkle chicken with salt, pepper, and garlic powder. Place eggs in a shallow bowl. Combine panko and cheese in another shallow bowl. Dip chicken in egg; dredge in breadcrumb mixture.
2. Heat a large nonstick skillet over medium-high heat. Add 1 tablespoon oil; swirl to coat. Add half of chicken; cook 3 to 4 minutes on each side or until browned and done. Remove from pan. Repeat procedure with remaining oil and chicken. Sprinkle with parsley, and serve with lemon quarters, if desired. Serves 4 (serving size: 3 chicken breast tenders)

CALORIES 314; FAT 11.2g (sat 2g, mono 5.5g, poly 2.6g); PROTEIN 42.6g; CARB 7.4g; FIBER 0g; CHOL 129mg; IRON 1.6mg; SODIUM 459mg; CALC 69mg

"I wish my mom would make nothing
but tomato sauce, tacos, ribs, and salmon!"
—Charlie, age 6

One of my favorite "fast foods," chicken soft tacos are a snap to prepare on a weeknight. You can customize them to your family's tastes and let your children build their own. Pulled Pork (page 225) would be a great substitute for chicken, or keep them vegetarian and bulk up on the beans! Strawberry-Lime Agua Fresca (page 103) would be a delicious drink for the kids. And parents, don't forget a cold Mexican beer to wash these down.

CHICKEN SOFT TACOS

HANDS-ON TIME: 10 MINUTES | TOTAL TIME: 50 MINUTES

1 teaspoon garlic powder

1 teaspoon ground cumin

½ teaspoon chipotle chile powder

2 (6-ounce) skinless, boneless chicken breast halves

Cooking spray

1 (15-ounce) can black beans, rinsed and drained

3 tablespoons fat-free, lower-sodium chicken broth

8 (6-inch) corn tortillas

½ cup Fresh Salsa (page 41) or commercial salsa

¼ cup reduced-fat sour cream

1 ounce shredded cheddar cheese (about ¼ cup)

1 ounce shredded Monterey Jack cheese (about ¼ cup)

2 cups shredded iceberg lettuce

1 lime, cut into 8 wedges

1. Preheat oven to 350°.

2. Combine first 3 ingredients in a medium bowl. Sprinkle chicken with 1¼ teaspoons spice mixture. Place chicken on a foil-lined baking sheet coated with cooking spray.

3. Bake at 350° for 30 minutes or until done. Cool slightly. Chop chicken into bite-sized pieces.

4. While chicken bakes, add beans and chicken broth to remaining spice mixture in bowl; mash with a potato masher until blended. Place bean mixture in a small skillet coated with cooking spray. Cook, stirring frequently, over medium heat 2 to 3 minutes or until thoroughly heated.

5. Warm tortillas according to package directions. Spread about 2 tablespoons bean mixture over each tortilla. Top each with about 3 tablespoons chicken, 1 tablespoon salsa, 1½ teaspoons sour cream, 1 tablespoon cheddar cheese, 1 tablespoon Monterey Jack cheese, and ¼ cup lettuce. Fold in half. Serve with lime wedges. Serves 4 (serving size: 2 tacos and 2 lime wedges)

CALORIES 391; **FAT** 10.1g (sat 4.3g, mono 2.2g, poly 0.8g); **PROTEIN** 30.1g; **CARB** 43.8g; **FIBER** 6.4g; **CHOL** 71mg; **IRON** 1.9mg; **SODIUM** 516mg; **CALC** 176mg

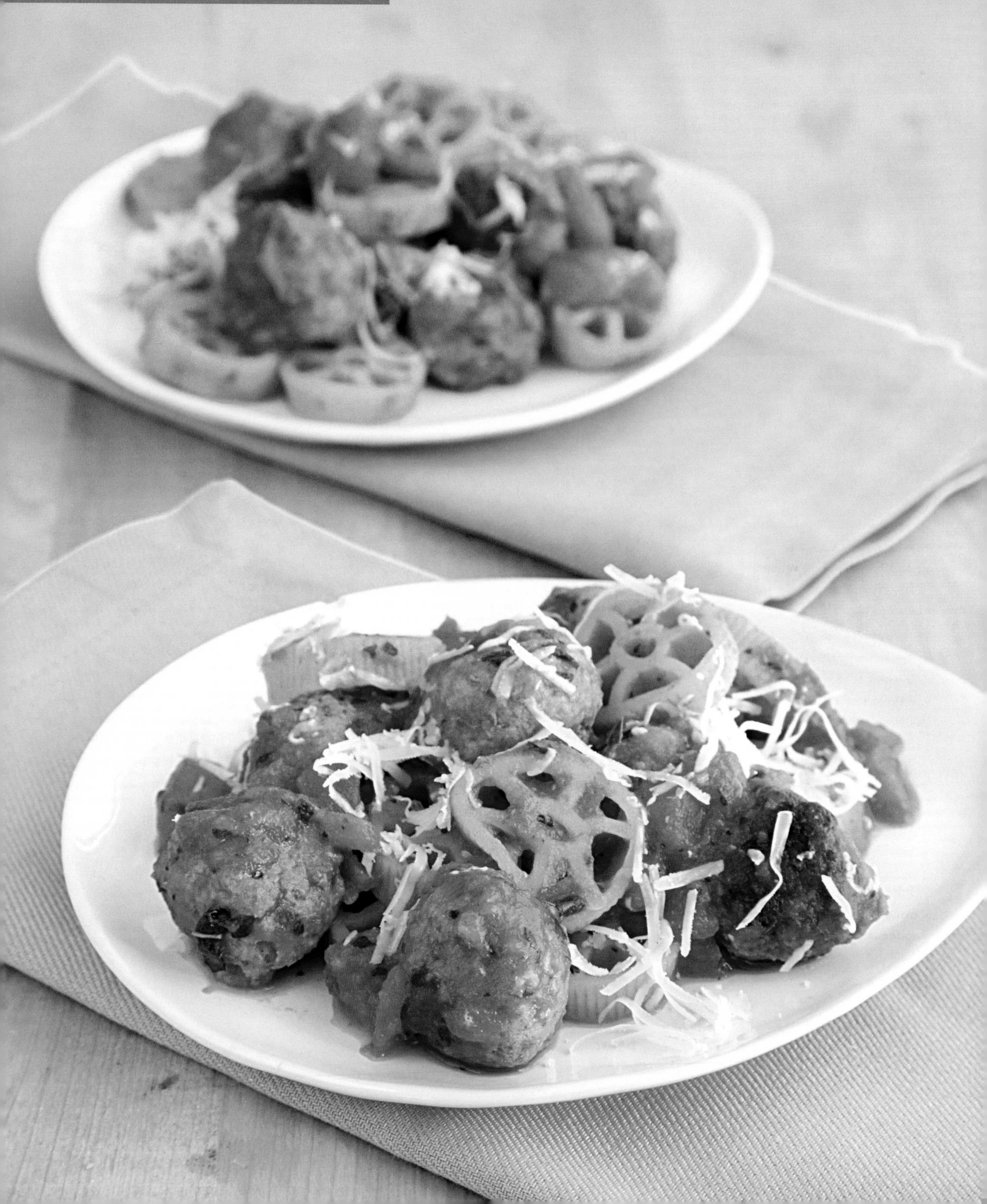

I have been so lucky to partner with the amazing women of Revolution Foods. (If you don't know their story, check them out online at revfoods.com.) Since their executive chef, Amy Klein, can get kids to eat pretty much anything, I asked her to share a few of her recipes. Here's one of them.

MINI TURKEY MEATBALLS WITH WAGON WHEEL PASTA

HANDS-ON TIME: 30 MINUTES | TOTAL TIME: 35 MINUTES

12 ounces uncooked wagon wheel pasta

½ cup fresh whole-wheat breadcrumbs

¼ cup 1% low-fat milk

1¼ pounds 97% lean ground turkey

1 tablespoon chopped fresh parsley

1 tablespoon chopped fresh basil

2 tablespoons olive oil, divided

½ teaspoon dried oregano

½ teaspoon ground fennel seed, crushed

½ teaspoon kosher salt

¼ teaspoon freshly ground black pepper

2 garlic cloves, minced

½ cup water

1 (25.5-ounce) jar organic pasta sauce

2 ounces finely grated fresh Parmesan cheese (about ½ cup)

1. Prepare pasta according to package directions, omitting salt and fat. Drain and place in a large bowl; keep warm.

2. While pasta cooks, combine breadcrumbs and milk. Let stand 5 minutes; squeeze out excess milk, and place in a large bowl. Add turkey, parsley, basil, 1 tablespoon oil, and next 5 ingredients (through garlic). Gently shape meat mixture into 48 (1-inch) balls (do not pack).

3. Heat a large nonstick skillet over medium heat. Add remaining 1 tablespoon oil; swirl to coat. Add half of meatballs to pan. Cook 1 to 2 minutes on each side or until browned. Remove from pan; keep warm. Repeat procedure with remaining meatballs. Return all meatballs to pan. Stir in ½ cup water, scraping pan to loosen browned bits. Stir in pasta sauce; cook, uncovered, over medium-high heat for an additional 3 minutes. Pour over pasta, tossing to coat. Sprinkle with cheese. Serves 8 (serving size: 1 cup pasta, 6 meatballs, and 1 tablespoon cheese)

CALORIES 363; **FAT** 8.9g (sat 2.2g, mono 3g, poly 0.8g); **PROTEIN** 26.9g; **CARB** 44.4g; **FIBER** 3.9g; **CHOL** 52mg; **IRON** 3.7mg; **SODIUM** 510mg; **CALC** 92mg

KIDS CAN HELP

With clean hands, kids can shape the meatballs.

This old-school, cheesy, meaty casserole is the most-requested recipe on my website (onefamilyonemeal.com) and is a favorite in my house! The best news is that it is quick and well balanced. The original recipe came from my friend Tori Ritchie, whose website, tuesdayrecipe.com, is chock-full of family-friendly recipes. Serve with corn chips for dipping, or roll this yummy mixture up in a tortilla with some chopped romaine lettuce for an amazing burrito.

MEXICAN SKILLET CASSEROLE

HANDS-ON TIME: 22 MINUTES | TOTAL TIME: 23 MINUTES

2 teaspoons canola oil
1³/₄ cups chopped onion
4 garlic cloves, minced
1 pound ground round
2 tablespoons chili powder
1 teaspoon ground cumin
³/₄ teaspoon kosher salt
1³/₄ cups hot cooked long-grain
    white rice
1 (14.5-ounce) can petite-cut diced
    tomatoes with jalapeños
1 (15-ounce) can black beans,
    rinsed and drained
2 ounces shredded reduced-fat sharp
    cheddar cheese (about ¹/₂ cup)

1. Heat a large skillet over medium-high heat. Add oil; swirl to coat. Add onion and garlic; sauté 3 minutes or until tender. Add beef; cook 4 minutes or until browned, stirring to crumble. Drain, and return to pan. Stir in chili powder, cumin, and salt. Add rice, tomatoes, and beans; cook over medium heat 2 minutes or until thoroughly heated, stirring occasionally. Sprinkle with cheese; cover and remove from heat. Let stand 1 minute or until cheese melts. Serves 8 (serving size: about 1 cup)

CALORIES 228; **FAT** 8.7g (sat 3.3g, mono 3.2g, poly 0.6g); **PROTEIN** 16.7g; **CARB** 20.4g; **FIBER** 3.3g; **CHOL** 42mg; **IRON** 2.5mg; **SODIUM** 532mg; **CALC** 146mg

This is the ideal weeknight meal. You can prep all your ingredients earlier in the day, and then it takes 10 minutes for it to come together. Center-cut loin pork chops are very lean, so they cook quickly and are a great alternative to chicken, but boneless, skinless chicken breast can certainly stand in for the pork, if you'd like. Serve with steamed jasmine or brown rice to round out the meal.

PORK AND MANGO STIR-FRY

HANDS-ON TIME: 16 MINUTES | TOTAL TIME: 16 MINUTES

4 (4-ounce) center-cut loin
   pork chops
1/2 cup all-purpose flour
1/4 cup lower-sodium soy sauce
3 tablespoons minced peeled fresh
   ginger
1/2 teaspoon grated orange rind
2 tablespoons fresh orange juice
2 teaspoons cornstarch
5 garlic cloves, minced
2 tablespoons canola oil
7 cups shredded napa (Chinese)
   cabbage
2 cups (1/4-inch) sliced ripe mango
1/4 cup chopped fresh mint or mint
   leaves
Grated orange rind (optional)

1. Place pork between 2 sheets of plastic wrap; pound to 1/4-inch thickness using a meat mallet or small heavy skillet. Cut pork into 1/4-inch strips. Place strips in a bowl; sprinkle with flour, tossing to coat.
2. Combine soy sauce and next 5 ingredients (through garlic), stirring with a whisk until cornstarch dissolves. Heat a large nonstick skillet over medium-high heat. Add oil; swirl to coat. Add pork; stir-fry 3 minutes or until browned. Add soy sauce mixture to pan. Cook, stirring constantly, 1 minute or until sauce thickens. Add cabbage; cook 30 seconds. Remove from heat. Stir in mango. Serve immediately. Garnish with mint and, if desired, grated orange rind. Serves 6 (serving size: about 1 1/2 cups)

CALORIES 255; FAT 8.9g (sat 1.6g, mono 4.4g, poly 1.8g); PROTEIN 17.7g; CARB 26.8g; FIBER 2.9g; CHOL 44mg; IRON 1.1mg; SODIUM 427mg; CALC 99mg

My dear friend Janis developed the Lime Crema, and it really makes the recipe! If you don't have any mango on hand, pineapple makes a good substitute. Add a side of Cilantro-Lime Rice (page 145) to complete your meal.

FISH TACOS WITH LIME CREMA AND MANGO SALSA

HANDS-ON TIME: 23 MINUTES | TOTAL TIME: 33 MINUTES

MANGO SALSA:
1¾ cups diced peeled mango (about 2 mangoes)
¼ cup diced red onion
2 tablespoons chopped fresh cilantro

LIME CREMA:
½ cup reduced-fat mayonnaise
½ cup fresh cilantro leaves
3 tablespoons fresh lime juice
½ ripe peeled avocado

TACOS:
1 pound mahimahi
⅛ teaspoon salt
⅛ teaspoon freshly ground black pepper
Cooking spray
8 (6-inch) gluten-free corn tortillas
2 cups shredded red cabbage

1. To prepare salsa, combine first 3 ingredients in a bowl. Cover and refrigerate until ready to serve.
2. To prepare Lime Crema, place mayonnaise and next 3 ingredients (through avocado) in a food processor; process until smooth. Cover and refrigerate up to 2 days.
3. To prepare tacos, preheat grill to medium-high heat. Sprinkle fish with salt and pepper. Place fish on grill rack coated with cooking spray; cook 5 minutes on each side or until fish flakes easily when tested with a fork. Remove from grill; break into chunks with a fork.
4. While fish cooks, warm tortillas according to package directions.
5. Spoon 3 ounces fish, ¼ cup salsa, 1½ tablespoons crema, and ¼ cup cabbage onto each tortilla; fold in half. Serves 4 (serving size: 2 tacos)

CALORIES 347; FAT 9.3g (sat 1.5g, mono 0.1g, poly 0.7g); PROTEIN 24.3g; CARB 45.4g; FIBER 4.6g; CHOL 83mg; IRON 1.8mg; SODIUM 454mg; CALC 57mg

My friend Sheila is one of my favorite cooks because we share the same philosophy: She, too, refuses to cook separate meals for her kids. The last time we had dinner at her place, she whipped up her version of fish tacos and used this recipe for the base. Guess what happened? All four of our children loved it. Some ate rice, some ate guacamole, and all of them ate the fish she put in the tacos. This fish is great on its own with Roasted Fingerling Fries (page 153), but if you want to make fish tacos, fill warmed tortillas with a piece of fish, a spoonful of guacamole, and some finely shredded romaine lettuce.

PARMESAN-CRUSTED TILAPIA

HANDS-ON TIME: 9 MINUTES | TOTAL TIME: 21 MINUTES

½ cup panko (Japanese breadcrumbs)
2 ounces grated fresh Parmesan cheese (about ½ cup)
¼ teaspoon kosher salt
¼ teaspoon freshly ground black pepper
2 large eggs, lightly beaten
4 (6-ounce) tilapia fillets
2 tablespoons canola oil, divided
8 lemon wedges

1. Combine first 4 ingredients in a shallow dish; place eggs in another shallow dish. Rinse fillets; pat dry with paper towels. Dip fillets in egg; dredge in panko mixture.
2. Heat a large nonstick skillet over medium heat. Add 1 tablespoon oil; swirl to coat. Add half of fillets to pan; cook 2 to 3 minutes on each side or until fish flakes easily when tested with a fork. Wipe pan with paper towels. Repeat procedure with remaining oil and fillets. Serve with lemon wedges. Serves 4 (serving size: 1 fillet and 2 lemon wedges)

CALORIES 305; FAT 13.6g (sat 3.5g, mono 6.5g, poly 2.9g); PROTEIN 39.5g; CARB 5.6g; FIBER 0g; CHOL 133mg; IRON 1.3mg; SODIUM 386mg; CALC 123mg

Let the kids dip the fish in the eggs and then into the panko mixture. It's messy, but fun!

"The parchment-wrapped fish was quite a hit at my house. Nick, my 8-year-old, said, 'Wow, this is the fanciest thing you have ever made!' It is now the dish I make when other families come for dinner. If they only knew how easy it is to make!"

—Valerie, mother of four

Cooking in parchment paper leaves you with food that is flavorful and tender. All you have to do is fill the pouch with your favorite fish—halibut, salmon, cod, or snapper—seasonal veggies, and seasonings, and twist the ends of the parchment. Presto! Dinner is served, and the kids—and adults—think it looks awesome.

TWISTED FISH

HANDS-ON TIME: 20 MINUTES | TOTAL TIME: 40 MINUTES

½ cup fresh corn kernels
½ cup shredded zucchini
1 pound asparagus spears, trimmed
4 (6-ounce) halibut fillets
1 lemon, cut into 12 thin slices
2 cups cherry tomatoes, halved
4 teaspoons butter, melted
½ teaspoon kosher salt
½ teaspoon freshly ground
    black pepper

1. Preheat oven to 400°.
2. Cut 4 (18-inch-long) pieces of parchment paper. Spoon corn and zucchini evenly onto center of each piece. Top evenly with asparagus, placing spears lengthwise on paper. Place fillets lengthwise over asparagus; top evenly with lemon slices. Place tomatoes around edges. Drizzle each serving with 1 teaspoon butter; sprinkle evenly with salt and pepper. Bring long sides of paper together; fold down tightly over fish and vegetables. Twist ends to enclose contents. Place packets on a large baking sheet.
3. Bake at 400° for 15 minutes. Place 1 packet on each of 4 plates. Let stand 5 minutes; cut open. Serves 4

CALORIES 281; **FAT** 8.3g (sat 3.1g, mono 2.4g, poly 1.6g); **PROTEIN** 39.4g; **CARB** 12.9g; **FIBER** 4.5g; **CHOL** 65mg; **IRON** 4.2mg; **SODIUM** 370mg; **CALC** 124mg

These burritos are so flavorful and simple to make. Dinner comes together in 20 minutes. The spinach-mushroom filling is packed with healthy ingredients, but the ooey-gooey cheese is what sells kids on this combo.

VEGETARIAN BURRITOS

HANDS-ON TIME: 22 MINUTES | TOTAL TIME: 22 MINUTES

Cooking spray
½ cup chopped onion
2 garlic cloves, minced
1 jalapeño pepper,
    seeded and chopped
1 (8-ounce) package sliced fresh
    mushrooms
1 (6-ounce) package fresh baby
    spinach leaves
1 tablespoon fresh lime juice
½ teaspoon kosher salt
½ teaspoon ground cumin
1½ cups cooked long-grain
    brown rice
1 (15-ounce) can black beans,
    rinsed and drained
4 ounces shredded reduced-fat
    4-cheese Mexican blend cheese
    (about 1 cup)
8 (8-inch) whole-wheat
    flour tortillas
Fresh salsa (optional)

1. Heat a large skillet over medium-high heat. Coat pan with cooking spray. Add onion, garlic, jalapeño, and mushrooms; sauté 5 minutes, stirring occasionally. Gradually add spinach; cook 1 to 2 minutes, stirring until wilted. Stir in lime juice, salt, and cumin. Add rice and beans; cook, stirring constantly, 1 minute or until thoroughly heated. Add cheese, stirring until melted.

2. Warm tortillas according to package directions. Spoon about ⅔ cup mushroom mixture down center of each tortilla; roll up. Serve with salsa, if desired. Serves 8 (serving size: 1 burrito)

CALORIES 229; FAT 4.6g (sat 1.6g, mono 0.1g, poly 0.2g); PROTEIN 11.5g; CARB 36.8g; FIBER 4.4g; CHOL 10mg; IRON 2mg; SODIUM 487mg; CALC 211mg

The kids can help scoop the mushroom mixture into the tortillas and then roll them up.

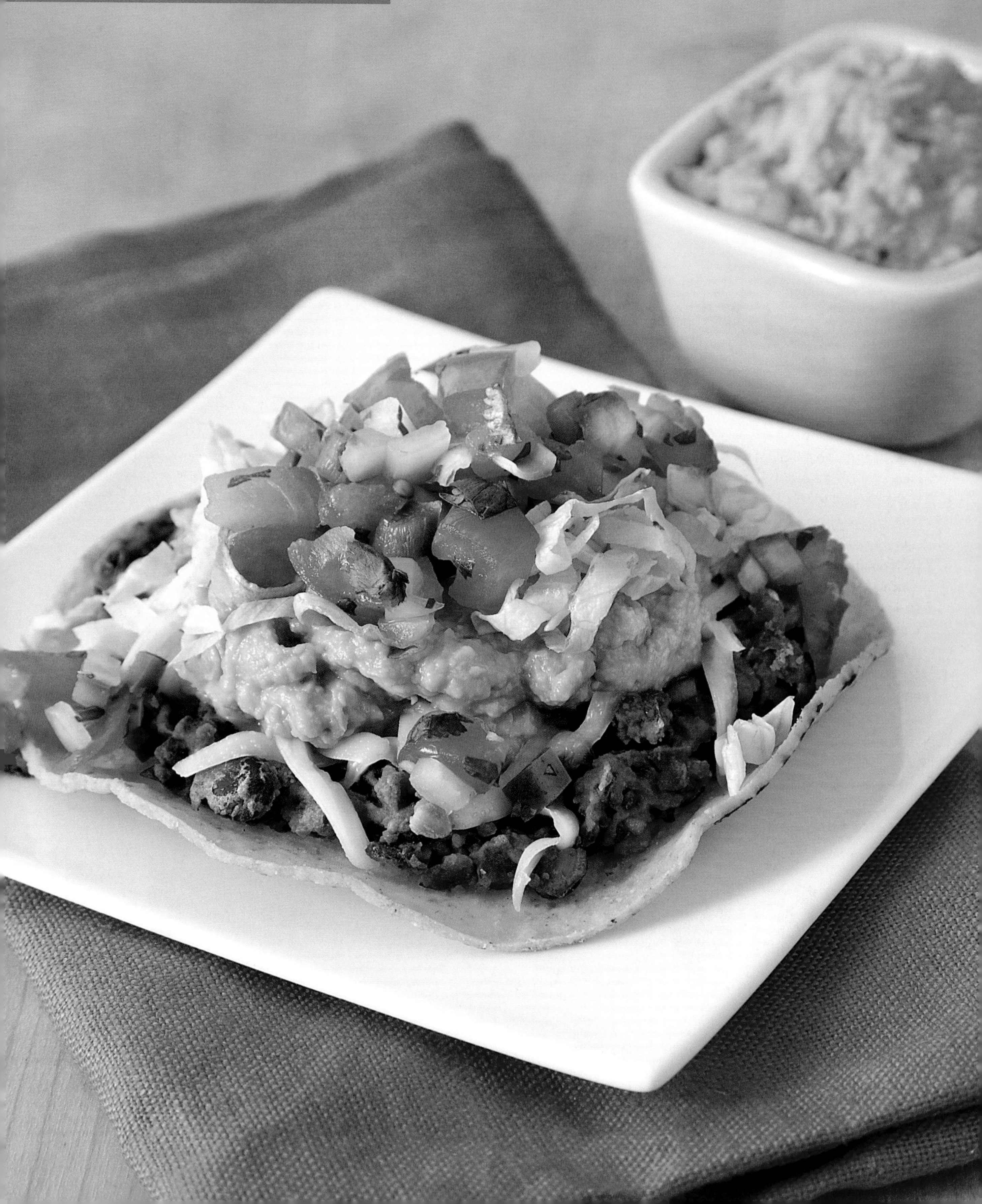

Here's another recipe that everyone in the family can customize to their own tastes.

VEGGIE TOSTADAS WITH BLACK BEANS AND EASY GUACAMOLE

HANDS-ON TIME: 17 MINUTES | TOTAL TIME: 22 MINUTES

2 ripe peeled avocados, coarsely mashed
2 tablespoons fresh lime juice
1/2 teaspoon salt
2 teaspoons olive oil
1 large garlic clove, minced
1/3 cup organic vegetable broth
2 (15.5-ounce) cans black beans, rinsed and drained
6 (6-inch) tostada shells, toasted
3 ounces shredded Monterey Jack cheese (about 3/4 cup)
1 1/2 cups shredded lettuce
3/4 cup Fresh Salsa (page 41)

1. Combine avocado, lime juice, and salt in a medium bowl. Cover surface of guacamole with plastic wrap.
2. Heat a medium saucepan over medium heat. Add oil; swirl to coat. Add garlic; cook 1 minute. Stir in vegetable broth and beans. Reduce heat to medium-low; cover and cook 5 minutes or until thoroughly heated. Remove pan from heat; mash beans to desired consistency.
3. Spread about 1/4 cup bean mixture on each tostada shell. Top each with 2 tablespoons cheese, about 1/3 cup guacamole, 1/4 cup lettuce, and 2 tablespoons Fresh Salsa. Serve immediately. Serves 6 (serving size: 1 tostada)

CALORIES 319; **FAT** 18.3g (sat 4.5g, mono 4.2g, poly 0.7g); **PROTEIN** 11.1g; **CARB** 30.1g; **FIBER** 6.6g; **CHOL** 13mg; **IRON** 2.2mg; **SODIUM** 613mg; **CALC** 165mg

Tip: You can make things even easier on yourself by purchasing store-bought salsa and guacamole if you can't find ripe avocados.

technique: how to prep an avocado

1. Hold the knife steady; rotate the fruit so the knife moves around the pit. Remove the knife, and slowly twist sides away from each other to separate.

2. Strike the pit, and pierce with the blade. Then twist and remove the knife; the pit will come with it.

3. Use the knife's tip to cut the flesh in horizontal and vertical rows. Be careful not to cut through the skin. Scoop out the diced pieces with a spoon.

When stuck in a rut with pasta and basic tomato sauce, turn to veggies. Sautéed in a little olive oil with lemon juice, this combination is great as a "sauce" on its own. It's a wonderful way to enjoy the flavors of spring and get some color into your family's diet. Make it a gluten-free option by using gluten-free pasta.

SPRING PASTA WITH ASPARAGUS AND GRAPE TOMATOES

HANDS-ON TIME: 17 MINUTES | TOTAL TIME: 17 MINUTES

8 ounces uncooked penne pasta
1 tablespoon olive oil, divided
1 cup chopped onion
2 cups (¹/₂-inch) sliced asparagus
1 teaspoon grated lemon rind
2 tablespoons fresh lemon juice, divided
2 cups grape tomatoes, halved
1 teaspoon kosher salt
¹/₂ teaspoon freshly ground black pepper
2.25 ounces grated fresh Parmigiano-Reggiano cheese (9 tablespoons)
6 tablespoons chopped fresh basil or small basil leaves (optional)

1. Cook pasta according to package directions, omitting salt and fat. Drain, reserving 2 tablespoons cooking liquid; return pasta to pan.
2. Heat a large skillet over medium heat. Add 1 teaspoon olive oil; swirl to coat. Add onion; cook 3 minutes. Add asparagus, lemon rind, and 1 tablespoon lemon juice; sauté 2 minutes. Stir in tomatoes; sauté 1 minute or just until tomatoes begin to soften. Add reserved cooking liquid, tomato mixture, remaining 2 teaspoons olive oil, remaining 1 tablespoon lemon juice, salt, and pepper to pasta. Toss well. Spoon 1 cup pasta mixture into each of 6 bowls, and sprinkle each serving with 1¹/₂ tablespoons cheese. Garnish with fresh basil, if desired. Serves 6

CALORIES 218; **FAT** 5.1g (sat 2g, mono 1.7g, poly 0.3g); **PROTEIN** 9.8g; **CARB** 35g; **FIBER** 3.3g; **CHOL** 6mg; **IRON** 2.3mg; **SODIUM** 371mg; **CALC** 141mg

DINNER TONIGHT

Loaded with surprising hits of curry powder, lime juice, and cilantro, this soup pairs perfectly with panini or with a salad for dinner. It also makes a wonderful first course for a fancier meal. Make this a vegetarian option by using vegetable broth instead of chicken broth.

CARROT-GINGER SOUP

HANDS-ON TIME: 17 MINUTES | TOTAL TIME: 1 HOUR AND 2 MINUTES

3 tablespoons unsalted butter
3 tablespoons olive oil
1 cup chopped onion
2 tablespoons finely chopped
  peeled fresh ginger
2 garlic cloves, finely minced
7 cups fat-free, lower-sodium
  chicken or vegetable broth
4 cups diced carrot (1½ pounds)
1 cup dry white wine
2 teaspoons fresh lime juice
¼ teaspoon curry powder
¼ teaspoon freshly ground
  black pepper
2 tablespoons chopped
  fresh cilantro

1. Heat a large saucepan over medium heat. Melt butter with olive oil in pan; cook 2 minutes or until butter melts. Add onion, ginger, and garlic. Cook 10 minutes or until onion is soft, stirring occasionally.
2. Stir in broth, carrot, and wine. Bring to a boil; reduce heat and simmer, uncovered, for 45 minutes.
3. Place half of carrot mixture in a blender. Remove center piece of blender lid (to allow steam to escape); secure blender lid on blender. Place a clean towel over opening in blender lid (to avoid splatters). Blend until smooth. Pour into a bowl. Repeat procedure with remaining carrot mixture. Stir in lime juice, curry powder, and pepper. Ladle about ²/₃ cup soup into each of 12 bowls. Sprinkle evenly with cilantro. Serves 12

CALORIES 88; **FAT** 6.4g (sat 2.3g, mono 3.2g, poly 0.5g); **PROTEIN** 1.2g; **CARB** 6g; **FIBER** 1.5g; **CHOL** 8mg; **IRON** 0.2mg; **SODIUM** 294mg; **CALC** 20mg

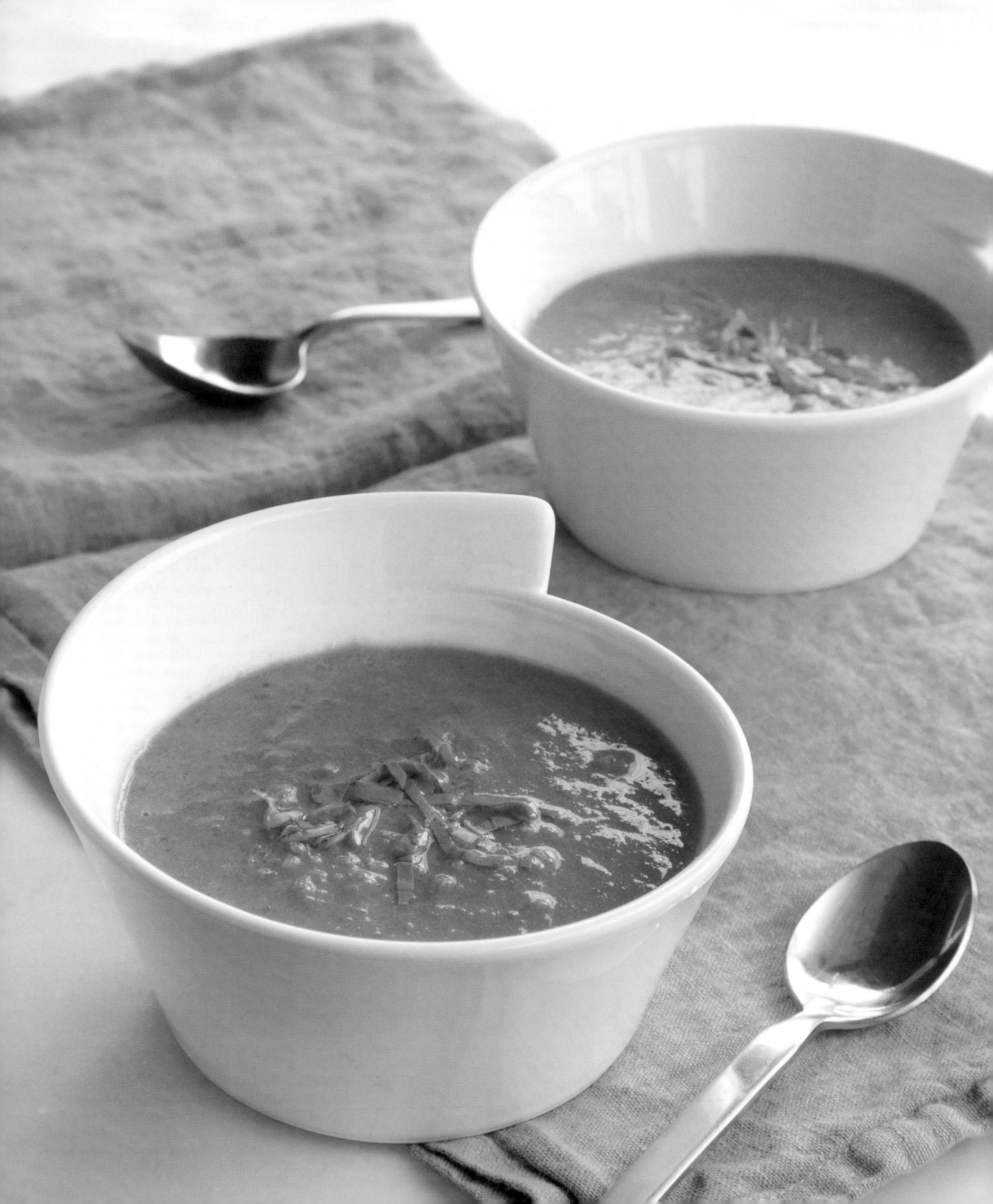

I was not a fan of tomato soup growing up—probably because I had eaten only the thin, sugary version out of a can. Then I ate the real deal, and it all made sense. I like to finish this soup with a little cream, but it is absolutely delicious without it, too. Serve with Parmesan Crisps (page 47) to round out your meal. Make this a vegetarian option by using vegetable broth instead of chicken broth.

CREAMY TOMATO SOUP

HANDS-ON TIME: 33 MINUTES | TOTAL TIME: 1 HOUR AND 3 MINUTES

3 tablespoons olive oil
1 cup chopped onion
³/₄ cup chopped celery
¹/₃ cup chopped carrot
¹/₂ teaspoon freshly ground
    black pepper
¹/₈ teaspoon kosher salt
3 garlic cloves, minced
1 tablespoon tomato paste
3 cups fat-free, lower-sodium
    chicken or vegetable broth
¹/₂ cup white wine
¹/₄ cup chopped fresh basil
1 (28-ounce) can no-salt-added
    tomatoes, undrained
¹/₄ cup whipping cream
Fresh basil (optional)

1. Heat a large saucepan over medium heat. Add oil; swirl to coat. Add onion and next 5 ingredients (through garlic) to pan; cook 10 minutes, stirring occasionally. Stir in tomato paste; cook 1 minute. Add broth and next 3 ingredients (through tomatoes). Bring to a boil; reduce heat and simmer, uncovered, 30 minutes.
2. Place one-third of tomato mixture in a blender. Remove center piece of blender lid (to allow steam to escape); secure blender lid on blender. Place a clean towel over opening in blender lid (to avoid splatters). Blend until smooth. Pour into a large bowl. Repeat procedure twice with remaining tomato mixture. Stir in cream. Garnish with basil, if desired. Serves 9 (serving size: about ³/₄ cup)

CALORIES 95; FAT 6.6g (sat 1.9g, mono 3.9g, poly 0.6g); PROTEIN 2.5g; CARB 6.4g; FIBER 1.4g; CHOL 7mg; IRON 2.2mg; SODIUM 271mg; CALC 19mg

This is a perfect cold-weather soup. Because it's pureed, the creamy texture and vibrant color make it appealing to most kids, and no cream is needed. It's an ideal make-ahead meal on a weekend when you have a little time to sit around and let it cook. Then on Monday night, all you have to do is reheat it and make some garlic bread.

CREAMY BROCCOLI SOUP

HANDS-ON TIME: 35 MINUTES | TOTAL TIME: 45 MINUTES

1 tablespoon olive oil
1 cup chopped onion
¾ cup chopped leek
2 garlic cloves, minced
3 cups organic vegetable broth
2 cups water
1½ cups (1-inch) cubed peeled
    red potato
½ teaspoon freshly ground
    black pepper
⅛ teaspoon kosher salt
1 (12-ounce) bag broccoli florets,
    coarsely chopped
1 (15-ounce) can no-salt-added
    cannellini beans, rinsed
    and drained
6 tablespoons grated fresh
    Parmesan cheese

1. Heat a large Dutch oven over medium heat. Add oil; swirl to coat. Add onion, leek, and garlic; cook 5 minutes or until tender, stirring frequently. Stir in broth and next 4 ingredients (through salt). Bring to a boil; reduce heat and simmer 10 minutes or just until potatoes are tender, stirring occasionally. Stir in broccoli and beans; cook 8 minutes or until broccoli is tender.

2. Place one-third of soup mixture in a blender. Remove center piece of blender lid (to allow steam to escape); secure blender lid on blender. Place a clean towel over opening in blender lid (to avoid splatters). Blend until smooth. Pour into a large bowl. Repeat procedure twice with remaining soup mixture. Wipe pan with paper towels.

3. Return soup to pan. Cook over medium-low heat 5 minutes or until thoroughly heated, stirring occasionally. Ladle soup into bowls; sprinkle evenly with cheese. Serves 4 (serving size: about 2 cups soup and 1½ tablespoons cheese)

CALORIES 231; FAT 6.5g (sat 1.9g, mono 3.1g, poly 0.7g); PROTEIN 10.5g; CARB 35g; FIBER 7.4g; CHOL 7mg; IRON 2.5mg; SODIUM 640mg; CALC 173mg

TOMATO-BASIL RISOTTO

SPRING VEGETABLE RISOTTO

Risotto is comforting, substantial, and so versatile. Plus, once you learn how to stir it and add the broth, you realize it's truly a cinch to make. Here are a few main-dish combinations that will take you through the seasons.

RISOTTO, RISOTTO, RISOTTO!
HANDS-ON TIME: 5 MINUTES | TOTAL TIME: 33 MINUTES

4 cups fat-free, lower-sodium chicken or vegetable broth
2 tablespoons butter, divided
2 tablespoons olive oil
1¼ cups chopped onion
2 (8-ounce) packages presliced fresh cremini mushrooms
1 cup uncooked Arborio rice
2 tablespoons dry sherry
1.3 ounces grated fresh Parmigiano-Reggiano cheese, divided (about ⅓ cup)
1 teaspoon fresh thyme leaves
¼ teaspoon freshly ground black pepper
⅛ teaspoon kosher salt

1. Bring broth to a simmer in a 3-quart saucepan (do not boil). Keep warm over low heat.
2. Heat a deep 10-inch skillet over medium heat. Melt 1 tablespoon butter with olive oil in pan; cook until butter melts. Add onion and mushrooms; sauté 5 minutes or until tender. Add rice; cook 1 minute, stirring constantly. Stir in sherry; cook 30 seconds or until liquid is nearly absorbed, stirring constantly. Stir in 1 cup broth; cook 5 minutes or until liquid is nearly absorbed, stirring constantly. Add remaining broth, ½ cup at a time, stirring constantly until each portion of broth is absorbed before adding the next (about 14 minutes). Remove from heat; stir in remaining 1 tablespoon butter, ¼ cup cheese, and remaining ingredients. Cover and let stand 2 minutes. Sprinkle with remaining cheese. Serve immediately. Serves 4 (serving size: 1 cup)

CALORIES 366; **FAT** 15.2g (sat 6g, mono 6.4g, poly 1g); **PROTEIN** 11.1g; **CARB** 47.5g; **FIBER** 3.6g; **CHOL** 21mg; **IRON** 0.8mg; **SODIUM** 600mg; **CALC** 131mg

Tomato-Basil Risotto: Omit mushrooms, sherry, thyme, and salt. Add ¼ cup white wine to sautéed onion, cooking as directed above. Add broth, and cook as directed above. Remove from heat; stir in 1 cup chopped drained San Marzano tomatoes, ½ cup grated fresh Parmigiano-Reggiano cheese, 2 tablespoons chopped fresh basil, and pepper. Cover and let stand 2 minutes before serving. Serves 4 (serving size: about 1 cup)

CALORIES 364; **FAT** 16.1g (sat 6.6g, mono 6.4g, poly 0.9g); **PROTEIN** 10.2g; **CARB** 45.4g; **FIBER** 3.4g; **CHOL** 23mg; **IRON** 0.7mg; **SODIUM** 683mg; **CALC** 170mg

Spring Vegetable Risotto: Omit mushrooms and sherry. Add ½ cup white wine to sautéed onion, cooking as directed above. Add broth, and cook as directed above, adding 1 cup chopped trimmed asparagus spears and ¾ cup frozen petite green peas, thawed, before adding last ½ cup broth. Remove from heat; stir in ⅓ cup grated fresh Parmigiano-Reggiano cheese, thyme, pepper, and salt. Cover and let stand 2 minutes. Serves 4 (serving size: 1 cup)

CALORIES 366; **FAT** 15.2g (sat 6g, mono 6.4g, poly 1g); **PROTEIN** 10.5g; **CARB** 48.2g; **FIBER** 5g; **CHOL** 21mg; **IRON** 1.5mg; **SODIUM** 595mg; **CALC** 125mg

What's not to love about stuffed shells? Loaded with cheese and tomato sauce, this pasta dish is a total crowd-pleaser. To change it up, you can add a little lean ground beef or different herbs to the sauce. Also, it's easy to double the recipe and freeze one batch.

CHEESY STUFFED SHELLS WITH MY SECRET TOMATO SAUCE

HANDS-ON TIME: 12 MINUTES | TOTAL TIME: 1 HOUR AND 4 MINUTES

30 uncooked jumbo shell pasta (about 8 ounces)

4 ounces shredded 6-cheese Italian-blend cheese, divided (about 1 cup)

8 ounces shredded part-skim mozzarella cheese (about 2 cups)

¼ cup chopped fresh flat-leaf parsley

¼ cup chopped fresh basil

½ teaspoon kosher salt

½ teaspoon freshly ground black pepper

1 (15-ounce) container part-skim ricotta cheese

Cooking spray

3 cups My Secret Tomato Sauce (page 25) or bottled pasta sauce

1. Preheat oven to 350°.
2. Cook pasta in boiling water 8 minutes or until almost al dente. Drain. Rinse with cold water; drain.
3. Combine ½ cup Italian-blend cheese and next 6 ingredients (through ricotta) in a bowl. Spoon about 1½ tablespoons cheese mixture into each pasta shell. Place shells, stuffed sides up, in a 13 x 9–inch glass or ceramic baking dish coated with cooking spray. Pour sauce over shells. Cover and bake at 350° for 30 minutes or until bubbly. Uncover; sprinkle with remaining ½ cup Italian-blend cheese. Bake 5 minutes or until cheese melts. Serves 10 (serving size: 3 stuffed shells)

CALORIES 285; **FAT** 13.1g (sat 6.5g, mono 4g, poly 0.6g); **PROTEIN** 17.5g; **CARB** 24.5g; **FIBER** 1.5g; **CHOL** 37mg; **IRON** 1.7mg; **SODIUM** 536mg; **CALC** 401mg

Tip: If you don't have any My Secret Tomato Sauce (page 25) prepared, the Organic Tomato Basil Sauce from Whole Foods Market is a great go-to option.

When I think of beef and broccoli, I think of oversalted Chinese takeout. But this version is fantastic. Loaded with the flavors you crave, but packed with enough broccoli and lean flank steak to make it nutritious, this is a great meal for any night of the week. Gluten-free tamari is a delicious stand-in for the soy sauce.

BEEF AND BROCCOLI

HANDS-ON TIME: 20 MINUTES | TOTAL TIME: 50 MINUTES

1 (1-pound) flank steak
1 tablespoon brown sugar
3 tablespoons lower-sodium soy sauce
2 tablespoons sherry
1 tablespoon oyster sauce
2 teaspoons cornstarch
2 teaspoons sambal oelek (chile paste with garlic)
1 tablespoon peanut oil
3 garlic cloves, thinly sliced
1 tablespoon minced peeled fresh ginger
1½ cups vertically sliced onion
1 (12-ounce) package broccoli florets
3 cups hot cooked brown rice

1. Freeze steak 30 minutes. Cut steak across grain into ¼-inch-thick strips.
2. Combine brown sugar and next 5 ingredients (through chile paste) in a small bowl, stirring with a whisk.
3. Place a wok or large frying pan over high heat until very hot. Drizzle oil around sides of wok to coat sides and bottom. When oil is very hot, but not smoking, add garlic; stir-fry 30 seconds or until golden. Remove garlic using slotted spoon; drain on paper towels. Add ginger, onion, and broccoli to pan; stir-fry 2 minutes. Add steak; stir-fry 2 minutes or just until no longer pink.
4. Stir in soy sauce mixture. Cook 1 minute or until sauce thickens, stirring constantly. Serve over rice. Top with garlic slices. Serves 6 (serving size: 1 cup beef mixture, ½ cup rice, and ½ garlic clove)

CALORIES 291; FAT 7.6g (sat 2.2g, mono 2.9g, poly 1.4g); PROTEIN 21.5g; CARB 32.6g; FIBER 4g; CHOL 25mg; IRON 2.3mg; SODIUM 378mg; CALC 69mg

"This is my favorite fancy dinner. I want my mom to make it every night!" —Paige, age 6

I prefer to grill everything, especially beef, but sometimes I enjoy the flavor of a pan-fried steak. A well-seasoned cast-iron skillet is my pan of choice, but any ovenproof skillet will work. Allowing the steaks to come to room temperature for an hour before cooking is the secret to evenly cooked meat. Plus, it gives them time to marinate.

PAN-FRIED BEEF TENDERLOIN

HANDS-ON TIME: 5 MINUTES | TOTAL TIME: 1 HOUR AND 16 MINUTES

2 tablespoons coarsely
   chopped fresh rosemary
2 tablespoons olive oil
1 teaspoon kosher salt
1 teaspoon grated lemon rind
2 garlic cloves, minced
4 (4-ounce) beef tenderloin
   steaks, trimmed

1. Combine first 5 ingredients in a small baking dish. Add steaks to marinade, turning to coat. Cover and marinate steaks at room temperature 1 hour, turning occasionally.
2. Heat a cast-iron skillet over medium-high heat. Remove steaks from dish; discard marinade. Place steaks in pan; cook, without disturbing, 2 minutes or until steaks release easily from bottom of pan. Turn steaks over; cook 2 minutes. Turn steaks over, and cook an additional 2 minutes or until desired degree of doneness. Let stand 5 minutes. Serves 4 (serving size: 1 steak)

CALORIES 237; FAT 14.2g (sat 3.7g, mono 7.9g, poly 1g); PROTEIN 25.2g; CARB 0.8g; FIBER 0.2g; CHOL 76mg; IRON 1.9mg; SODIUM 544mg; CALC 34mg

Rosemary is a fragrant and easy herb for kids to handle. They can pick the leaves off for you by pulling them in the opposite direction in which they grow. Voilà! It's ready to use.

My friend and mentor Tori Ritchie is a fabulous cook. Of all the things she makes, this has to be my favorite. I like to serve it over egg noodles, as Tori recommends; as a sandwich; or simply on its own with some juices from the pot. Perfection!

POT ROAST

HANDS-ON TIME: 24 MINUTES | TOTAL TIME: 3 HOURS AND 24 MINUTES

2 tablespoons olive oil

3 pounds boneless sirloin tip roast, trimmed and tied

2 1/2 cups thinly sliced onion

6 small carrots, cut into 1-inch chunks

3 garlic cloves, sliced

2 rosemary sprigs

1 1/2 teaspoons kosher salt

1 teaspoon freshly ground black pepper

1/2 cup water

1/4 cup reduced-fat sour cream

2 tablespoons prepared horseradish

2 tablespoons chopped fresh flat-leaf parsley (optional)

1. Preheat oven to 325°.
2. Heat an ovenproof 6-quart Dutch oven over medium heat. Add oil; swirl to coat. Add roast to pan. Cook 10 minutes, turning to brown on all sides. Remove from heat. Add onion, carrot, garlic, and rosemary to pan. Sprinkle roast and vegetables with salt and pepper. Add 1/2 cup water to pan. Cover and bake at 325° for 3 to 3 1/2 hours or until meat is fork-tender, turning roast halfway through cooking time.
3. While roast bakes, combine sour cream and horseradish in a small bowl.
4. Skim fat from drippings. Break roast into large chunks with 2 forks. Serve roast with vegetables, pan drippings, and horseradish cream. Garnish with parsley, if desired. Serves 12 (serving size: 3 ounces beef, 1/12 of vegetables, and 1 1/2 teaspoons horseradish cream)

CALORIES 231; FAT 11.7g (sat 3.9g, mono 6g, poly 0.7g); PROTEIN 24.3g; CARB 6.2g; FIBER 1.4g; CHOL 68mg; IRON 1.9mg; SODIUM 333mg; CALC 55mg

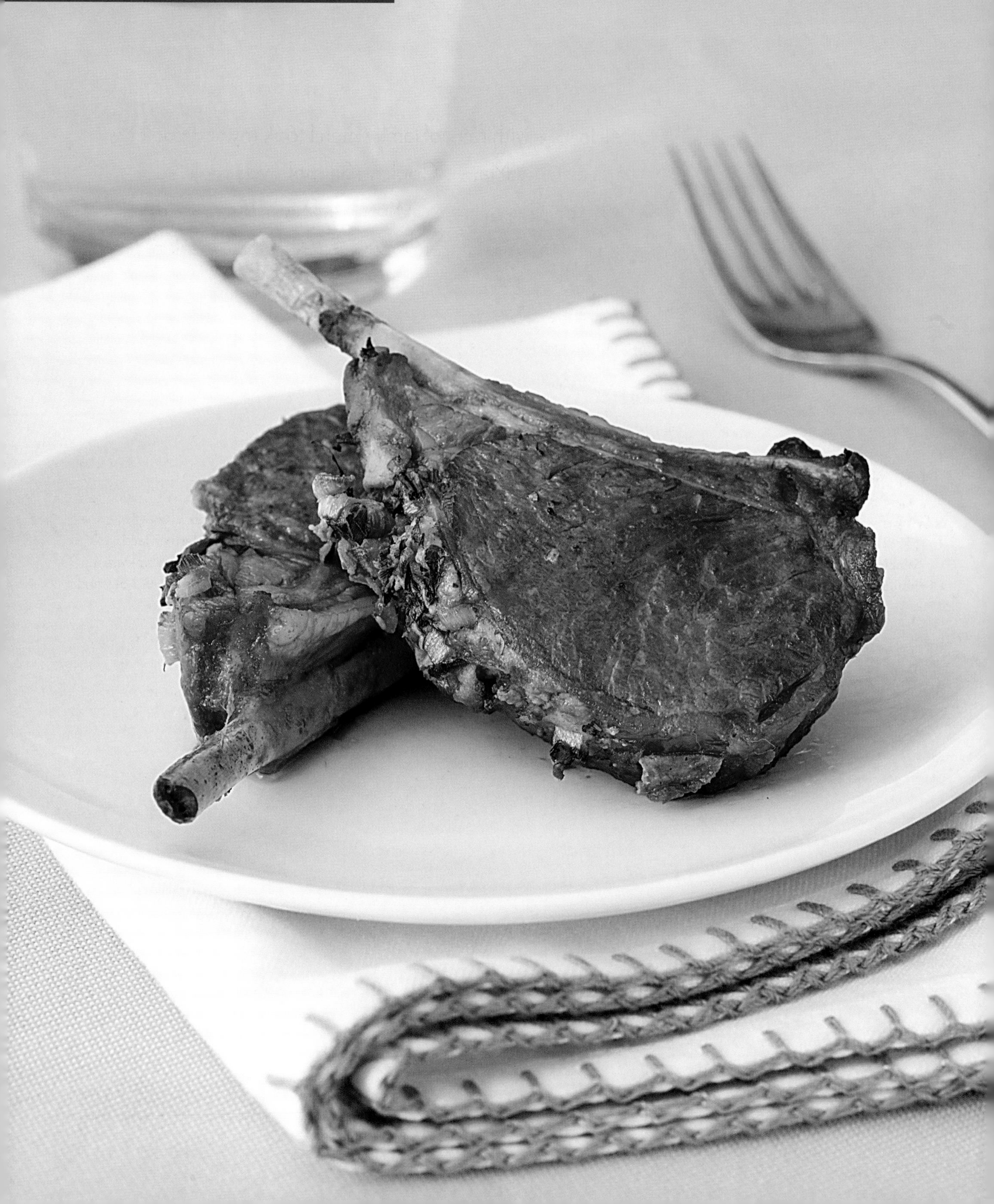

I fell in love with rack of lamb when I took my first cooking class at Tante Marie's Cooking School. I've simplified it a bit so it's easy enough for a weeknight but still special. While it's cooking, make a side of polenta and a salad.

HERBED RACK OF LAMB

HANDS-ON TIME: 12 MINUTES | TOTAL TIME: 47 MINUTES

1½ teaspoons olive oil
1 (1½-pound) rack of lamb (8 ribs), trimmed
½ teaspoon kosher salt
½ teaspoon freshly ground black pepper
1 tablespoon Dijon mustard
¼ cup minced shallots
1 tablespoon minced fresh chives
1 tablespoon chopped fresh flat-leaf parsley
1 tablespoon chopped fresh mint

1. Preheat oven to 450°.
2. Lightly brush a small roasting pan and rack with olive oil.
3. Place lamb, fat side up, on rack in prepared pan. Score outside of lamb in a diamond pattern. Sprinkle lamb with salt and pepper; brush with mustard. Combine shallots and remaining ingredients in a small bowl. Pat shallot mixture into mustard on lamb.
4. Bake at 450° for 25 minutes or until a thermometer registers 145° (medium-rare) or until desired degree of doneness. Remove lamb from pan; cover with foil, and let stand 10 minutes. Cut into chops. Serves 4 (serving size: 2 chops)

CALORIES 300; **FAT** 15.7g (sat 6.3g, mono 6.8g, poly 0.7g); **PROTEIN** 34.6g; **CARB** 2.8g; **FIBER** 0.2g; **CHOL** 112mg; **IRON** 2.9mg; **SODIUM** 470mg; **CALC** 25mg

Tip: If it hasn't already been done, ask the butcher to trim the rack for you and score it, too.

"My mom makes this chicken as my special dinner. I like the sauce that she puts on it—even the green stuff." —Matt, age 9

When you make this recipe the first time, give yourself a little extra time. For kids, consider cutting up the juicy chicken, and putting it on their plates with the sauce on the side so they can control how much they try. Once again, I owe chef and cookbook author Joey Altman for this recipe. Serve with couscous.

LEMON CHICKEN WITH CURRANTS AND PINE NUTS

HANDS-ON TIME: 15 MINUTES | TOTAL TIME: 1 HOUR AND 21 MINUTES

¼ cup fresh lemon juice
1 tablespoon minced garlic
1 tablespoon honey
½ teaspoon kosher salt
½ teaspoon freshly ground
    black pepper
3 tablespoons extra-virgin
    olive oil, divided
4 (6-ounce) skinless, boneless
    chicken breast halves
¼ cup fat-free, lower-sodium
    chicken broth
2 tablespoons dried currants
2 tablespoons butter
1 tablespoon capers,
    rinsed and drained
¼ cup coarsely chopped
    fresh basil
⅓ cup pine nuts, toasted

1. Combine first 5 ingredients and 2 tablespoons oil in a large zip-top plastic bag; seal and shake to blend. Add chicken to bag; seal, turning to coat. Refrigerate 1 hour.
2. Preheat oven to 375°.
3. Heat a large ovenproof skillet over medium-high heat. Add remaining 1 tablespoon oil; swirl to coat. Remove chicken from bag, draining well and reserving marinade. Add chicken to pan; cook 2 minutes or until browned. Turn chicken over. Place skillet in oven; bake at 375° for 15 minutes or until a thermometer registers 160°. Remove chicken from pan; let stand 5 minutes.
4. While chicken cooks, pour reserved marinade into a medium saucepan. Add chicken broth and next 3 ingredients (through capers). Bring to a boil; reduce heat and simmer, uncovered, 2 minutes or until sauce is reduced to about ¾ cup. Remove from heat; stir in basil.
5. Place 1 chicken breast on each of 4 plates. Drizzle evenly with sauce, and sprinkle evenly with pine nuts. Serves 4 (serving size: 1 chicken breast, 3 tablespoons sauce, and 4 teaspoons pine nuts)

CALORIES 454; FAT 26.5g (sat 6.2g, mono 12.2g, poly 5.5g); PROTEIN 41.3g; CARB 11.5g; FIBER 1g; CHOL 114mg; IRON 2.1mg; SODIUM 484mg; CALC 35mg

Tip: This is one of those recipes where you need to have all your ingredients prepped and ready so you're not running around at the end.

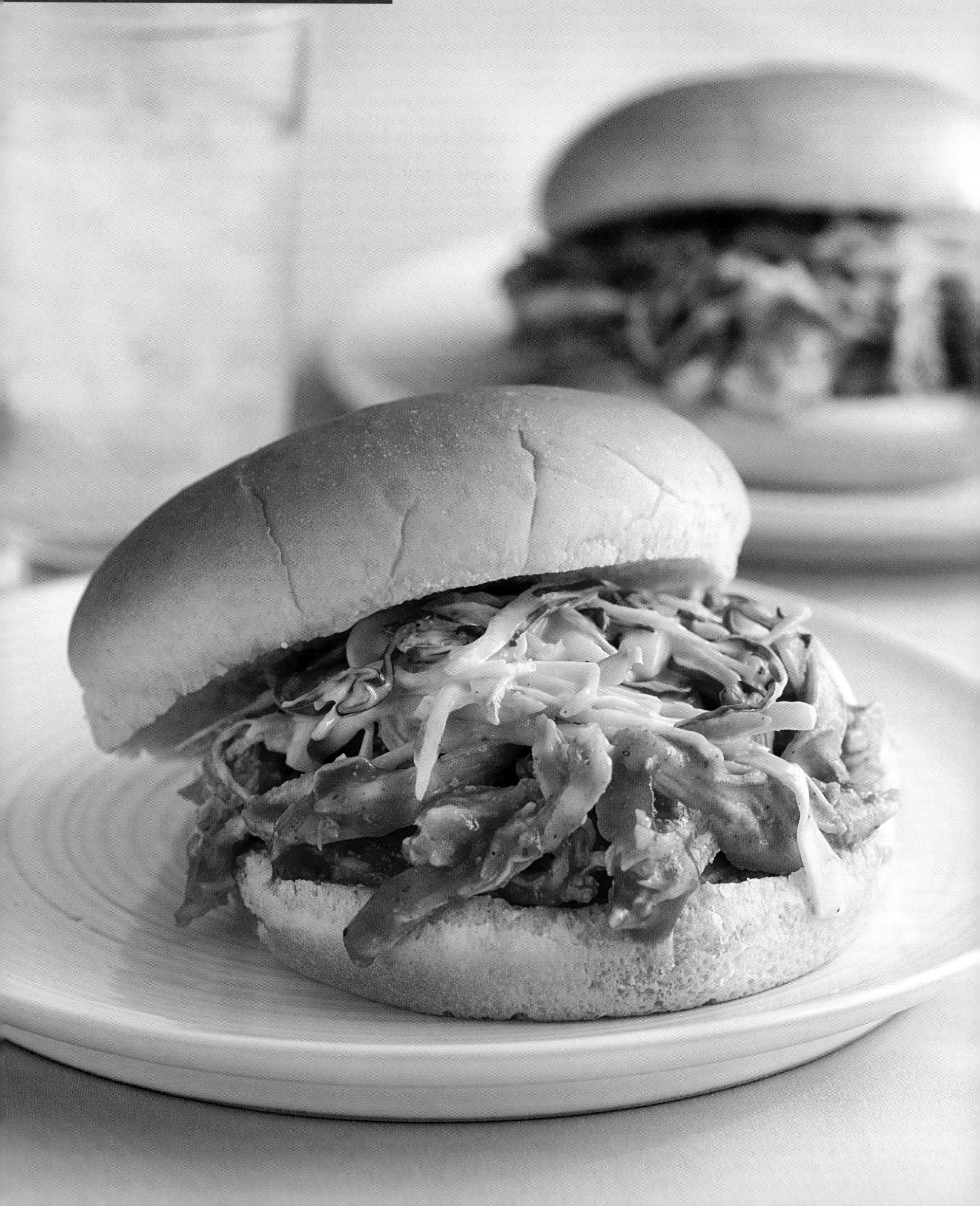

Pulled pork is outstanding, but pulled chicken is a perfect substitute on a weeknight. Everyone will go nuts for this sandwich topped with Crunchy, Creamy Coleslaw (page 125). Simmering the chicken in my homemade Barbecue Sauce (page 29) makes all the difference.

PULLED BARBECUE CHICKEN AND COLESLAW SANDWICHES

HANDS-ON TIME: 11 MINUTES | TOTAL TIME: 42 MINUTES

4 (6-ounce) skinless, boneless chicken breast halves
1⅓ cups Barbecue Sauce (page 29)
1 cup water
¼ cup cider vinegar
¼ teaspoon freshly ground black pepper
10 (1.9-ounce) hamburger buns
2½ cups Crunchy, Creamy Coleslaw (page 125)
Hot pepper sauce (optional)

1. Combine first 5 ingredients in a 3-quart saucepan. Bring to a boil; cover, reduce heat, and simmer 18 to 20 minutes or until chicken is tender. Remove chicken from sauce, reserving sauce. Place chicken on a plate, and cool 15 minutes. Shred chicken with 2 forks.
2. While chicken cools, return sauce to heat. Bring to a boil; boil, uncovered, 15 minutes or until reduced by half. Stir chicken into sauce. Cook 1 to 2 minutes or until thoroughly heated.
3. Spoon ½ cup chicken mixture onto bottom half of each bun. Top each serving with ¼ cup Crunchy, Creamy Coleslaw. Cover with bun tops. Serve with hot pepper sauce, if desired. Serves 10 (serving size: 1 sandwich)

CALORIES 296; **FAT** 4.4g (sat 1.2g, mono 0.8g, poly 1.3g); **PROTEIN** 21.2g; **CARB** 41.6g; **FIBER** 1.7g; **CHOL** 40mg; **IRON** 2.7mg; **SODIUM** 686mg; **CALC** 103mg

Tip: You can make the chicken up to two days in advance on the stove or in a slow cooker.

Kids can measure the ingredients for the barbecue sauce. Once the chicken has cooled, they can also shred the chicken and build the sandwiches.

"Sometimes I try to skip my vegetables, but for some reason I'll eat them in here!"

—Ella, age 11

In college, I spent a semester in the South of France. Once a week, we'd splurge on couscous. My version combines chicken, an assortment of the best root vegetables, and an aromatic broth to create an amazing stew served over couscous. I can taste it already.

COUSCOUS WITH CHICKEN AND ROOT VEGETABLES

HANDS-ON TIME: 22 MINUTES | TOTAL TIME: 32 MINUTES

1 tablespoon olive oil
2 cups chopped onion
2 garlic cloves, coarsely chopped
1/2 teaspoon salt
1 1/2 teaspoons curry powder
1 1/2 teaspoons ground cumin
1 teaspoon turmeric
1/2 teaspoon freshly ground
   black pepper
2 (3-inch) cinnamon sticks
1 tablespoon tomato paste
2 cups fat-free, lower-sodium
   chicken broth
1 (14.5-ounce) can diced tomatoes,
   drained
2 (6-ounce) skinless, boneless
   chicken breast halves,
   cut into 1-inch pieces
1 1/4 cups diced peeled turnips
   (about 2 small)
1 cup chopped carrot
   (about 3 medium)
1/4 cup diced parsnip
1 cup raisins
3 cups hot cooked couscous
2 tablespoons chopped fresh
   flat-leaf parsley

1. Heat a large nonstick skillet over medium-high heat. Add oil; swirl to coat. Add onion to pan; sauté 5 minutes or until tender. Add garlic; sauté 1 minute. Stir in salt and next 5 ingredients (through cinnamon sticks); cook 30 seconds. Stir in tomato paste. Stir in chicken broth and tomatoes; bring to a boil. Stir in chicken and next 3 ingredients (through parsnip). Bring to a boil. Reduce heat; simmer, uncovered, 5 minutes. Stir in raisins, and cook 5 minutes or until vegetables are tender and chicken is done. Discard cinnamon sticks.

2. Spoon 1/2 cup couscous into each of 6 bowls. Ladle 1 cup stew evenly over couscous. Sprinkle with parsley. Serves 6 (serving size: 1 cup)

CALORIES 310; **FAT** 3.6g (sat 0.6g, mono 1.9g, poly 0.5g); **PROTEIN** 19.1g; **CARB** 52g; **FIBER** 5.9g; **CHOL** 33mg; **IRON** 2.4mg; **SODIUM** 555mg; **CALC** 77mg

Tip: Do yourself a favor and prep all your ingredients first. It saves so much time and makes the recipe come together in a snap.

My friend Jenny Hill is a fantastic home cook and an enthusiastic follower of One Family One Meal. Because she is my biggest fan, I had to ask her for her favorite recipe. Her husband, Wayne, said this is it by far. The simple ones are so often the best. Thank you, Jenny!

SPINACH AND FETA–STUFFED CHICKEN

HANDS-ON TIME: 15 MINUTES | TOTAL TIME: 43 MINUTES

1 tablespoon butter
1 garlic clove, minced
6 cups fresh baby spinach leaves
1/8 teaspoon salt
1/8 teaspoon freshly ground
   black pepper
4 (6-ounce) skinless, boneless
   chicken breast halves
2 ounces feta cheese, crumbled
   (about 1/2 cup)
2 cups grape tomatoes
2 tablespoons grated fresh
   Parmesan cheese
1/4 cup dry white wine

1. Preheat oven to 425°.
2. Melt butter in a large cast-iron skillet over medium heat. Add garlic; cook 30 seconds. Gradually add spinach to pan, turning with tongs. Sprinkle with salt and pepper; cook 2 minutes or until spinach wilts, stirring frequently. Remove from pan; cool.
3. Place chicken between 2 sheets of plastic wrap; pound to 1/2-inch thickness using a meat mallet or small heavy skillet.
4. Crumble one-fourth of feta cheese over each chicken breast half; divide spinach mixture evenly among chicken breast halves. Roll up, jelly-roll fashion. Tuck in sides; secure each roll with wooden picks. Place chicken in skillet. Cook over medium-high heat 3 minutes. Turn chicken over; cook 2 minutes or until browned. Add tomatoes to skillet; sprinkle chicken with Parmesan cheese. Transfer skillet to oven.
5. Bake at 425° for 25 minutes or until chicken is done and tomatoes begin to burst. Transfer chicken and tomatoes to a serving platter. Add wine to skillet, scraping pan to loosen browned bits. Remove wooden picks from chicken; cut into slices. Serve with tomatoes and pan juices. Serves 4 (serving size: 1 stuffed chicken breast, about 6 tablespoons tomatoes, and 3 tablespoons sauce)

CALORIES 299; **FAT** 8.7g (sat 4.9g, mono 2.1g, poly 0.7g); **PROTEIN** 43.7g; **CARB** 8.1g; **FIBER** 2.8g; **CHOL** 121mg; **IRON** 2.5mg; **SODIUM** 463mg; **CALC** 157mg

Tip: You can prep in the morning, and then pop it in the oven when you're ready.

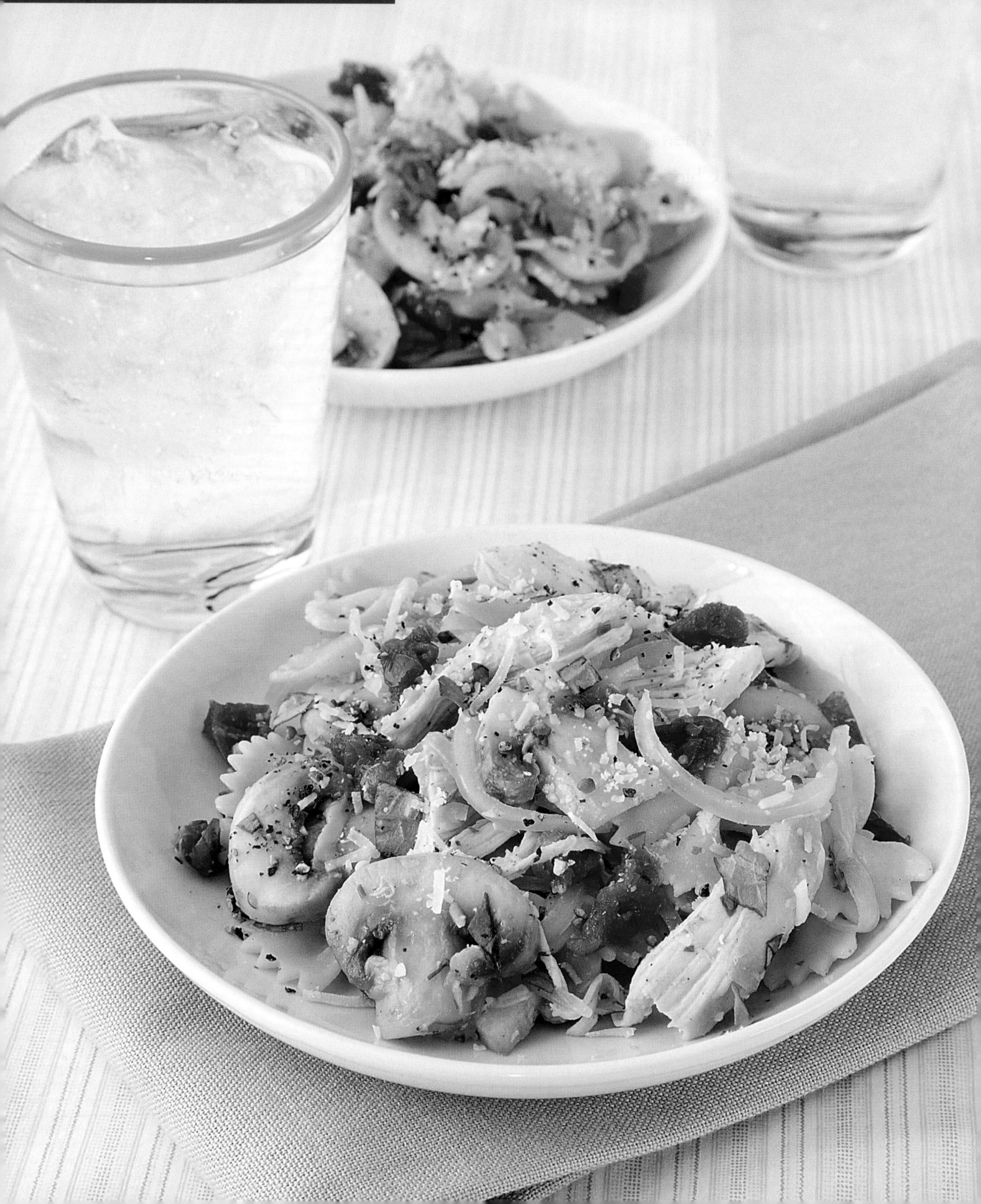

If you have leftover chicken, put it to use in this pasta recipe. Feel free to add anything you have that sounds good to you.

FARFALLE WITH CHICKEN AND SUN-DRIED TOMATOES

HANDS-ON TIME: 15 MINUTES | TOTAL TIME: 30 MINUTES

8 ounces uncooked farfalle (bow tie pasta)

2 tablespoons oil from sun-dried tomatoes packed in oil

1³/₄ cups vertically sliced onion

¹/₄ teaspoon crushed red pepper

2 garlic cloves, minced

1 (8-ounce) package presliced mushrooms

¹/₂ teaspoon kosher salt

¹/₄ teaspoon freshly ground black pepper

1 tablespoon fresh lemon juice

2 cups shredded rotisserie chicken breast

¹/₃ cup sun-dried tomatoes, diced

1.3 ounces grated fresh Parmesan cheese (about ¹/₃ cup)

¹/₄ cup coarsely chopped fresh basil leaves

1. Cook pasta according to package directions, omitting salt and fat; drain.
2. While pasta cooks, heat a large nonstick skillet over medium heat. Add sun-dried tomato oil; swirl to coat. Add onion; sauté 5 minutes or until tender. Add red pepper and garlic; cook 1 minute. Add mushrooms, salt, and black pepper; sauté 4 minutes. Stir in lemon juice. Stir in pasta, chicken, and tomatoes. Reduce heat to low; cook 2 minutes or until thoroughly heated, stirring frequently. Add cheese and basil; toss gently. Serves 8 (serving size: about 1 cup)

CALORIES 230; **FAT** 6.5g (sat 1.6g, mono 3.4g, poly 0.8g); **PROTEIN** 17.4g; **CARB** 25.7g; **FIBER** 1.9g; **CHOL** 33mg; **IRON** 1.6mg; **SODIUM** 209mg; **CALC** 59mg

KIDS CAN HELP

Teaching kids how to gather all their ingredients together before cooking is a great way to set good habits. They can collect everything while you start the pasta water.

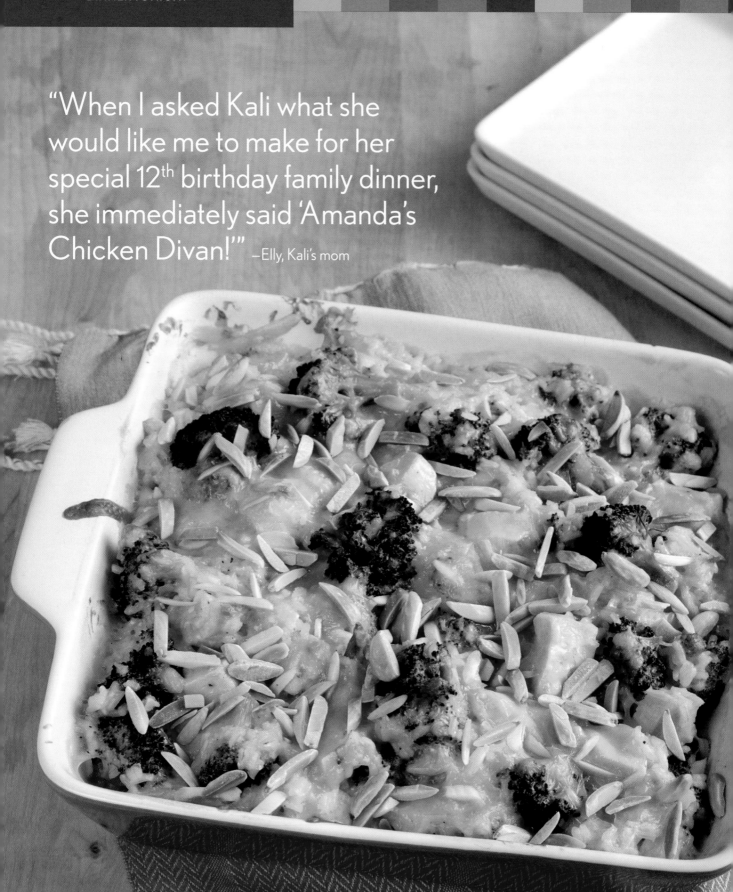

"When I asked Kali what she would like me to make for her special 12th birthday family dinner, she immediately said 'Amanda's Chicken Divan!'" —Elly, Kali's mom

After having my second son, the first thing I wanted when I got home from the hospital was my Grandma Marty's Chicken Divan. As I sit here looking at the recipe, I can see why: It's the ultimate comfort food. The original recipe called for two cans of cream of chicken soup and a cup of mayonnaise. Ugh. So I tinkered around for months, trying to create a lighter version. It still has all its cheesy, creamy goodness—but without any of the guilt.

CHICKEN DIVAN

HANDS-ON TIME: 15 MINUTES | TOTAL TIME: 55 MINUTES

4 cups broccoli florets,
   cut into (1-inch) pieces
6 tablespoons all-purpose flour
1½ cups fat-free, lower-sodium
   chicken broth
2 tablespoons unsalted butter
2 ounces grated fresh Parmesan
   cheese (about ½ cup)
⅓ cup half-and-half
2 tablespoons dry sherry
½ teaspoon kosher salt
½ teaspoon freshly ground
   black pepper
4 ounces shredded reduced-fat
   sharp cheddar cheese, divided
   (about 1 cup)
4 cups cooked long-grain
   brown rice
2 cups chopped cooked
   chicken breast
Cooking spray
½ cup slivered almonds,
   toasted

1. Preheat oven to 375°.
2. Cook broccoli in boiling water to cover 5 minutes; drain.
3. While broccoli cooks, place flour in a Dutch oven or large saucepan. Gradually add broth, stirring with a whisk until blended. Bring to a boil, stirring with a whisk; reduce heat to medium, and cook 5 minutes or until mixture thickens. Add butter, stirring with a whisk until melted. Add Parmesan cheese, next 4 ingredients (through pepper), and ½ cup cheddar cheese, stirring until cheeses melt. Stir in broccoli, rice, and chicken.
4. Spoon rice mixture into a 9-inch square glass or ceramic baking dish coated with cooking spray. Top with remaining cheddar cheese, and sprinkle with almonds. Cover and bake at 375° for 20 minutes. Uncover and bake 15 additional minutes or until bubbly and top is browned. Serves 6 (serving size: about 1 cup)

CALORIES 458; **FAT** 19g (sat 8g, mono 5.8g, poly 2.3g); **PROTEIN** 29.9g; **CARB** 41.9g; **FIBER** 5.1g; **CHOL** 74mg; **IRON** 2.2mg; **SODIUM** 588mg; **CALC** 424mg

My friend and an amazing cook Donata Maggipinto shared this soup with me. My kids love it as much as we do!

MINI MEATBALL MINESTRONE

HANDS-ON TIME: 25 MINUTES | TOTAL TIME: 1 HOUR AND 5 MINUTES

SOUP:
1 tablespoon olive oil
2 cups diced onion
3/4 cup (1/2-inch) sliced carrot
3/4 cup (1/2-inch) sliced celery
3/4 cup (1/2-inch) cubed parsnip
2 garlic cloves, minced
3 cups chopped Swiss chard
1 cup dry red wine
1/2 teaspoon freshly ground
**   black pepper**
1/4 teaspoon kosher salt
1 (32-ounce) container
**   lower-sodium beef broth**
1 (14.5-ounce) can no-salt-added
**   diced tomatoes with basil,**
**   garlic, and oregano**

MINI MEATBALLS:
1 pound ground turkey
3 tablespoons dry breadcrumbs
1 tablespoon chopped fresh basil
1 tablespoon olive oil
1/2 teaspoon freshly ground
**   black pepper**
1/4 teaspoon kosher salt
1 large egg, lightly beaten

REMAINING INGREDIENTS:
1 (15-ounce) can chickpeas
**   (garbanzo beans),**
**   rinsed and drained**
1/4 cup chopped fresh basil
1 ounce grated fresh Parmesan
**   cheese (optional)**

1. To prepare soup, heat a large Dutch oven over medium-high heat. Add oil; swirl to coat. Add onion and next 4 ingredients (through garlic); sauté 6 minutes or until vegetables are tender. Add chard; sauté 1 minute or until wilted. Stir in wine and next 4 ingredients (through tomatoes). Bring to a boil; reduce heat and simmer 10 minutes.
2. To prepare meatballs, combine turkey and next 6 ingredients (through egg) in a bowl. Shape meat mixture by tablespoonfuls into 30 meatballs. Add meatballs and chickpeas to soup. Bring to a boil over medium-high heat. Cover and cook 12 minutes or until meatballs are done. Remove from heat; stir in 1/4 cup basil.
3. Ladle soup into bowls, and sprinkle evenly with Parmesan cheese, if desired. Serves 8 (serving size: 1 cup soup and about 4 meatballs)

CALORIES 249; **FAT** 11.5g (sat 2.9g, mono 2.9g, poly 0.6g); **PROTEIN** 16.2g; **CARB** 18.4g; **FIBER** 4.2g; **CHOL** 74mg; **IRON** 1.5mg; **SODIUM** 614mg; **CALC** 93mg

Tip: If your family loves this recipe as much as ours does, make a double batch on the weekend, and use it all week long.

With clean hands, kids can help make the meatballs.

Thanksgiving dinner is my favorite meal of the year. But I'm not a fan of trying to turn leftover turkey into a million different recipes—it dilutes the memory of how great the original meal was. If you're like me and need a way to eat leftover turkey other than on a sandwich, try this turkey-penne bake with a glass of pinot noir and a mixed greens salad.

BAKED PENNE WITH TURKEY

HANDS-ON TIME: 18 MINUTES | TOTAL TIME: 1 HOUR AND 10 MINUTES

12 ounces uncooked penne (tube-shaped pasta)
1 tablespoon olive oil
2 (8-ounce) packages presliced mushrooms
2 tablespoons dry sherry
1 cup chopped onion
2 teaspoons minced garlic
1 tablespoon water
5 tablespoons all-purpose flour
3 cups organic vegetable broth
1 cup milk
1 tablespoon fresh thyme leaves
¾ teaspoon salt
½ teaspoon freshly ground black pepper
¼ cup unsalted butter
4 cups chopped cooked turkey breast
1 cup frozen petite green peas, thawed
4 ounces grated fresh Parmesan cheese (about 1 cup), divided
Cooking spray
Thyme leaves (optional)

1. Preheat oven to 350°.
2. Cook pasta according to package directions, omitting salt and fat. Drain and return to pan. Cover and keep warm.
3. Heat a large nonstick skillet over medium-high heat. Add oil; swirl to coat. Add mushrooms; cook 8 minutes or until browned and tender, stirring occasionally. Stir in sherry, scraping pan to loosen browned bits. Cook 1 minute or until liquid evaporates. Remove mushrooms from pan. Add onion and garlic to pan; sauté over medium heat 4 minutes. Add 1 tablespoon water; cook 1 minute or until tender, stirring constantly.
4. Place flour in a large saucepan; gradually add vegetable broth and next 4 ingredients (through pepper), stirring with a whisk until blended. Place over medium heat; cook until thick (about 5 minutes), stirring constantly. Add butter, stirring until melted. Add sauce, mushrooms, onion mixture, turkey, peas, and ½ cup cheese to pasta, stirring until cheese melts. Pour mixture into a 13 x 9-inch glass or ceramic baking dish coated with cooking spray. Sprinkle with remaining ½ cup cheese.
5. Bake, uncovered, at 350° for 25 minutes. Let stand 5 minutes. Garnish with thyme, if desired. Serves 10

CALORIES 374; FAT 11.3g (sat 5.9g, mono 3.4g, poly 0.7g); PROTEIN 31g; CARB 36.2g; FIBER 2.7g; CHOL 76mg; IRON 2.9mg; SODIUM 563mg; CALC 180mg

KIDS CAN HELP

Kids can combine the sauce, turkey, peas, onion mixture, and mushrooms with the pasta, and then sprinkle the cheese on top before it bakes.

SLOW COOKING
& FAST SERVING

My family could eat pizza every day. With a make-ahead dough and a simple sauce, this pizza is an option any night of the week. Just make the dough in the morning; then shape it an hour before you're ready to eat. If homemade dough is not your thing, just buy the premade dough at Trader Joe's or Whole Foods Market, and shape it as you would the scratch dough. Then let the kids add their own toppings.

MOZZARELLA AND BASIL PIZZA

HANDS-ON TIME: 10 MINUTES | TOTAL TIME: 1 HOUR AND 15 MINUTES

1 (8-ounce) ball Pizza Dough (page 45)
½ cup Pizza Sauce (page 27)
4 ounces fresh mozzarella cheese, sliced
12 fresh basil leaves

1. Place Pizza Dough on a large sheet of parchment paper. Cover with a damp towel; let rise in a warm place (85°), free from drafts, 45 minutes.
2. Preheat oven to 500°.
3. Roll dough into a 12-inch circle on parchment paper. Crimp edges of dough to form a ½-inch border. Slide dough and parchment paper onto a large baking sheet. Place on bottom rack in oven. Bake at 500° for 5 minutes.
4. Spread Pizza Sauce evenly onto crust, leaving a ½-inch border. Top with cheese slices. Bake an additional 10 minutes or until crust is golden and cheese melts. Remove from oven; let stand 5 minutes. Top with basil leaves; cut into wedges. Serves 6 (serving size: 1 wedge)

CALORIES 169; **FAT** 5.9g (sat 2.9g, mono 0.9g, poly 0.2g); **PROTEIN** 6.2g; **CARB** 22g; **FIBER** 0.9g; **CHOL** 15mg; **IRON** 1.5mg; **SODIUM** 116mg; **CALC** 9mg

Note: If using refrigerated Pizza Dough (page 45), let dough rise as directed in step 1 for 1 hour. Proceed as directed in recipe.

I usually eat half of these onions before they ever make it to the pizza! This is a classic combination that pleases everyone in my house.

CARAMELIZED ONION AND TURKEY SAUSAGE PIZZA

HANDS-ON TIME: 28 MINUTES | TOTAL TIME: 1 HOUR AND 5 MINUTES

1 (8-ounce) ball Pizza Dough (page 45)

1 tablespoon olive oil

1 1/2 cups vertically sliced onion

1 teaspoon sugar

1/8 teaspoon kosher salt

5 ounces sweet turkey Italian sausage links

1/2 cup Pizza Sauce (page 27)

8 ounces shredded part-skim mozzarella cheese (about 2 cups)

1. Place Pizza Dough on a large sheet of parchment paper. Cover with a damp towel; let rise in a warm place (85°), free from drafts, 45 minutes.
2. Preheat oven to 500°.
3. While dough rises, heat a large nonstick skillet over medium-high heat. Add oil; swirl to coat. Add onion; cook 5 minutes, stirring frequently. Sprinkle with sugar and salt. Continue cooking 15 to 20 minutes or until deep golden brown, stirring frequently.
4. Remove casings from sausage. Cook sausage in a large nonstick skillet over medium-high heat until browned, stirring to crumble. Drain well.
5. Roll dough into a 12-inch circle on parchment paper. Crimp edges of dough with fingers to form a rim. Slide dough and parchment paper onto a large baking sheet. Place on bottom rack in oven. Bake at 500° for 5 minutes.
6. Spoon Pizza Sauce onto crust, spreading to rim. Top with cheese, onion, and sausage. Bake an additional 10 minutes or until crust is golden and cheese melts. Remove from oven; let stand 5 minutes. Cut into wedges. Serves 6 (serving size: 1 wedge)

CALORIES 299; **FAT** 13.5g (sat 5.9g, mono 4.7g, poly 0.7g); **PROTEIN** 16.9g; **CARB** 26.8g; **FIBER** 1.4g; **CHOL** 35mg; **IRON** 1.8mg; **SODIUM** 487mg; **CALC** 295mg

Note: If using refrigerated Pizza Dough (page 45), let dough rise as directed in step 1 for 1 hour. Proceed as directed in recipe.

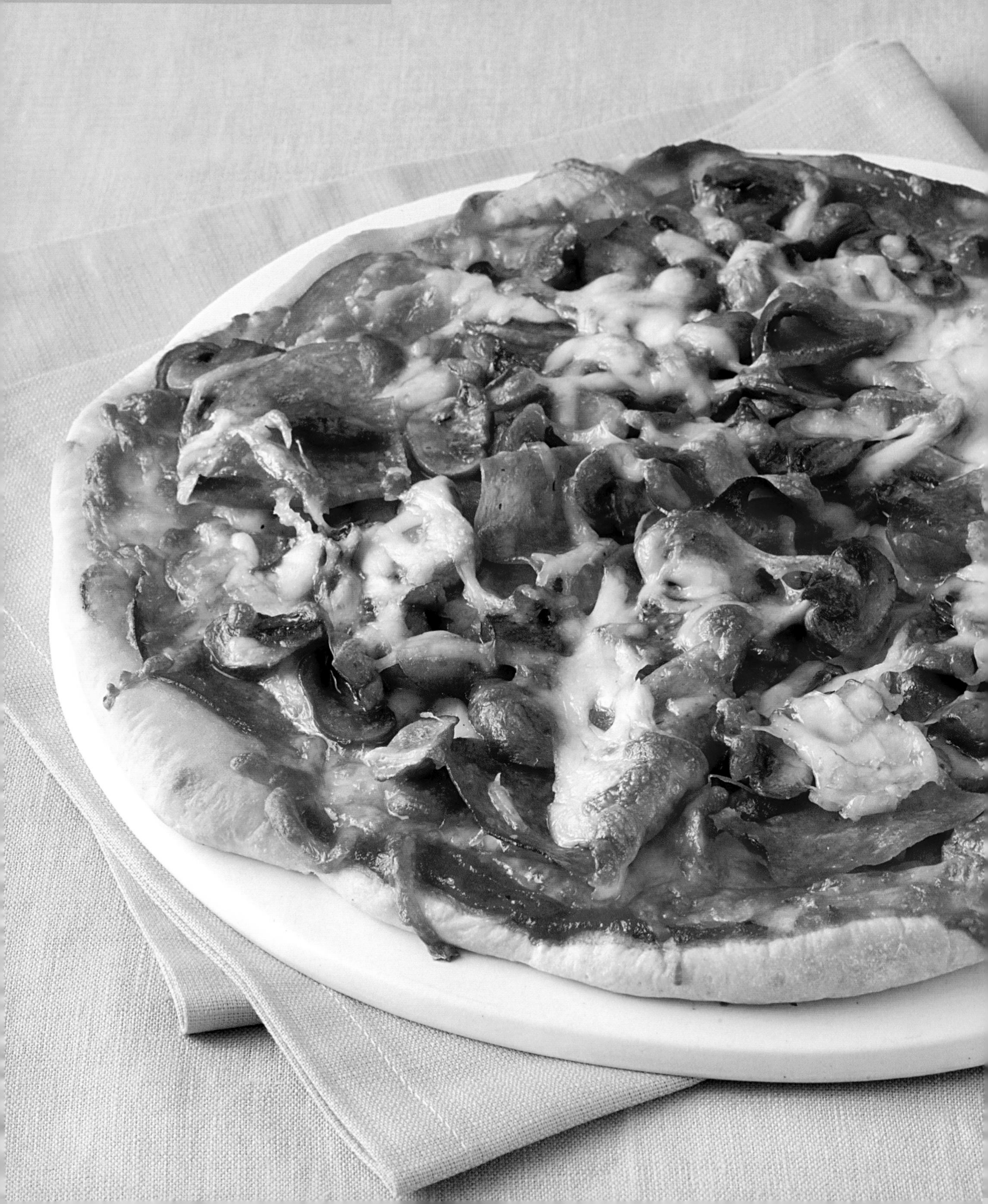

A better option than straight pepperoni, this mushroom and salami combination is still very kid friendly. Pair it with a glass of red wine for the adults.

SALAMI AND MUSHROOM PIZZA

HANDS-ON TIME: 16 MINUTES | TOTAL TIME: 1 HOUR AND 21 MINUTES

1 (8-ounce) ball Pizza Dough (page 45)
1 teaspoon olive oil
1 (8-ounce) package presliced mushrooms
1/2 cup Pizza Sauce (page 27)
2 ounces thinly sliced Genoa salami
8 ounces shredded part-skim mozzarella cheese (about 2 cups)

1. Place Pizza Dough on a large sheet of parchment paper. Cover with a damp towel; let rise in a warm place (85°), free from drafts, 45 minutes.
2. Preheat oven to 500°.
3. While dough rises, heat a large nonstick skillet over medium-high heat. Add oil; swirl to coat. Add mushrooms; cook 6 minutes or until tender, stirring frequently.
4. Roll dough into a 12-inch circle on parchment paper. Crimp edges of dough with fingers to form a rim. Slide dough and parchment paper onto a large baking sheet. Place on bottom rack in oven. Bake at 500° for 5 minutes.
5. Spoon Pizza Sauce onto crust, spreading to rim. Top with salami, cheese, and mushrooms. Bake an additional 10 minutes or until crust is golden and cheese melts. Remove from oven; let stand 5 minutes. Cut into wedges. Serves 6 (serving size: 1 wedge)

CALORIES 281; FAT 13.1g (sat 6.3g, mono 5.2g, poly 0.9g); PROTEIN 16g; CARB 24.8g; FIBER 1.3g; CHOL 30mg; IRON 1.8mg; SODIUM 479mg; CALC 287mg

Note: If using refrigerated Pizza Dough (page 45), let dough rise as directed in step 1 for 1 hour. Proceed as directed in recipe.

Angie, a mom who has cooked from One Family One Meal for nearly two years, was afraid to make pizza from scratch. But since she finds every OFOM recipe so easy to follow and so tasty, she took the plunge—with amazing results!

CARAMELIZED ONION AND PROSCIUTTO PIZZA

HANDS-ON TIME: 30 MINUTES | TOTAL TIME: 1 HOUR AND 35 MINUTES

1 (8-ounce) ball Pizza Dough
   (page 45)
1 tablespoon olive oil
1½ cups vertically sliced onion
1 teaspoon sugar
⅛ teaspoon kosher salt
½ cup Pizza Sauce (page 27)
3 ounces thinly sliced prosciutto
8 ounces shredded part-skim
   mozzarella cheese (about 2 cups)

1. Place Pizza Dough on a large sheet of parchment paper. Cover with a damp towel; let rise in a warm place (85°), free from drafts, 45 minutes.
2. Preheat oven to 500°.
3. While dough rises, heat a large nonstick skillet over medium-high heat. Add oil; swirl to coat. Add onion; cook 5 minutes, stirring frequently. Sprinkle with sugar and salt. Continue cooking 15 to 20 minutes or until deep golden brown, stirring frequently.
4. Roll dough into a 12-inch circle on parchment paper. Crimp edges of dough with fingers to form a rim. Slide dough and parchment paper onto a large baking sheet. Place on bottom rack in oven. Bake at 500° for 5 minutes.
5. Spoon Pizza Sauce onto crust, spreading to rim. Top with prosciutto, cheese, and onion. Bake an additional 10 minutes or until crust is golden and cheese melts. Remove from oven; let stand 5 minutes. Cut into wedges. Serves 6 (serving size: 1 wedge)

CALORIES 294; FAT 12.8g (sat 5.8g, mono 4.7g, poly 0.7g); PROTEIN 17.3g; CARB 27.3g; FIBER 1.4g; CHOL 32mg; IRON 1.8mg; SODIUM 726mg; CALC 290mg

Note: If using refrigerated Pizza Dough (page 45), let dough rise as directed in step 1 for 1 hour. Proceed as directed in recipe.

KIDS CAN HELP

Older kids can help stir the onions while they caramelize, and then everyone can top their own pizzas with the sauce, prosciutto, onions, and cheese.

This is the number-one recipe requested by my girlfriends because it's an easy make-ahead option and ideal for a crowd. You can make it ahead of time, and kids love it, so don't even think about making a separate kids' meal!

CITRUS-MARINATED PORK TACOS WITH PICKLED ONIONS

HANDS-ON TIME: 21 MINUTES | TOTAL TIME: 12 HOURS AND 22 MINUTES

PULLED PORK:
1 cup fresh orange juice
1/2 cup fresh lime juice
2 teaspoons ground annatto
    (achiote seed)
1 teaspoon salt
1 teaspoon ancho chile powder
1/2 teaspoon freshly ground
    black pepper
1/2 teaspoon ground cumin
1/4 teaspoon dried oregano
2 garlic cloves, crushed
1 (3 1/2-pound) bone-in pork
    shoulder (Boston butt), trimmed
    and cut in half crosswise

PICKLED ONIONS:
1 medium red onion, halved vertically
1/4 cup fresh lime juice
1/4 cup fresh orange juice
1/2 teaspoon salt
1 jalapeño pepper, seeded and minced

REMAINING INGREDIENTS:
18 (6-inch) gluten-free corn tortillas
1 cup Guacamole (page 39)

1. To prepare pulled pork, combine first 9 ingredients in a large heavy-duty zip-top plastic bag. Add pork to bag. Seal bag, turning to coat. Marinate in refrigerator overnight, turning occasionally.
2. Preheat oven to 325°.
3. Remove pork from marinade, reserving marinade. Place pork in a large Dutch oven; pour marinade over pork. Cover and bake at 325° for 4 hours or until pork is fork-tender.
4. To prepare pickled onions, while pork cooks, place red onion and next 4 ingredients (through jalapeño pepper) in a medium bowl, tossing to coat. Cover and marinate in refrigerator at least 2 hours.
5. Remove pork from pan, and place on a cutting board. Reserve 1/2 cup cooking liquid; discard remaining cooking liquid. Remove pork from bones; place in a large bowl. Shred pork with 2 forks. Stir in reserved cooking liquid.
6. Place 1/4 cup pork mixture on each tortilla. Top with about 1 tablespoon Guacamole and about 3 tablespoons pickled onions. Serves 9 (serving size: 2 tacos)

CALORIES 388; **FAT** 17g (sat 4.3g, mono 4.9g, poly 1.7g); **PROTEIN** 33.3g; **CARB** 28.3g; **FIBER** 3.7g; **CHOL** 101mg; **IRON** 2.6mg; **SODIUM** 635mg; **CALC** 54mg

Tip: This pork is best when made ahead and refrigerated for a few days to blend the flavors. Then you can scrape off any excess fat before reheating it on the cooktop over low heat.

Brining your meat is certainly not necessary, but it adds so much moisture to lean cuts like pork and chicken. I guarantee it's worth it if you have the time.

BRINED PORK CHOPS WITH APPLE COMPOTE

HANDS-ON TIME: 42 MINUTES | TOTAL TIME: 25 HOURS AND 12 MINUTES

Master Brine (recipe below)
4 (6-ounce) bone-in center-cut
    pork chops (about ½ inch thick)
Cooking spray
1½ pounds Granny Smith apples,
    peeled, cored, and cut into
    ³/₈-inch wedges
²/₃ cup apple cider
3 tablespoons brown sugar
2 teaspoons grated peeled
    fresh ginger

1. Prepare Master Brine. Add pork to brine; seal bag. Let stand in refrigerator 24 hours.
2. Remove pork from brine; rinse and pat dry. Let stand 30 minutes.
3. Heat a large cast-iron skillet over medium-high heat until very hot. Coat pan with cooking spray. Add pork; cook 3 to 4 minutes on each side or until done. Transfer chops to a plate; cover and keep warm.
4. Add apples to pan; sauté 5 minutes. Add cider, brown sugar, and ginger, scraping pan to loosen browned bits. Reduce heat to low; cook 5 minutes until apple is tender, stirring frequently. Serves 4 (serving size: 1 pork chop and ²/₃ cup apple compote)

CALORIES 271; FAT 4.3g (sat 1.3g, mono 1.5g, poly 0.5g); PROTEIN 24.7g; CARB 34.2g; FIBER 1.9g; CHOL 76mg; IRON 0.9mg; SODIUM 341mg; CALC 36mg

MASTER BRINE

HANDS-ON TIME: 7 MINUTES | TOTAL TIME: 7 MINUTES

BASIC BRINE:
6 cups water
4½ tablespoons kosher salt
3 tablespoons granulated sugar
6 teaspoons black peppercorns

SPICE FLAVORING:
2 cinnamon sticks
10 whole cloves
4 star anise

HERB FLAVORING:
8 thyme sprigs
4 bay leaves

1. To prepare basic brine, combine first 4 ingredients in a large heavy-duty zip-top plastic bag. Add ingredients for either the spice flavoring or the herb flavoring; seal bag, shaking until salt and sugar dissolve. Makes 6 cups (enough for 1½ pounds of meat or poultry—a small chicken, a turkey breast, or about 4 pork chops)

CALORIES 2; FAT 0g; PROTEIN 0g; CARB 0.4g; FIBER 0g; CHOL 0mg; IRON 0mg; SODIUM 270mg; CALC 0mg

Tip: For larger cuts of meat or a larger bird like a turkey, triple or quadruple the mixture.

My mom, a wonderful cook, was fanatical about our health while we were growing up. So it was a huge treat when she cooked red meat, especially with a rich, sweet barbecue sauce to go with it. Serve with Crunchy, Creamy Coleslaw (page 125).

MOM'S BRISKET

HANDS-ON TIME: 16 MINUTES | TOTAL TIME: 3 HOURS AND 16 MINUTES

1 (2¹/₂-pound) flat-cut beef brisket, trimmed
¹/₂ teaspoon garlic salt
¹/₂ teaspoon onion salt
¹/₂ teaspoon celery seed
¹/₂ teaspoon freshly ground black pepper
1 tablespoon canola oil
¹/₂ cup water
¹/₂ cup Barbecue Sauce (page 29)

1. Preheat oven to 325°.
2. Rinse brisket, and pat dry. Combine garlic salt and next 3 ingredients (through pepper); sprinkle evenly over brisket.
3. Heat a 4- to 6-quart ovenproof Dutch oven over medium heat. Add oil; swirl to coat. Add brisket; cook 5 minutes on each side or until browned. Add ¹/₂ cup water to pan. Cover and bake at 325° for 3 hours or until tender.
4. Remove brisket from drippings, reserving drippings. Skim fat from drippings. Serve brisket with drippings, if desired, and Barbecue Sauce. Serves 7 (serving size: 3 ounces brisket and about 1 tablespoon sauce)

CALORIES 247; FAT 8.3g (sat 2.5g, mono 3.9g, poly 0.8g); PROTEIN 35g; CARB 5.8g; FIBER 0g; CHOL 66mg; IRON 3.4mg; SODIUM 477mg; CALC 34mg

Chasen's was an Old Hollywood restaurant frequented by Elizabeth Taylor and many other stars. The chili was Liz's favorite. I've made the recipe my own with some tweaks, including streamlining the process to speed it up. If you want to skip the dried-bean step, you can substitute two (15-ounce) cans of pinto beans that have been drained and rinsed. Add some cornbread and a salad for the perfect casual dinner on a cold night.

CHASEN'S FAMOUS CHILI

HANDS-ON TIME: 28 MINUTES | TOTAL TIME: 3 HOURS AND 22 MINUTES

1 cup dried pinto beans
3 cups water
1 (28-ounce) can crushed tomatoes
1 tablespoon canola oil
2 cups chopped red bell pepper
2 cups chopped onion
¼ cup chopped fresh flat-leaf parsley
2 garlic cloves, minced
1¼ pounds ground round
½ pound lean ground pork
3 tablespoons chili powder
1 teaspoon salt
1 teaspoon ground cumin
½ teaspoon freshly ground
    black pepper

1. Sort and wash beans; place in a Dutch oven. Cover with water to 2 inches above beans; bring to a boil. Cook 2 minutes; remove from heat. Cover and let stand 1 hour. Drain beans.

2. Add 3 cups water. Bring to a boil; cover, reduce heat, and simmer 1 hour and 30 minutes or until beans are tender. Stir in tomatoes; cook 5 minutes.

3. While beans cook, heat a large nonstick skillet over medium-high heat. Add oil; swirl to coat. Add bell pepper and onion; cook 8 minutes or until tender, stirring frequently. Add parsley and garlic; cook 1 minute. Add ground round and remaining ingredients; cook 8 minutes or until browned, stirring to crumble. Add meat mixture to bean mixture. Bring to a boil; cover, reduce heat, and simmer 30 minutes. Serves 10 (serving size: 1 cup)

CALORIES 282; FAT 12.1g (sat 4.3g, mono 4.9g, poly 1.6g); PROTEIN 20.9g; CARB 21.2g; FIBER 6.6g; CHOL 53mg; IRON 3.9mg; SODIUM 486mg; CALC 75mg

KIDS CAN HELP

Let the kids stir the pot while the meat is browning and the tomatoes are cooking. They'll feel like real cooks. Just make sure you stay close.

"Along with pizza, lasagna is a regular on our weekly menu. Amanda's recipes are the glue that keeps my family coming together during dinnertime!" —Jessica, mother of two

Lasagna is love on a plate. The homemade sauce, the layering of noodles with cheese . . . it's pretty much perfection. So how do you pull it off on a weeknight? No-boil noodles. You can make the lasagna in the morning, cover and refrigerate it, and then bake it just before dinnertime. Serve it with a crunchy romaine salad and garlic bread, and your kids might think you're the best cook ever.

TURKEY SAUSAGE LASAGNA

HANDS-ON TIME: 27 MINUTES | TOTAL TIME: 1 HOUR AND 21 MINUTES

2 tablespoons olive oil
1/2 cup finely chopped onion
5 garlic cloves, minced
1/4 teaspoon kosher salt
1/4 teaspoon freshly ground
    black pepper
1 pound mild turkey Italian sausage
1 (28-ounce) can crushed tomatoes
    with basil
1 (14.5-ounce) can no-salt-added
    diced tomatoes with basil,
    garlic, and oregano
6 ounces shredded part-skim
    mozzarella cheese (about 1 1/2 cups),
    divided
2 ounces grated fresh Parmesan
    cheese (about 1/2 cup)
1 (16-ounce) container 2% low-fat
    cottage cheese
2 large eggs, lightly beaten
Cooking spray
12 no-boil lasagna noodles

1. Preheat oven to 350°.
2. Heat a large skillet over medium-high heat. Add oil; swirl to coat. Add onion; cook 3 minutes, stirring occasionally. Add garlic, salt, and pepper; cook 1 minute. Remove casings from sausage. Add sausage to pan; cook 5 minutes or until browned, stirring to crumble. Add tomatoes. Bring to a boil; reduce heat, and simmer, uncovered, 10 minutes. Remove from heat.
3. While sauce simmers, combine 1 cup mozzarella cheese, Parmesan cheese, cottage cheese, and eggs.
4. Spoon 1/2 cup meat sauce into a 13 x 9-inch baking dish coated with cooking spray. Place 4 noodles over sauce. Spread half of cheese mixture over noodles; top with 2 cups sauce. Repeat procedure with 4 noodles, remaining half of cheese mixture, and 2 cups sauce. Top with remaining 4 noodles; spread remaining sauce over noodles. Sprinkle with remaining 1/2 cup mozzarella cheese.
5. Cover and bake at 350° for 40 minutes or until bubbly and noodles are tender. Uncover and bake an additional 10 minutes. Let stand 5 minutes before serving. Serves 10

CALORIES 339; FAT 14.7g (sat 4.1g, mono 3.9g, poly 0.7g); PROTEIN 24.2g; CARB 29g; FIBER 3.1g; CHOL 87mg; IRON 3.1mg; SODIUM 765mg; CALC 248mg

Serve this chicken on top of Herbed Brown Rice Pilaf (page 143), and drizzle a little bit of the sauce over the chicken.

I recently read about a guy who roasted a chicken in a pan with nothing but salt and pepper. I mean nothing. After all the lemon-stuffing, bacon-wrapping, and herb-buttering I've put myself through to create the perfect roast chicken, I had to try it. One word: heaven. Another word: easy.

SIMPLEST ROAST CHICKEN EVER

HANDS-ON TIME: 21 MINUTES | TOTAL TIME: 1 HOUR AND 21 MINUTES

1 (4-pound) whole chicken
³⁄₄ teaspoon kosher salt, divided
¹⁄₄ teaspoon freshly ground
    black pepper
2 tablespoons unsalted butter
2 teaspoons fresh lemon juice
2 teaspoons chopped fresh herbs,
    such as chives, tarragon, and basil
Herbed Brown Rice Pilaf
    (page 143)

1. Preheat oven to 425°.

2. Remove and discard giblets and neck from chicken. Trim excess fat. Tie ends of legs together with twine. Lift wing tips up and over back; tuck under chicken. Sprinkle with ¹⁄₂ teaspoon salt and pepper.

3. Place chicken, breast side down, in a shallow roasting pan. Bake at 425° for 30 minutes. Turn chicken over. Baste chicken with pan drippings. Bake an additional 20 minutes or until a thermometer inserted into meaty part of leg registers 165°. Remove chicken from pan; let stand 10 minutes. Discard skin. Carve chicken.

4. Combine butter and lemon juice in a small saucepan; cook over low heat 2 minutes or until butter melts. Remove from heat; stir in remaining ¹⁄₄ teaspoon salt and herbs. Serve chicken with sauce and Herbed Brown Rice Pilaf. Serves 4 (serving size: 1 breast half or 1 leg quarter, about 2 teaspoons sauce, and ¹⁄₂ cup rice)

CALORIES 431; **FAT** 15g (sat 5.7g, mono 5.3g, poly 2.3g); **PROTEIN** 49.5g; **CARB** 22g; **FIBER** 1.8g; **CHOL** 166mg; **IRON** 3mg; **SODIUM** 699mg; **CALC** 49mg

My kids have always loved black beans, so I was looking to find a way to make them a more substantial meal instead of a side dish. This simple soup hits the spot. For richer flavor, you could use some chicken stock, but I like this version because it is completely vegetarian.

BLACK BEAN SOUP

HANDS-ON TIME: 30 MINUTES | TOTAL TIME: 3 HOURS AND 10 MINUTES

1¼ cups dried black beans
1 tablespoon olive oil
3 cups chopped onion
1 cup chopped red bell pepper
1 tablespoon ground cumin
1 teaspoon dried oregano
4 garlic cloves, minced
2 cups organic vegetable broth
2 cups water
2 tablespoons fresh lime juice
1 teaspoon hot pepper sauce
½ teaspoon kosher salt
¼ teaspoon freshly ground
     black pepper
8 teaspoons shredded Monterey
     Jack cheese
2 tablespoons finely chopped onion
     (optional)
¼ cup light sour cream (optional)
2 tablespoons chopped fresh cilantro
     (optional)

1. Sort and wash beans; place in a large saucepan. Cover with water to 2 inches above beans; bring to a boil. Cook 2 minutes; remove from heat. Cover and let stand 1 hour. Drain beans.
2. Heat a large saucepan over medium-high heat. Add oil; swirl to coat. Add onion and bell pepper; cook 8 minutes or until tender, stirring frequently. Add cumin, oregano, and garlic; sauté 1 minute. Add beans, vegetable broth, and water. Bring to a boil; partially cover, reduce heat, and simmer 1 hour and 30 minutes or until beans are tender.
3. Place half of bean mixture in a blender. Remove center piece of blender lid (to allow steam to escape); secure blender lid on blender. Place a clean towel over opening in blender lid (to avoid splatters). Blend until smooth. Return pureed soup to pan. Stir in lime juice and next 3 ingredients (through black pepper). Ladle soup into bowls; top evenly with cheese, and if desired, onion, sour cream, and cilantro. Serves 6 (serving size: 1⅓ cups soup)

CALORIES 219; FAT 3.6g (sat 1g, mono 1.9g, poly 0.3g); PROTEIN 10g; CARB 36g; FIBER 5.7g; CHOL 3mg; IRON 3mg; SODIUM 460mg; CALC 59mg

"Mommy, Aunt Amanda's
Chicken Enchiladas are
better than the restaurant's!"
—Jack, age 12

I was raised in Arizona on ridiculous amounts of Mexican food, and it remains my favorite comfort food today. These chicken enchiladas come together in the time it takes for me to make a salad and a batch of homemade margaritas. And they're not too spicy for the kids.

CHICKEN ENCHILADAS

HANDS-ON TIME: 20 MINUTES | TOTAL TIME: 1 HOUR AND 10 MINUTES

1 cup finely chopped onion
½ teaspoon ground cumin
2 garlic cloves, minced
2 cups shredded cooked chicken
3 ounces ⅓-less-fat cream cheese
    (⅓ cup), softened
4 ounces shredded reduced-fat white
    cheddar cheese with jalapeño
    peppers (about 1 cup), divided
¼ teaspoon freshly ground
    black pepper
1 cup fat-free, lower-sodium
    chicken broth, divided
12 (6-inch) corn tortillas
Cooking spray
1 cup commercial salsa verde
½ cup chopped fresh cilantro

1. Preheat oven to 350°.
2. Heat a large nonstick skillet over medium-high heat. Add onion and cumin; sauté 4 minutes or until tender, stirring frequently. Add garlic; cook 1 minute. Remove from heat.
3. Combine chicken and cream cheese in a large bowl. Stir in onion mixture, 3 ounces cheddar cheese, pepper, and ½ cup broth.
4. Bring remaining ½ cup broth to a simmer in a medium skillet; remove from heat. Dip 1 tortilla in broth 1 to 2 seconds on each side or just until slightly softened. Place tortilla on work surface. Spoon about 2 tablespoons chicken mixture down center of tortilla; roll up. Place tortilla, seam side down, in a 13 x 9-inch baking dish coated with cooking spray. Repeat procedure with remaining tortillas, broth, and chicken mixture.
5. Pour salsa over enchiladas; sprinkle evenly with remaining ¼ cup cheddar cheese. Cover and bake at 350° for 30 minutes. Uncover and bake an additional 10 minutes or until cheese melts. Let stand 5 minutes. Sprinkle with cilantro. Serves 6 (serving size: 2 enchiladas)

CALORIES 335; FAT 23.5g (sat 4.5g, mono 0.6g, poly 0.4g); PROTEIN 23.5g; CARB 35g; FIBER 2.6g; CHOL 60mg; IRON 0.6mg; SODIUM 658mg; CALC 162mg

KIDS CAN HELP

The kids can fill each tortilla, roll them up, and place them seam side down in the pan. Then they can top with the sauce and cheese.

GET GRILLING

I am loving the trend of sliders—mini burgers that satiate your craving for beef without the guilt of a ½-pound serving. Plus, kids love making their own. Cook the burgers in a pan or on a grill over medium-high heat. Mini hamburger buns or Parker House Rolls are perfect.

SLIDERS WITH CHEDDAR AND ONIONS

HANDS-ON TIME: 11 MINUTES | TOTAL TIME: 26 MINUTES

1 teaspoon canola oil
½ cup vertically sliced onion
1 pound 93% lean ground beef
¼ teaspoon salt
¼ teaspoon freshly ground black pepper
2 (1-ounce) slices reduced-fat cheddar cheese, quartered
8 (1.4-ounce) slider rolls
Toppings (optional): lettuce, ketchup, canola mayonnaise, prepared mustard

1. Heat a large nonstick skillet over medium-high heat. Add oil; swirl to coat. Add onion; cook 5 minutes or until tender, stirring frequently. Remove onion from pan; do not wipe pan.
2. While onion cooks, combine beef, salt, and pepper; shape into 8 (½-inch-thick) patties. Add patties to drippings in pan. Cook 4 minutes on each side or until done, topping each patty with 1 cheese quarter during last 2 minutes of cooking time. Remove from pan. Add 4 rolls, cut sides down, to drippings in pan. Cook 1 minute or until toasted. Repeat procedure with remaining 4 rolls.
3. Place patties on bottom halves of rolls; top patties evenly with onion. Cover with top halves of buns. Serve with desired toppings. Serves 4 (serving size: 2 sliders)

CALORIES 382; **FAT** 11.9g (sat 3.1g, mono 2.7g, poly 2.8g); **PROTEIN** 34.2g; **CARB** 38g; **FIBER** 2.3g; **CHOL** 68mg; **IRON** 3.3g; **SODIUM** 618mg; **CALC** 184mg

Tip: You can season the beef and shape the patties in the morning; then when you get home they're ready to go.

"Can I have this steak for my special birthday dinner this year?" –Izzy, age 12

Skirt steak is packed with flavor and is a great alternative to more expensive cuts. You'll love it in steak tacos or served on its own with this delicious herb sauce. The most important thing about preparing skirt steak is to slice it against the grain. The grain in the skirt steak is obvious—it looks like big lines running across the meat. Cut the slices perpendicular to those lines, and you're left with very tender, flavorful meat.

SKIRT STEAK WITH CHIMICHURRI SAUCE

HANDS-ON TIME: 8 MINUTES | TOTAL TIME: 46 MINUTES

1½ pounds skirt steak
1 teaspoon freshly ground
black pepper, divided
½ teaspoon kosher salt
1 garlic clove
½ cup fresh parsley leaves
⅓ cup fresh cilantro leaves
⅓ cup fresh mint leaves
2 tablespoons extra-virgin olive oil
1 tablespoon Dijon mustard
1 tablespoon fresh lime juice
1½ teaspoons drained capers
Cooking spray

1. Let steak stand 30 minutes at room temperature. Sprinkle steak with ½ teaspoon pepper and salt.
2. Preheat grill to high heat.
3. Place garlic in food processor; process until minced. Add parsley, cilantro, and mint; process until coarsely chopped. Add oil, next 3 ingredients (through capers), and remaining ½ teaspoon pepper; process until finely chopped.
4. Place steak on grill rack coated with cooking spray. Grill 2 minutes; turn steak over. Grill 2 to 3 minutes or until desired degree of doneness. Let stand 5 minutes. Cut steak across grain into thin slices. Serve with sauce. Serves 6 (serving size: 3 ounces steak and 1 tablespoon sauce)

CALORIES 236; **FAT** 14.1g (sat 4.2g, mono 8.4g, poly 0.9g); **PROTEIN** 24.2g; **CARB** 1.7g; **FIBER** 0.4g; **CHOL** 65mg; **IRON** 3mg; **SODIUM** 321mg; **CALC** 22mg

KIDS CAN HELP

Like with most of my sauces, kids can do practically all the work. They can pick the stems off the herbs or use a child-safe knife to cut them. Kids can also measure out all the ingredients and dump them directly into the food processor.

My first friend when I moved to San Francisco almost 20 years ago was Jennifer King. Her family invited me over and made this awesome steak. Now Jen and I are all grown up, and we serve it to our kids. Thanks, King family, for a total crowd-pleaser.

GINGER-SOY FLANK STEAK

HANDS-ON TIME: 8 MINUTES | TOTAL TIME: 9 HOURS AND 25 MINUTES

⅓ cup lower-sodium soy sauce
2 tablespoons canola oil
2 tablespoons honey
1 tablespoon red wine vinegar
½ teaspoon grated peeled fresh ginger
1 garlic clove, pressed
1 (3-pound) flank steak, trimmed
Cooking spray

1. Combine first 6 ingredients in a heavy-duty zip-top plastic bag. Add steak. Seal bag, and turn to coat steak. Marinate in refrigerator overnight, turning occasionally.
2. Remove bag from refrigerator, and let stand at room temperature 1 hour.
3. Preheat grill to high heat.
4. Remove steak from bag; discard marinade. Place steak on grill rack coated with cooking spray. Grill 6 minutes on each side or to desired degree of doneness. Let stand 5 minutes. Cut steak diagonally across grain into thin slices. Serves 12 (serving size: 3 ounces)

CALORIES 174; **FAT** 7.1g (sat 2.5g, mono 2.4g, poly 0.8g); **PROTEIN** 24.7g; **CARB** 1.4g; **FIBER** 0g; **CHOL** 37mg; **IRON** 1.8mg; **SODIUM** 132mg; **CALC** 28mg

technique: how to prepare fresh ginger

1. Use a vegetable peeler to remove the tough skin and reveal the yellowish flesh.

2. For chopped or minced ginger, place a peeled piece on a cutting board. Cut with the grain into thin strips; stack the slices. Cut across the pile into small pieces.

3. For grated ginger, rub a peeled piece of ginger across a fine grater, such as a Microplane®.

"When Amanda is working late, this is one of my favorite things to cook. I always make double because the boys and I always want more the next day."

—Kyle (my husband)

Quite honestly, I've never been a big fan of turkey burgers. But when I saw Oprah raving about a turkey burger she ate at Mar-a-Lago, I was intrigued. We all agree—with crunchy apple and tangy mango chutney, it's one delicious burger! I've sped up the recipe and added more of what we love to it. I buy Udi's Gluten Free Hamburger Buns at Whole Foods Market for this recipe.

THE ULTIMATE TURKEY BURGER

HANDS-ON TIME: 43 MINUTES | TOTAL TIME: 2 HOURS AND 43 MINUTES

2 teaspoons canola oil
1¹/₃ cups finely chopped peeled
   Granny Smith apple
1 cup finely chopped celery
¹/₄ cup finely chopped onion
1 lemon
1¹/₂ pounds ground turkey
1 teaspoon salt
1 teaspoon freshly ground
   black pepper
1 large egg white
1 teaspoon hot pepper sauce
   (optional)
Cooking spray
6 (1.6-ounce) whole-wheat
   hamburger buns
¹/₂ cup plain 2% reduced-fat
   Greek yogurt
2 tablespoons mango chutney
1¹/₂ cups fresh baby spinach

1. Heat a large nonstick skillet over medium-high heat. Add oil; swirl to coat. Add apple, celery, and onion; sauté 5 minutes or until tender. Remove from heat, and cool completely.
2. Grate rind and squeeze juice from lemon to measure 2 teaspoons rind and 1 tablespoon juice. Combine apple mixture, lemon rind, lemon juice, and turkey. Sprinkle with salt and pepper. Add egg; mix gently just until combined. Add hot pepper sauce, if desired. Shape into 6 (¹/₂-inch-thick) patties. Cover and refrigerate 2 hours or until thoroughly chilled.
3. Preheat grill to high heat. Place patties on grill rack coated with cooking spray. Grill 5 minutes on each side or until done. Place buns, cut side down, on grill rack. Grill 1 minute or until toasted.
4. Combine yogurt and chutney. Place patties on bottom halves of buns; top each patty with ¹/₄ cup spinach and about 4 teaspoons sauce. Cover with top halves of buns. Serves 6 (serving size: 1 burger)

CALORIES 341; FAT 11.2g (sat 2.8g, mono 1.5g, poly 1.4g); PROTEIN 28.6g; CARB 33.8g; FIBER 4.5g; CHOL 66mg; IRON 3.2mg; SODIUM 786mg; CALC 77mg

KIDS CAN HELP

With clean hands, kids can mix the ingredients into the ground turkey, and then shape the patties.

This chicken tastes great with a romaine salad and a side of corn, or sliced and turned into tacos with rice and beans.

HONEY-LIME CHICKEN

HANDS-ON TIME: 15 MINUTES | TOTAL TIME: 24 HOURS AND 8 MINUTES

3 tablespoons honey, divided
2 tablespoons fresh lime juice
1 tablespoon olive oil
1 teaspoon ground cumin
½ teaspoon kosher salt
¼ teaspoon ground red pepper
¼ teaspoon freshly ground
    black pepper
3 garlic cloves, minced
4 (6-ounce) skinless, boneless
    chicken breast halves
½ teaspoon grated lime rind
Cooking spray

1. Combine 2 tablespoons honey and next 7 ingredients (through garlic) in a large heavy-duty zip-top plastic bag. Add chicken; seal bag. Marinate in refrigerator overnight, turning occasionally.
2. Preheat grill to high heat.
3. Combine remaining 1 tablespoon honey and lime rind. Remove chicken from bag; discard marinade. Place chicken on grill rack coated with cooking spray. Grill 5 minutes on each side, basting with reserved honey mixture during last 2 minutes of cooking time. Cover and let stand 5 minutes. Serves 4 (serving size: 1 chicken breast half)

CALORIES 239; **FAT** 4g (sat 0.8g, mono 1.7g, poly 0.7g); **PROTEIN** 39.5g; **CARB** 9.4g; **FIBER** 0.2g; **CHOL** 99mg; **IRON** 1.4mg; **SODIUM** 232mg; **CALC** 24mg

technique: how to juice a lime

To get the most juice out of a fresh lime, bring it to room temperature, and then use the palm of your hand to roll the lime on a countertop a few times, applying a bit of pressure. Cut the fruit in half, and then squeeze. Or, for easier work, use a handheld press to release the most juice while safely trapping the seeds. Place the lime half, cut side down, in the press, and lower the handle.

My kids love chicken *pho*—the advantage of growing up in a place like the San Francisco Bay Area—so we set out to make a tweaked version of it at home.

THAI CHICKEN NOODLE BOWLS

HANDS-ON TIME: 24 MINUTES | TOTAL TIME: 8 HOURS AND 52 MINUTES

MARINADE:
½ cup chopped fresh cilantro
2 tablespoons brown sugar
2 tablespoons minced peeled fresh
  ginger
2 tablespoons lower-sodium soy sauce
2 tablespoons rice vinegar
1 tablespoon fresh lime juice
1½ teaspoons roasted red chile paste
⅓ cup finely chopped green onions
  (4 onions)
3 garlic cloves, minced
6 (6-ounce) skinless, boneless
  chicken breast halves
6 ounces uncooked rice sticks
  (rice-flour noodles)

SAUCE:
¼ cup rice vinegar
2 tablespoons brown sugar
2 tablespoons chopped fresh cilantro
2 tablespoons fresh lime juice
1 tablespoon fish sauce
1 tablespoon minced peeled fresh
  ginger
1 teaspoon roasted red chile paste
Cooking spray

TOPPINGS:
2 carrots, peeled and cut into ribbons
  (about 2 cups)
½ English cucumber, halved
  lengthwise and thinly sliced
  (about 1¼ cups)
¼ cup chopped fresh basil
2 tablespoons finely chopped
  unsalted dry-roasted peanuts

ADDITIONAL INGREDIENTS:
6 lime wedges

1. To prepare marinade, combine first 9 ingredients in a large heavy-duty zip-top plastic bag; add chicken. Seal bag; marinate in refrigerator overnight.
2. Remove chicken from bag; discard marinade. Let stand at room temperature 30 minutes.
3. While chicken stands, cook noodles according to package directions, omitting salt and fat. Drain.
4. To prepare sauce, combine ¼ cup rice vinegar and next 6 ingredients (through chile paste) in a small bowl.
5. Preheat grill to medium-high heat.
6. Place chicken on grill rack coated with cooking spray. Cook 6 minutes on each side or until done. Let stand 5 minutes. Cut chicken crosswise into slices.
7. Place ¾ cup noodles and slices from 1 chicken breast half in each of 6 bowls. Top each serving with ⅓ cup carrot, about 3 tablespoons cucumber, 2 teaspoons basil, and 1 teaspoon peanuts. Drizzle each serving with 1½ teaspoons sauce, and serve with 1 lime wedge. Serves 6

CALORIES 356; **FAT** 3.9g (sat 0.8g, mono 1.3g, poly 1g); **PROTEIN** 41.1g; **CARB** 37.3g; **FIBER** 1.7g; **CHOL** 99mg; **IRON** 2.3mg; **SODIUM** 469mg; **CALC** 54mg

Tips: To make carrot ribbons, use a vegetable peeler.

This recipe was originally for a whole chicken, but I decided to speed it up for a weeknight and turn it into kebabs. You can make this super spicy with hot pepper sauce or omit it altogether and enjoy the milder spices of the Caribbean that are totally kid friendly. If you use wooden skewers, make sure to soak them in water first, or you'll set them on fire. Serve with some Greek yogurt and chopped cilantro as a dipping sauce, if desired.

CARIBBEAN-SPICED CHICKEN KEBABS

HANDS-ON TIME: 12 MINUTES | TOTAL TIME: 4 HOURS AND 24 MINUTES

³/₄ cup diced onion
¹/₄ cup lower-sodium soy sauce
¹/₄ cup canola oil
1 tablespoon brown sugar
2 tablespoons apple cider vinegar
2 tablespoons fresh lime juice
2 teaspoons ground allspice
2 teaspoons fresh thyme leaves
1 teaspoon ground coriander
1 teaspoon hot pepper sauce
¹/₂ teaspoon ground ginger
¹/₄ teaspoon kosher salt
¹/₄ teaspoon freshly ground
    black pepper
¹/₄ teaspoon ground cinnamon
¹/₄ teaspoon ground cloves
3 garlic cloves, minced
3 green onions, minced
4 (6-ounce) skinless, boneless
    chicken breast halves,
    cut into 1-inch pieces
Cooking spray

1. Place all ingredients except chicken and cooking spray in food processor; process until smooth. Pour marinade into a large heavy-duty zip-top plastic bag. Add chicken; seal bag, turning to coat. Marinate in refrigerator 4 hours, turning occasionally.
2. Preheat grill to medium-high heat.
3. Remove chicken from bag; discard marinade. Pat chicken dry with paper towels. Thread chicken evenly onto 4 metal skewers. Place on grill rack coated with cooking spray. Cook 10 minutes or until done, turning after 5 minutes. Serves 4 (serving size: 1 kebab)

CALORIES 364; FAT 16.6g (sat 1.6g, mono 9.5g, poly 4.5g); PROTEIN 41.2g; CARB 11.7g; FIBER 2g; CHOL 99mg; IRON 1.9mg; SODIUM 656mg; CALC 57mg

KIDS CAN HELP

Another way to get kids excited about cooking is to let them in the spice cabinet! Spices like ginger, cinnamon, and cloves all smell wonderful. Kids can measure the spices for you before sprinkling them into the food processor.

A regular little sandwich can go from good to spectacular simply by grilling it. I'm hungry just thinking about it! Favorite Pesto (page 33) is a wonderful addition to this sandwich.

CAPRESE SANDWICHES

HANDS-ON TIME: 10 MINUTES | TOTAL TIME: 10 MINUTES

1 (8½-ounce) French bread baguette, cut crosswise into 4 pieces
1 tablespoon olive oil
2 (8-ounce) heirloom tomatoes, cut into ½-inch slices
4 ounces fresh mozzarella cheese, cut into ¼-inch slices
12 fresh basil leaves
½ teaspoon freshly ground black pepper
¼ teaspoon kosher salt
1 teaspoon balsamic vinegar (optional)

1. Preheat panini grill.
2. Cut bread pieces in half horizontally. Brush uncut sides of halves evenly with oil. Layer bottom halves of bread evenly with tomato slices, cheese, and basil leaves. Sprinkle with pepper, salt, and, if desired, vinegar. Cover with top halves.
3. Place sandwiches on panini grill; cook 2 minutes or until golden brown and cheese melts. Cut sandwiches in half, if desired. Serves 4 (serving size: 1 sandwich)

CALORIES 289; **FAT** 10.2g (sat 4.5g, mono 2.5g, poly 0.5g); **PROTEIN** 11g; **CARB** 40.6g; **FIBER** 2.5g; **CHOL** 23mg; **IRON** 2.3mg; **SODIUM** 533mg; **CALC** 15mg

KIDS CAN HELP

Another way to involve kids in cooking is to take them shopping with you. When it's tomato season, most farmers' markets have an amazing selection. Let your kids smell and touch the tomatoes before asking them to choose their favorites. Chances are greater that they'll eat them when they've been a part of the process!

"My mom makes this salmon almost every week, and I always eat the whole thing. It's my favorite dinner!" —Owen, age 9

My kids are hooked on this salmon. If you've been afraid to give your kids fish, start here. Salmon is firm-fleshed, flavorful, and the most kid-friendly fish I know.

GRILLED ASIAN SALMON

HANDS-ON TIME: 15 MINUTES | TOTAL TIME: 1 HOUR AND 15 MINUTES

3 tablespoons lower-sodium soy sauce
1 tablespoon light brown sugar
2 teaspoons fresh lime juice
1 teaspoon grated peeled fresh ginger
1/2 teaspoon dark sesame oil
1/2 teaspoon Sriracha (hot chile sauce)
1 (1 1/2-pound) salmon fillet, cut lengthwise and crosswise into 4 pieces
Cooking spray

1. Combine first 6 ingredients in a large heavy-duty zip-top plastic bag. Seal bag; shake to dissolve sugar. Add salmon to bag. Seal bag, turning to coat salmon. Marinate in refrigerator 1 hour.
2. Preheat grill to high heat. Remove salmon from bag; reserve marinade. Place salmon on grill rack coated with cooking spray. Grill 4 to 5 minutes on each side or until desired degree of doneness. Place marinade in a microwave-safe bowl. Microwave at HIGH 1 minute and 30 seconds or until boiling. Serve salmon with sauce. Serves 4 (serving size: 1 fillet and 2 teaspoons sauce)

CALORIES 226; **FAT** 6.6g (sat 1g, mono 1.8g, poly 2.6g); **PROTEIN** 34.7g; **CARB** 4.6g; **FIBER** 0g; **CHOL** 88mg; **IRON** 1.4mg; **SODIUM** 420mg; **CALC** 27mg

Tip: Buying good fish is really important to the final taste of the recipe. Fish should never smell "fishy." It should smell like the sea or the stream. Also, the flesh should be brightly colored. Don't be afraid to smell it or ask the fishmonger when it arrived. If he can't tell you, then it's time to find a different place to buy it!

SWEET TREATS

A good homemade piecrust is too tedious for a weeknight, so a delicious crisp is a wonderful dessert alternative. Once you've mastered this recipe, use it as your base to create any flavor you like. Some of my favorites include pear, nectarine, blackberry, peach, and plum. If you add 1/4 cup of fat-free vanilla frozen yogurt, keep in mind that it will add an additional 50 calories.

APPLE CRISP

HANDS-ON TIME: 16 MINUTES | TOTAL TIME: 1 HOUR AND 26 MINUTES

3 ounces all-purpose flour
    (about 2/3 cup)
3/4 cup packed brown sugar
1/2 cup old-fashioned rolled oats
2 teaspoons ground cinnamon,
    divided
1/4 teaspoon salt
Dash of freshly ground nutmeg
    (optional)
6 tablespoons chilled butter,
    cut into pieces
7 cups sliced peeled Fuji apple
1 teaspoon grated lemon rind
1 tablespoon fresh lemon juice
1/4 cup granulated sugar
Cooking spray

1. Preheat oven to 400°.
2. Weigh or lightly spoon flour into dry measuring cups; level with a knife. Combine flour, brown sugar, oats, 1 teaspoon cinnamon, salt, and, if desired, nutmeg, in a bowl. Add butter; beat with a mixer at low speed 3 minutes or until moist and crumbly.
3. Place apple in a large bowl; sprinkle with lemon rind and lemon juice, and toss well. Sprinkle with granulated sugar and remaining 1 teaspoon cinnamon; toss well. Spoon apple mixture into an 8-inch square glass or ceramic baking dish coated with cooking spray. Sprinkle brown sugar mixture over apple mixture. Bake, uncovered, at 400° for 15 minutes. Reduce oven temperature to 350°.
4. Bake an additional 40 to 50 minutes or until apples are tender and topping is crisp and brown. Let stand 15 minutes. Serves 8 (serving size: 3/4 cup)

CALORIES 298; FAT 9.3g (sat 5.5g, mono 2.3g, poly 0.4g); PROTEIN 2.4g; CARB 54g; FIBER 2.7g; CHOL 23mg; IRON 1mg; SODIUM 141mg; CALC 37mg

For kids with gluten intolerance, I think it's important to create a few desserts that taste as good as the real thing. This one sure does. I rely on Cup4Cup flour and S'moreables gluten-free graham crackers for the best results.

GLUTEN-FREE S'MORE BARS

HANDS-ON TIME: 20 MINUTES | TOTAL TIME: 3 HOURS AND 35 MINUTES

5 gluten-free graham cracker
  sheets, broken
3.38 ounces gluten-free flour
  (about ¾ cup)
½ cup packed brown sugar
¼ cup chilled unsalted butter,
  cut into ½-inch pieces
1 large egg
6 tablespoons heavy whipping
  cream
2 (4-ounce) bars semisweet
  chocolate, chopped
2 cups miniature marshmallows

1. Preheat oven to 350°.
2. Line an 8-inch square metal baking pan with aluminum foil, allowing foil to extend over edge of pan.
3. Place graham crackers in a food processor; process until finely ground. Weigh or lightly spoon flour into dry measuring cups; level with a knife. Add flour and sugar to crumbs; pulse until combined. Add butter; pulse 15 times or until blended. Add egg; process until moist. Press crumb mixture into bottom of prepared pan.
4. Bake at 350° for 15 minutes. Cool completely in pan on a wire rack.
5. Cook cream in a heavy saucepan over medium-high heat to 180° or until tiny bubbles form around edge (do not boil). Remove from heat. Add chocolate, stirring until smooth. Fold in marshmallows. Spread chocolate mixture over cooled crust. Cover and chill 2 hours and 30 minutes or until firm. Holding edges of foil, lift mixture from pan, and carefully peel off foil. Place on a cutting board. Cut into bars. Serves 24 (serving size: 1 bar)

CALORIES 138; FAT 6.7g (sat 3.9g, mono 1g, poly 0.2g); PROTEIN 1.5g; CARB 19.1g; FIBER 0.9g; CHOL 19mg; IRON 0.2mg; SODIUM 24mg; CALC 10mg

My kids love pressing the crumb mixture into the pan, and then melting the chocolate and stirring in the marshmallows.

"This cookie is what Mandy has been making me for 20 years. It is the best!"

—Steve, 41, friend and favorite critic of my food

My goal with gluten-free desserts is to make them taste so good that no one notices the difference. That happened here!

CHEWY CARAMEL APPLE COOKIES

HANDS-ON TIME: 21 MINUTES | TOTAL TIME: 1 HOUR AND 28 MINUTES

½ cup plus 2 tablespoons unsalted butter, softened

1 cup plus 2 tablespoons packed brown sugar

1 large egg

2 tablespoons milk

¾ teaspoon vanilla extract

6.75 ounces gluten-free flour (about 1½ cups)

¾ teaspoon baking soda

¼ teaspoon salt

1½ cups gluten-free old-fashioned rolled oats

2 chopped peeled apples

20 caramel candies

2 tablespoons water

1. Preheat oven to 325°.

2. Beat butter and brown sugar with a mixer at medium speed until creamy. Add egg, milk, and vanilla; beat 2 minutes or until light and fluffy.

3. Weigh or lightly spoon flour into dry measuring cups; level with a knife. Combine flour, baking soda, and salt in a bowl, stirring with a whisk. Stir in oats. Add oat mixture to butter mixture, beating at low speed until blended. Stir in apples.

4. Drop dough by 1½ tablespoonfuls 2 inches apart onto baking sheets lined with parchment paper.

5. Bake at 325° for 14 minutes or until golden. Transfer cookies to wire racks; cool completely.

6. Place caramels and water in a small saucepan. Cook over low heat 7 minutes, stirring until smooth. Remove from heat. Drizzle warm glaze over cookies. Let stand 15 minutes or until caramel is completely set. Store in an airtight container for up to 5 days. Serves 36 (serving size: 1 cookie)

CALORIES 115; FAT 4g (sat 2.3g, mono 1g, poly 0.3g); PROTEIN 1.6g; CARB 18.4g; FIBER 1g; CHOL 15mg; IRON 0.4mg; SODIUM 61mg; CALC 22mg

"My mom is
the best ice-cream
maker ever!"
—Charlie, age 6

Ice cream and sorbets are convenient go-tos when you want an easy dessert. Use this custard as a base for many flavors by adding your favorite ingredients when it's almost frozen. Our family favorites are strawberries, crushed peaches, or a little crushed toffee with chocolate syrup. Yum!

FROZEN VANILLA CUSTARD

HANDS-ON TIME: 16 MINUTES | TOTAL TIME: 4 HOURS AND 39 MINUTES

2 cups milk
¹⁄₂ cup half-and-half
¹⁄₂ cup sugar
5 large egg yolks
¹⁄₈ teaspoon salt
¹⁄₂ teaspoon vanilla extract

1. Cook milk and half-and-half in a heavy saucepan over medium-high heat to 180° or until tiny bubbles form around edge (do not boil). Remove from heat.
2. Combine sugar and egg yolks in a large bowl, stirring with a whisk until thick and pale. Gradually add hot milk mixture to egg mixture, stirring constantly with a whisk. Return milk mixture to pan. Stir in salt; cook over medium heat 10 minutes or until thick, stirring constantly. Remove from heat; stir in vanilla.
3. Place pan in a large ice-filled bowl until custard is chilled (about 1 hour), stirring occasionally.
4. Pour mixture into the freezer can of an ice-cream freezer; freeze according to manufacturer's instructions. Spoon frozen custard into a freezer-safe container; cover and freeze 3 hours or until firm. Serves 8 (serving size: ¹⁄₂ cup)

CALORIES 139; **FAT** 6.5g (sat 3.2g, mono 2.2g, poly 0.6g); **PROTEIN** 4.1g; **CARB** 16.4g; **FIBER** 0g; **CHOL** 143mg; **IRON** 0.3mg; **SODIUM** 73mg; **CALC** 99mg

KIDS CAN HELP

I love making our sweet treats really count, so when we're at the store, I ask my kids to pick out the fruit they'd like to add to this base. Then they're really excited to eat it, plus they're getting a great dose of fruit. Kids can also help by measuring all the ingredients for you.

"My mom caught me trying to eat the whole pan of these! I love how lemony they are." —Laney, age 9

It's no coincidence that citrus is in season when it's cold and snowing in most places. I'm convinced Mother Nature designed it that way so we could enjoy something other than chocolate in the middle of a drab winter. Promise me you'll use fresh lemon juice in this recipe. It's not worth it without it. Substitute gluten-free all-purpose flour for a gluten-free option.

MY FAVORITE LEMON BARS

HANDS-ON TIME: 10 MINUTES | TOTAL TIME: 1 HOUR AND 55 MINUTES

6.75 ounces all-purpose flour
   (about 1¹/₂ cups)
¹/₂ cup powdered sugar
³/₄ cup butter, softened
Cooking spray
1¹/₂ cups granulated sugar
1¹/₂ tablespoons all-purpose flour
1 tablespoon grated lemon rind
¹/₂ cup fresh lemon juice
4 large eggs
2 tablespoons powdered sugar

1. Preheat oven to 350°.
2. Weigh or lightly spoon 6.75 ounces (about 1¹/₂ cups) flour into dry measuring cups; level with a knife. Combine 6.75 ounces flour and ¹/₂ cup powdered sugar in a large bowl, stirring with a whisk. Work in butter with hands until mixture resembles coarse meal that comes together like dough when pinched. Press mixture into bottom of a 13 x 9-inch baking pan coated with cooking spray.
3. Bake at 350° for 15 minutes or until golden brown. Cool 5 minutes on a wire rack.
4. Combine granulated sugar, 1¹/₂ tablespoons flour, and lemon rind in a medium bowl, stirring with a whisk. Add lemon juice and eggs, beating with a whisk until blended; pour over crust.
5. Bake at 350° for 20 to 25 minutes or until filling is set. Cool completely. Sift 2 tablespoons powdered sugar over top. Cut into bars. Serves 24 (serving size: 1 bar)

CALORIES 156; **FAT** 6.7g (sat 3.9g, mono 1.8g, poly 0.4g); **PROTEIN** 2g; **CARB** 22.7g; **FIBER** 0.3g; **CHOL** 51mg; **IRON** 0.6mg; **SODIUM** 53mg; **CALC** 8mg

Summertime means berries and stone fruits. You can take advantage of the abundance and low prices of the season, and serve them for a quick and easy dessert. Any combination of berries will work; even add a sliced nectarine or two.

MIXED BERRIES WITH ORANGE MASCARPONE CREAM

HANDS-ON TIME: 20 MINUTES | TOTAL TIME: 20 MINUTES

¹/₄ cup mascarpone cheese
¹/₄ cup vanilla 2% reduced-fat
   Greek yogurt
¹/₂ teaspoon grated orange rind
2 cups quartered strawberries
1 cup blueberries
1 cup raspberries
1 cup blackberries
1 tablespoon sugar
1 tablespoon chopped fresh mint
1 tablespoon fresh orange juice
Orange curls (optional)
Mint leaves (optional)

1. Combine first 3 ingredients in a small bowl.
2. Combine strawberries and next 3 ingredients (through blackberries) in a medium bowl. Gently stir in sugar, mint, and orange juice. Spoon fruit mixture into bowls; top evenly with mascarpone cream. Garnish with orange curls and mint leaves, if desired. Serves 6 (serving size: ³/₄ cup fruit mixture and 4 teaspoons mascarpone cream)

CALORIES 149; FAT 9.3g (sat 4.8g, mono 0.1g, poly 0.3g); PROTEIN 3.2g; CARB 15.8g; FIBER 4.1g; CHOL 24mg; IRON 0.6mg; SODIUM 15mg; CALC 64mg

Tip: Don't wash your berries until you're ready to use them; otherwise they can go bad quickly. Once you wash them, dry them gently on paper towel–lined jelly-roll pans. Give them a gentle shake to remove excess water. Also, I buy organic when possible because berries easily absorb pesticides.

KIDS CAN HELP

When washing berries, line baking sheets with paper towels. Then let kids rinse the berries in a colander, dump them onto the baking sheets, and give them a shake to dry them.

This no-fuss dessert requires less than 15 minutes of prep time, and the finished product is sure to draw oohs and aahs from guests of all ages. You can make it the morning of the party, and everyone will think you worked all day.

CHOCOLATE POTS DE CRÈME

HANDS-ON TIME: 12 MINUTES | TOTAL TIME: 8 HOURS AND 12 MINUTES

¼ cup sugar
⅛ teaspoon salt
2 large eggs
1¼ cups milk
9 ounces semisweet chocolate, finely chopped
2 teaspoons vanilla extract
1½ tablespoons dark rum or brandy (optional)
Raspberries (optional)
Mint leaves (optional)

1. Combine first 3 ingredients in a medium bowl, stirring with a whisk. Gradually add milk, stirring with a whisk. Set bowl over a saucepan of simmering water. Cook, stirring constantly, 8 minutes or until a thermometer registers 160°. Remove bowl from heat; add chocolate, vanilla, and, if desired, rum, stirring until chocolate melts and mixture is smooth.
2. Pour chocolate mixture evenly into 10 (4-ounce) ramekins or small glasses. Cover and chill 8 hours. Garnish with raspberries and mint, if desired. Serves 10 (serving size: ¼ cup)

CALORIES 177; FAT 9.6g (sat 5.4g, mono 3.2g, poly 0.4g); PROTEIN 3.3g; CARB 22.7g; FIBER 1.5g; CHOL 45mg; IRON 1mg; SODIUM 59mg; CALC 48mg

Tip: Mixing in a splash of rum or brandy for adults adds a little touch of sophistication.

Kids can stir the chocolate with the help of a parent and watch it transform into this delicious dessert. They can also garnish the top with the raspberries and mint.

Believe it or not, banana splits are a great way for children to have a well-balanced sweet treat. My secret? Go heavy on the fruit!

BANANA SPLIT SUNDAES

HANDS-ON TIME: 10 MINUTES | TOTAL TIME: 10 MINUTES

1/4 cup whipping cream
1 1/2 teaspoons granulated sugar
1/4 teaspoon vanilla extract
4 cups vanilla light ice cream
2 cups diced strawberries
1 1/4 cups sliced banana (2 bananas)
1/4 cup Dark Chocolate Sauce
    (page 49), warmed
1/4 cup bottled caramel sauce,
    warmed
1/2 cup coarsely chopped
    dry-roasted almonds

1. Combine first 3 ingredients in a bowl. Beat with mixer at medium speed until soft peaks form.
2. Scoop 1/2 cup ice cream into each of 8 bowls. Top each with 1/4 cup strawberries and 2 1/2 tablespoons banana. Drizzle 1 1/2 teaspoons each of Dark Chocolate Sauce and caramel sauce over each serving. Top each with 1 tablespoon sweetened whipped cream and 1 tablespoon almonds. Serves 8 (serving size: 1 sundae)

CALORIES 296; **FAT** 12.3g (sat 4.5g, mono 4.7g, poly 1.4g); **PROTEIN** 6.8g; **CARB** 42.4g; **FIBER** 2.9g; **CHOL** 31mg; **IRON** 0.9mg; **SODIUM** 85mg; **CALC** 163mg

Tip: For portion control, scoop the ice cream for the kids, and then let them assemble everything else themselves.

My friend Denise and I have a terrible sweet tooth. The last time she made these, I was eating so many of them that I had to hide from my kids! One (or two) is the perfect treat.

CHOCOLATE-BUTTERSCOTCH-NUT CLUSTERS

HANDS-ON TIME: 24 MINUTES | TOTAL TIME: 54 MINUTES

1½ cups semisweet chocolate chips
½ cup butterscotch chips
¼ cup whole natural almonds, toasted
¼ cup unsalted dry-roasted peanuts
¼ cup lightly salted cashews

1. Place chocolate chips and butterscotch chips in top of a double boiler. Cook over simmering water until chips melt (about 10 minutes), stirring frequently. Remove from heat; stir in remaining ingredients.

2. Drop by 2 level teaspoonfuls onto 2 large baking sheets lined with wax paper. Chill 30 minutes or until firm. Store, covered, in refrigerator. Serves 30 (serving size: 1 cluster)

CALORIES 82; FAT 5.3g (sat 2.7g, mono 1.8g, poly 0.5g); PROTEIN 1.1g; CARB 8.6g; FIBER 0.8g; CHOL 0mg; IRON 0.4mg; SODIUM 12mg; CALC 7mg

Tip: If you store nuts in the freezer, bring them to room temperature before stirring them into the chocolate mixture.

KIDS CAN HELP

This is an ideal recipe for older children to make themselves. For younger children, they'll just need a hand at the stove while melting the chocolate and butterscotch chips.

Now that I've accepted that I have a severe gluten intolerance, I've started enjoying food a lot more. Thanks to people like Lena Kwak—the co-founder of Cup4Cup—we all have better gluten-free options. She has developed a gluten-free flour that can be used interchangeably with all-purpose flour. So grab a bag and start baking these awesome cookies. Like the name suggests, I put just about everything in them—it just depends what I have on hand.

KITCHEN SINK OATMEAL COOKIES

HANDS-ON TIME: 15 MINUTES | TOTAL TIME: 40 MINUTES

3.45 ounces gluten-free flour (about ¾ cup)
½ teaspoon baking soda
½ teaspoon ground cinnamon
¼ teaspoon salt
½ cup unsalted butter, softened
½ cup packed brown sugar
¼ cup granulated sugar
1 large egg
1½ cups gluten-free old-fashioned rolled oats
½ cup chocolate chips
¼ cup chopped walnuts or almonds

1. Preheat oven to 350°.
2. Weigh or lightly spoon flour into dry measuring cups; level with a knife. Combine flour, baking soda, cinnamon, and salt in a bowl, stirring with a whisk.
3. Place butter and sugars in a large bowl; beat with a mixer at medium speed until well blended. Add egg, beating well. Add flour mixture; beat. Stir in oats, chocolate chips, and nuts.
4. Drop dough by 2 level teaspoonfuls onto a baking sheet lined with parchment paper. Bake at 350° for 10 minutes. Remove cookies from pan; cool on wire racks. Serves 48 (serving size: 1 cookie)

CALORIES 60; **FAT** 3.2g (sat 1.6g, mono 0.8g, poly 0.4g); **PROTEIN** 1g; **CARB** 7.7g; **FIBER** 0.6g; **CHOL** 9mg; **IRON** 0.3mg; **SODIUM** 28mg; **CALC** 7mg

Tip: Choose your brand of chocolate chips carefully. Read the label to make sure you select a truly safe gluten-free option.

My ice-cream maker gets a ton of use, but not just for ice cream. Sorbet and frozen yogurt are in the rotation, as well. Depending on how sweet your mangoes are, you can add more or less lime and more or less simple syrup. To make simple syrup, combine equal parts water and granulated sugar in a saucepan; stir over low heat until the sugar dissolves. Allow to cool before using.

MANGO-LIME SORBET

HANDS-ON TIME: 6 MINUTES | TOTAL TIME: 2 HOURS AND 36 MINUTES

2¼ cups mango puree (4 mangoes)
½ cup plain simple syrup
1 teaspoon grated lime rind
2 teaspoons fresh lime juice
Lime zest (optional)

1. Combine all ingredients in a bowl. Cover and chill 1 hour.
2. Pour mixture into the freezer can of an ice-cream freezer; freeze according to manufacturer's instructions. Spoon sorbet into a freezer-safe container; cover and freeze 1 hour or until firm. Garnish with lime zest, if desired. Serves 8 (serving size: about ⅓ cup)

CALORIES 93; **FAT** 0.3g (sat 0.1g, mono 0.1g, poly 0.1g); **PROTEIN** 0.5g; **CARB** 24.7g; **FIBER** 1.9g; **CHOL** 0mg; **IRON** 0.1mg; **SODIUM** 2mg; **CALC** 11mg

technique: how to cut a mango

1. Use a sharp knife to trim half an inch from the top and bottom. Hold the mango in one hand, and use a vegetable peeler to slice the skin from the flesh.

2. Cut flesh from around the pit with two curved cuts down the plumpest sides, then trim remaining sides.

3. Cut the fruit's flesh according to your desire—diced or sliced.

"I can make this dessert all by myself. It's like a frozen strawberry lemonade." —Jack, age 11

Making lemon ice always feels like a fun science project. You pour cooled, sweet liquid into a shallow container and wait for ice crystals to form. Then you scrape it with a fork until you have chunky crystals of juicy ice. It's kind of a mix between a snow cone and a fancy sorbet.

TART LEMON ICE WITH CRUSHED STRAWBERRIES

HANDS-ON TIME: 24 MINUTES | TOTAL TIME: 8 HOURS AND 30 MINUTES

1 cup sugar
1 cup water
1 cup fresh lemon juice
1½ cups quartered strawberries
1 teaspoon sugar
2 tablespoons chopped fresh mint
Lemon zest (optional)

1. Combine 1 cup sugar and 1 cup water in a 2-cup glass measure. Microwave at HIGH 3 to 5 minutes or until sugar dissolves and mixture boils; stir well. Cool completely. Cover and refrigerate simple syrup until thoroughly chilled.

2. Combine lemon juice and simple syrup in a 13 x 9-inch baking dish. Cover and freeze at least 3 hours or until firm. Scrape frozen mixture with the tines of a fork.

3. Place strawberries and 1 teaspoon sugar in a medium bowl. Mash strawberry mixture slightly with a potato masher to release juice. Stir in mint. Cover and let stand at room temperature 30 minutes.

4. Spoon ½ cup lemon mixture into each of 7 bowls; top each serving with about 2 tablespoons strawberry mixture. Garnish with lemon zest, if desired. Serves 7

CALORIES 133; **FAT** 0.1g (sat 0g, mono 0g, poly 0.1g); **PROTEIN** 0.4g; **CARB** 35g; **FIBER** 0.8g; **CHOL** 0mg; **IRON** 0.2mg; **SODIUM** 1mg; **CALC** 9mg

nutritional analysis

HOW TO USE IT AND WHY   Glance at the end of any *Cooking Light* recipe, and you'll see how committed we are to helping you make the best of today's light cooking. With chefs, registered dietitians, home economists, and a computer system that analyzes every ingredient we use, *Cooking Light* gives you authoritative dietary detail like no other magazine. We go to such lengths so you can see how our recipes fit into your healthful eating plan. If you're trying to lose weight, the calorie and fat figures will probably help most. But if you're keeping a close eye on the sodium, cholesterol, and saturated fat in your diet, we provide those numbers, too. And because many women don't get enough iron or calcium, we can help there, as well. Finally, there's a fiber analysis for those of us who don't get enough roughage.

Here's a helpful guide to put our nutritional analysis numbers into perspective. Remember, one size doesn't fit all, so take your lifestyle, age, and circumstances into consideration when determining your nutrition needs. For example, pregnant or breast-feeding women need more protein, calories, and calcium. And women older than 50 need 1,200mg of calcium daily, 200mg more than the amount recommended for younger women.

IN OUR NUTRITIONAL ANALYSIS, WE USE THESE ABBREVIATIONS

sat	saturated fat	**CHOL**	cholesterol
mono	monounsaturated fat	**CALC**	calcium
poly	polyunsaturated fat	**g**	gram
CARB	carbohydrates	**mg**	milligram

DAILY NUTRITION GUIDE

	Women ages 25 to 50	Women over 50	Men ages 24 to 50	Men over 50
Calories	2,000	2,000 or less	2,700	2,500
Protein	50g	50g or less	63g	60g
Fat	65g or less	65g or less	88g or less	83g or less
Saturated Fat	20g or less	20g or less	27g or less	25g or less
Carbohydrates	304g	304g	410g	375g
Fiber	25g to 35g	25g to 35g	25g to 35g	25g to 35g
Cholesterol	300mg or less	300mg or less	300mg or less	300mg or less
Iron	18mg	8mg	8mg	8mg
Sodium	2,300mg or less	1,500mg or less	2,300mg or less	1,500mg or less
Calcium	1,000mg	1,200mg	1,000mg	1,000mg

The nutritional values used in our calculations either come from The Food Processor, Version 8.9 (ESHA Research), or are provided by food manufacturers.

metric equivalents

The information in the following charts is provided to help cooks outside the United States successfully use the recipes in this book. All equivalents are approximate.

COOKING/OVEN TEMPERATURES

	Fahrenheit	Celsius	Gas Mark
Freeze Water	32° F	0° C	
Room Temp.	68° F	20° C	
Boil Water	212° F	100° C	
Bake	325° F	160° C	3
	350° F	180° C	4
	375° F	190° C	5
	400° F	200° C	6
	425° F	220° C	7
	450° F	230° C	8
Broil			Grill

LIQUID INGREDIENTS BY VOLUME

1/4 tsp	=						1 ml	
1/2 tsp	=						2 ml	
1 tsp	=						5 ml	
3 tsp	=	1 tbl	=	1/2 fl oz	=		15 ml	
2 tbls	=	1/8 cup	=	1 fl oz	=		30 ml	
4 tbls	=	1/4 cup	=	2 fl oz	=		60 ml	
5 1/3 tbls	=	1/3 cup	=	3 fl oz	=		80 ml	
8 tbls	=	1/2 cup	=	4 fl oz	=		120 ml	
10 2/3 tbls	=	2/3 cup	=	5 fl oz	=		160 ml	
12 tbls	=	3/4 cup	=	6 fl oz	=		180 ml	
16 tbls	=	1 cup	=	8 fl oz	=		240 ml	
1 pt	=	2 cups	=	16 fl oz	=		480 ml	
1 qt	=	4 cups	=	32 fl oz	=		960 ml	
				33 fl oz	=	1000 ml	=	1 l

DRY INGREDIENTS BY WEIGHT

To convert ounces to grams, multiply the number of ounces by 30.

1 oz	=	1/16 lb	=	30 g
4 oz	=	1/4 lb	=	120 g
8 oz	=	1/2 lb	=	240 g
12 oz	=	3/4 lb	=	360 g
16 oz	=	1 lb	=	480 g

LENGTH

To convert inches to centimeters, multiply the number of inches by 2.5.

1 in	=				2.5 cm	
6 in	=	1/2 ft		=	15 cm	
12 in	=	1 ft		=	30 cm	
36 in	=	3 ft	= 1 yd	=	90 cm	
40 in	=				100 cm	= 1 m

EQUIVALENTS FOR DIFFERENT TYPES OF INGREDIENTS

Standard Cup	Fine Powder (ex. flour)	Grain (ex. rice)	Granular (ex. sugar)	Liquid Solids (ex. butter)	Liquid (ex. milk)
1	140 g	150 g	190 g	200 g	240 ml
3/4	105 g	113 g	143 g	150 g	180 ml
2/3	93 g	100 g	125 g	133 g	160 ml
1/2	70 g	75 g	95 g	100 g	120 ml
1/3	47 g	50 g	63 g	67 g	80 ml
1/4	35 g	38 g	48 g	50 g	60 ml
1/8	18 g	19 g	24 g	25 g	30 ml

index

D

E

F

G

acknowledgments

I'm so grateful for the support I've received while dreaming up the idea of One Family One Meal. To watch it come to life in a book is amazing!

To my "One Family"—Kyle, Connor, and Charlie: Thank you so much for your love, support, and willingness to eat my food. None of this would have happened without you three.

To the team who made this book happen: **Jim Childs, Felicity Keane, Michelle Aycock, Heather Averett, Cathy Robbins, Allison Potter, Perri Hubbard,** and the **Oxmoor House Test Kitchen and Photo staff.** Thank you so much.

James Carriere: Thank you for bringing my food and family to life with your beautiful photography. **Mindi Shapiro:** Your styling made my house a home! You're amazing. **Robyn Valarik:** You made my food look better than I ever could. **Kurt Lundquist, Brett Levine,** and **Jason Wheeler:** You all were such a help at the shoot, too.

My Mentors. **Tori Ritchie:** Every wonderful blessing in my career has come from your encouragement, Tori. Thank you. **Mary Risley:** Thank you for giving the world Tante Marie's Cooking School and for supporting my career. **Chef Todd English:** I still can't believe I was hired to watch one of my favorite chefs cook in his own kitchen. It was truly a gift! My favorite recipes are from you. **Chef Matthew Accarrino:** I may not be your next butcher, but because of you, my family understands the magic of inspired cooking. I can't wait for the world to see what you can do. **Katherine Cobbs:** Your work made my work so much better. **The Women of Revolution Foods—Kristin, Kirsten,** and **Amy:** Our world is a better place with you leading the charge for better food in our schools.

The other amazing foodies whose work inspires me: **Shelley Lindgren, Jason Wallis, Jodi Liano, Farina Achuck, Michael Coon, Joey Altman, Kate Leahy, Donata Maggipinto, Sheila Middleton, Nate Appleman, Chuck Williams, Mourad Lahlou, Michael Mina, Gib Dyer,** and **Whole Foods Market.**

My One Family One Meal "Family"—**Inken Chrisman:** You are the magic behind One Family One Meal! None of this would have been possible without your hard work and talent. **Jennifer Aaker-Smith, Andy Smith, Dave Gravano, SolutionSet, Stasia Huiner,** and **John Hassig:** Thank you for bringing One Family One Meal to life. And to **all my readers:** Thank you for encouraging me to go for it.

Williams-Sonoma, Inc.: I feel lucky to have found my way back to the place where I discovered my passion for cooking 20 years ago. **Sandra, Melissa,** and **Angela:** You are the best. I love working with you. **Jean:** Thank you for leading me back.

My Family: Thanks to all of my family for encouraging me to do this from the very beginning. **Mom, Dad,** and **Wendy:** With my life-long love of eating, I'm sure you're not surprised by my career path! Thanks for your love and support. And **Madison, Kaleigh, Lily,** and **Addison:** I'm counting on you to keep this family cooking!

My Girlfriends: You all have something in common—you're all amazing cooks!

resources

I reached out to the few companies where I buy most everything for my home, and they all generously agreed to donate or lend items for the photo shoot. Here is where you can find my favorite things:

- **Whole Foods Market:** I buy every ingredient I need here, including tamari (gluten-free soy sauce), gluten-free pasta and bread, and the best produce and meat around. Thank you for your generous grocery donation for the photo shoot, and for supporting One Family One Meal. Most importantly, thank you for giving our country a wonderful place to shop for healthful food.

- **Williams-Sonoma, Inc.:** Most everything you see in my kitchen comes from this store, from the cookware to the knives to the mixer to the French porcelain. I can't live without their Olio Santo olive oil and Cup4Cup flour. They generously contributed Apilco Zen Dinnerware (my absolute favorite!), aprons, and linens for the shoot.

- **West Elm:** My 20X200 artwork, Andalusia rug, Blue Dot dinnerware, and Zigzag rug all come from West Elm. Thank you for contributing the vases and other fun objects that made my house feel so chic for the shoot!

- **Pottery Barn Kids:** Thank you so much for the lunchbox storage pieces, Spiderman Dinnerware, striped flatware, and water bottles. You make setting the table and packing lunches fun for our family!